HEALTHY
DEMOCRACIES

HEALTHY
DEMOCRACIES

◇◇◇◇◇◇◇◇◇◇◇◇◇◇◇◇◇◇◇◇◇◇◇◇◇◇◇◇◇◇ ◆◇◆ ◇◇◇◇◇◇◇◇◇◇◇◇◇◇◇◇◇◇◇◇◇◇◇◇◇◇◇◇◇◇

WELFARE POLITICS IN TAIWAN
AND SOUTH KOREA

JOSEPH WONG

CORNELL UNIVERSITY PRESS

ITHACA AND LONDON

First published 2004 by Cornell University Press
First printing, Cornell Paperbacks, 2006

Printed in the United States of America

Library of Congress Cataloging-in-Publication Data

Wong, Joseph, 1973–
    Healthy democracies : welfare politics in Taiwan and South
Korea / Joseph Wong.
        p. cm.
    Includes bibliographical references and index.
    ISBN-13: 978-0-8014-4300-8 (cloth : alk. paper)
    ISBN-10: 0-8014-4300-8 (cloth : alk. paper)
    ISBN-13: 978-0-8014-7349-4 (pbk.: alk.paper)
    ISBN-10: 0-8014-7349-7 (pbk.: alk.paper)

    1. Taiwan—Social policy. 2. Public welfare—Taiwan.
3. Democracy—Taiwan. 4. South Korea (South)—Social policy.
5. Public welfare—Korea (South) 6. Democracy—Korea (South)
I. Title.
    HN748.5.W66   2004
    361.6'1'0951249—dc22   2004012141

Cloth printing   10 9 8 7 6 5 4 3 2 1
Paperback printing   10 9 8 7 6 5 4 3 2 1

For my mother and father,
and for Jen and Anita

CONTENTS

PREFACE

We just might be witnessing another East Asian miracle in the making. At a time when governments around the world are facing fiscal constraints and are thus clawing back public expenditures, governments in Taiwan and South Korea have increased their spending. In an ideological climate in which economic crisis invites neoliberal economic restructuring, Taiwan and South Korea expanded their social safety nets after the 1997 Asian financial crisis. Indeed, when the conventional wisdom suggests the inevitability of welfare state retrenchment, democratizing states in Taiwan and South Korea have legislated new social security programs, broadened the scope of family care policies, and universalized medical care insurance. Though the social policy "race to the bottom" is becoming the norm in most advanced industrial countries, a "race to the top" dominates social policy agendas in Taiwan and South Korea. This book endeavors to understand how these two countries embarked on this new social welfare trajectory despite overwhelming odds. It does so by tracing the development of health care policy in Taiwan and South Korea from the authoritarian period through the present day.

The short answer to this puzzle is that democracy has mattered very much in shaping social policy reform. In the area of health care—the focus of this book—Taiwan and South Korea first moved toward universal medical insurance during the late 1980s, around the time of democratic transition. During the 1990s, Taiwan and Korea maintained or even deepened health care reform despite strong economic pressures to scale back existing social policy measures. Health care policy in democratic Taiwan and Korea has become an instrument for socioeconomic redistribution, a significant departure from the authoritarian developmental state in which selective social policy was used by elites essentially to buy off key distributional coalitions.

Welfare reform in Taiwan and South Korea has been the product of intense political conflict, though recent social policy contestation has been mediated through increasingly democratic institutions and practices. Political competition, the emergence of new actors, the expansion of health care policy networks, and changing conceptions about democratic citizenship have together delivered burgeoning welfare states in Northeast Asia. This book tells this counterintuitive story of health care reform. It is a tribute to the people of Taiwan and South Korea, who gave me such a fascinating story to tell in the first place, and holds lessons that may be useful for others struggling to make democracy just.

There are so many people I need to thank; too many, unfortunately, to fit in these few pages. You know who you are. Nonetheless, there are some individuals I absolutely must acknowledge here. My colleagues in Taiwan—Yun-Han Chu, Chang-Ling Huang, Yeun-Wen Ku, Zong-Rong Lee, Jih-Wen Lin, Liang-Rong Lin, Tien-Haw Peng, and Bo Tedards—lent me their expertise, their ear, and their insights throughout the research and writing of this manuscript. Thanks to Hung-Mao Tien and the staff at the Institute for National Policy Research in Taipei, where I was a research fellow in 1999. Peter Wen-Hui Cheng, Tony Tung-Liang Chiang, Kai-Hsun Wu, and Chi-Liang Yaung helped me navigate the ins and outs of health care policy in Taiwan, and for that I am deeply indebted. In Korea, Seoul National University (SNU) professors Soon-Man Kwon, Ok-Ryun Moon, and Bong-Min Yang were generous with their time, teaching me about health care policy in South Korea, past and present..Thanks also to Yong-Duck Jung of SNU's School of Public Administration for inviting me to be a visiting fellow at the university in 2000 and for supplying me with a stream of contacts in the Korean bureaucracy. Several friends and colleagues have been extremely supportive throughout the writing of this book, most notably Chang-Bae Chun, Byung-Kook Kim, and Huck-Ju Kwon. I also extend my sincerest appreciation to Sejin Kim, my research assistant in Korea, without whom my fieldwork would have been nonexistent. She worked tirelessly with me throughout the spring and summer of 2000.

I was the fortunate recipient of several grants that supported my research and writing. Thanks to the Association of Asian Studies, the Chiang Ching-Kuo Foundation, the Institute for the Study of World Politics, the Irving Louis Horowitz Foundation, the MacArthur Foundation, the Social Sciences and Humanities Research Council of Canada, and the University of Wisconsin-Madison. Subsequent grants from the University of Toronto and the Connaught Foundation were very helpful when I was preparing the final manuscript.

Over the past several years, I have been affiliated with many of the top research institutions in North America and have benefited from the teaching and wisdom of some fine scholars. While I was at the University of Wisconsin-Madison, Michael Barnett, Donald Emmerson, Edward Friedman, Paul Hutchcroft, and Graham Wilson not only taught me political science but also extended their support and encouragement, and have continued to do so. Between 1999 and 2001, I was a visiting research associate at the Fairbank Center, Harvard University. During that time I learned from colleagues at Harvard and from those in the larger Boston-Cambridge area. I owe special thanks to Joseph Fewsmith, William Grimes, Roderick MacFarquhar, Robert Ross, and Ezra Vogel, who helped make my time there enjoyable and intellectually fruitful. Since I joined the faculty of the Political Science Department at the University of Toronto, my colleagues have supported me in my research and writing. Sylvia Bashevkin, Jacques Bertrand, Michael Donnelly, Richard Iton, Jeffrey Kopstein, Louis Pauly, Ito Peng, Grace Skogstad, and Linda White have all read drafts of various chapters, and their comments have been very helpful. I am fortunate to be a part of such a high-caliber community of scholars, whom I also consider good friends. At Toronto, I have also had the luxury of working with absolutely first-rate research assistants, Nina Mansoori and Uyen Quach.

Roger Haydon of Cornell University Press has been fantastic. Over the past four years or so, he has helped me hone my ideas and arguments. Like all those authors who have worked with Roger before me, I especially appreciate his honesty, perseverance, and ability to squeeze the best writing out of me. Two anonymous reviewers provided excellent feedback, dissecting both the empirical and theoretical aspects of the manuscript. Their insights have made for a much better book.

Writing a book is terribly taxing. One needs constant encouragement and affirmation from others. Indeed, we ask friends and colleagues to read the work in progress and to offer constructive criticisms, and then we demand that they rebuild our confidence so we can go on. In addition to all those people I have already mentioned, I extend my appreciation to Steven Bernstein, John C. Campbell, Tun-Jen Cheng, John Fieno, Stephan Haggard, John Fu-Hseng Hsieh, Evelyne Huber, Robert Kaufman, Jay Krishnan, Chen-Wei Lin, Deborah Milly, Chris Murray, Bert Rockman, Edward Schatz, Gay Seidman, and Victor Shih, for reading, for constructively criticizing, and then for reassuring me that all will be well. A special mention of Edward Friedman, my mentor and good friend, is needed here. Ed has been a constant source of encouragement to me for the past ten years or so, particularly when I was a graduate student at Wisconsin. He challenged me in my work then and still does. From the very first paper I submitted to him in my first semester of graduate school to the most recent paper I finished, Ed dutifully splashes the pages with his red ink. I will forever be his student.

Finally, I thank my family for unconditionally supporting me in my intellectual and professional endeavors. Thank you, Frank, Diane, and Lisa. My parents, Pak and Lucia, my sister, Anita, and my wife, Jennifer, have from the beginning encouraged me to pursue my dreams. Well, here is one of those dreams. And for that, this book is dedicated to the four of you.

HEALTHY
DEMOCRACIES

CHAPTER 1

DEMOCRATIZATION AND THE WELFARE STATE

This book is about the politics of social welfare in Taiwan and South Korea. Few studies have investigated welfare reform in East Asia, and even fewer have taken seriously the role of democratic transition in welfare state development.[1] For good reason, it seems. Cultural interpretations of welfare in Confucian societies suggest that social protection is generally provided by the family and extended social networks, drawn together through ties of kinship and communitarianism.[2] Statist solutions for social welfare are understood to be incompatible with Asian culture. Democratic transition is furthermore supposed to have weakened the developmental state by undermining its institutional capacity to direct policy change. Democracy, in this respect, should hinder, not facilitate, welfare state development. Finally, theories of economic globalization teach us that the welfare state is in decline. Market fitness and productive efficiency have won out over redistributive equity. In the current era, the race to the bottom in social policy legislation has become the norm.[3] Indeed, welfare is believed to be inimical to economic growth.[4]

Yet the experiences of democratizing Taiwan and South Korea defy these well-reasoned expectations. They suggest that we need to go beyond social, political, and economic determinism. Beginning in the late 1980s, democratic regimes in Taiwan and South Korea increased public social spending and legislated new social welfare programs, creating more socially inclusive regimes. Moreover, social policy reform is no longer motivated by productivist or human capital development goals, as was the case in the not-so-distant past.[5] Rather, policymakers have begun to embrace the idea of welfare as an entitlement by right of citizenship, and they have turned to social policy for the purposes of redistributing wealth.

How can we explain these remarkable—and counterintuitive—developments in Taiwan and South Korea? Policymakers there offer a tentative explanation. According to elite survey data collected in 1999 and 2000, 77 percent of legislators and bureaucrats in Taiwan (n = 111) and 75 percent of elite respondents in Korea (n = 130) agreed with the following statement: "In Taiwan/Korea, there would be no improvement in social welfare without the transition to democracy."[6] Building on this insight, this book offers a political explanation for welfare state development in the region. Specifically, I contend that the politics of democratization fundamentally altered the dynamics of social policymaking in Taiwan and South Korea.

DEMOCRACY AND WELFARE

Public spending in Taiwan and South Korea has increased since the mid-1970s, with the most significant jumps occurring in the late 1980s and into the 1990s, around the time that democratic transition was initiated in both places. In Korea, central government expenditures as a percentage of gross domestic product (GDP) increased from 17.9 percent in 1975 to 21.4 percent twenty years later. Central and provincial government spending in Taiwan increased from 21.4 percent of GDP in 1975 to just over 30 percent in 1995.[7] Though only a rough indicator of state involvement in the financing and delivery of social services, these significant increases in public spending, and their timing, suggest that the democratizing governments in Taiwan and South Korea have taken on a larger role in the provision of public goods, such as in social welfare. They have, in short, become more interventionist, not less, as the globalization and democratization theses would suggest.

When we break down public spending patterns in Taiwan and South Korea by regime, the relationship between democratic reform and increased public spending becomes even clearer. Central government expenditures in South Korea increased from 16.6 percent of GDP under authoritarian president Chun Doo-Hwan (1983–87) to an average of 18.5 percent between 1988 and 1992 under democratically elected Roh

Tae-Woo. After the election of Korea's first civilian president, Kim Young-Sam, public spending rose to 20.4 percent of GDP in the years 1993 to 1997, and again increased substantially to 23.8 percent after Kim Dae-Jung took the presidency in late 1997. We find a similar pattern in Taiwan. Between 1983 and 1988, total government spending averaged 22.1 percent of the GDP. After the introduction of supplemental elections for Taiwan's central legislature in 1989 and with the continued expansion of national and presidential elections, government expenditures jumped to an average of 28.9 percent between 1989 and 1998.[8] Again, though only a crude indicator, the general upward trends in public spending, combined with a proportionate decrease in military expenditures, strongly suggest that the introduction of democracy in Taiwan and South Korea shifted government priorities.[9]

This shift is not just about public spending. Both governments legislated new social welfare programs predicated on the principles of socioeconomic redistribution, social protection, and universal entitlement.[10] The South Korean government implemented an unemployment insurance program in 1995. A national pension program was initiated by the Kim Dae-Jung regime during the late 1990s. The Roh Moo-Hyun regime, elected December 2002, has promised to carry out these reforms. In Taiwan, a new unemployment insurance scheme and a publicly financed old-age assistance program are being implemented. As in Korea, a national pension program is in the works. In short, the more vulnerable sectors of Korean and Taiwanese society have begun to enjoy greater social protection.

In the area of health care policy—arguably the most developed aspect of each emerging welfare regime—governments in Taiwan and South Korea have implemented universal, redistributive, and publicly administered medical insurance programs. Universalizing health care was a major social policy achievement in both places. Universal medical insurance was implemented in South Korea during the late 1980s, almost immediately after President Roh Tae-Woo announced the first direct presidential elections in the summer of 1987. In Taiwan, planning for the National Health Insurance (NHI) program was initiated in 1988, one year after martial law was lifted and just two years after the Democratic Progressive Party (DPP) formed in opposition to the ruling Kuomintang (KMT). Into the 1990s, health care reform in South Korea and Taiwan continued along this same trajectory, with new reform efforts in Korea aimed at increasing redistribution and a concerted resistance to retrenchment in Taiwan.

The deepening of social welfare occurred in Taiwan and South Korea in spite of factors that would seem to mitigate such developments. One might be tempted to conclude that these two cases should simply be dismissed as anomalies. I contend, however, that they are important examples of how the political imperatives of democratic transition can elude the economic logic of globalization and its overdetermined consequences for the welfare state. Cultural expectations of social welfare in Asian societies also do not hold up. The dynamics of welfare reform in Taiwan and South Korea therefore demand a political explanation. Indeed, the fact that major welfare reforms were initiated *after* democratic transition began in Taiwan and South Korea is no coincidence.

This book examines health policy reform in the context of political change, from the authoritarian period through the late 1990s, roughly a decade after democratic breakthrough in Taiwan and South Korea. In these accounts, the introduction of democracy and the dynamics of political change thereafter emerge and reemerge as key variables in health care policy reform. Indeed, the promotion of equity is critical to democracy's chances for survival.[11] Counter to the economic determinism of the globalization thesis, there is a political functionalist imperative that ties together the fates of democracy and the welfare state. The introduction of democracy also reconstitutes politics and thus social policymaking processes. Political competition undermines the insularity of the previously authoritarian states. New actors emerge on the political stage as entrenched hierarchies within the state and between state and society are gradually dismantled with democratic reform. Institutional change creates new strategic contexts in which actors maneuver and new institutional channels through which they can gain access to previously closed policy processes.

Democratic reform also cultivates new expectations for governance and new norms of political legitimacy, particularly when it comes to the aims and goals of the democratic state. In this respect, the developmental state in Taiwan and South Korea is not dead. The objectives of development, however, have been radically redefined through the interaction of state and society. Social welfare has provided a new and legitimate rationale for state intervention. In this way, democracy revalues the state, and for a short time after the moment of democratic breakthrough, the democratizing state enjoys a policy capacity for building democratic legitimacy that even the pressures of globalization cannot overpower. Rather than erode state capacity, democratization can actually revitalize the state. In the cases of Taiwan and South Korea, democratic change has been an effective antidote to economic globalization and related notions of the anachronistic welfare state.

The introduction of democracy clearly mattered for welfare state development in Taiwan and South Korea. However, the arguments developed in this book go beyond what I and others think is the simple teleology of the "democratic class struggle" thesis.[12] The introduction of democracy, broadly conceived, is not a panacea for proponents of social policy reform. As Robert Jackman teaches us, democracies, and the institutions that give shape to democratic governance, are variable across cases and thus weaken the generalized claims of the democratic class struggle thesis.[13] Indeed, it is precisely this variability in the pathways of democratization that has made it difficult for scholars to fashion theories that adequately explain the transition from minimalist conceptions of "procedural democracy" to more equitable forms of "substantive democracy."[14] In terms of theory building, then, this book seeks to identify the factors and sequences that facilitated welfare state formation in Taiwan and South Korea and, in so doing, inductively generate causal connections between democratic change and welfare reform. The comparative scope of this book allows us to examine both similarities and differences between the two countries' experiences in health care policy reform. Its longitudinal scope helps us distill certain pathways of democratic change and social policy reform over time. Using an inductive framework of analysis (introduced in Chapter 2), I develop arguments that provide explanations for welfare reform in Taiwan and South Korea, generate hypotheses to explore in larger comparative settings, and thus offer important lessons for health care policymakers in other national contexts.

HEALTH CARE IN TAIWAN AND SOUTH KOREA

A significant portion of this book is devoted to assessing the details of health care policy outcomes, for policy evaluation is central to and feeds back into the dynamic politics of health care reform. I am especially interested in the degree to which health care policies and programs promote equitable outcomes, and thus I focus on the redistributive consequences of health policy. Given the proportion of annual health care expenditures as a percentage of GDP—around 14 percent in the United States and 6–10 percent among other advanced industrial countries—health care policy as a mechanism for the provision of medical services and the collection and allocation of finances has the potential to be very redistributive. Offsetting the costs of expensive and/or repeated treatments through socialized medicine helps mitigate the effects of income disparities and other determinants of quality of life.[15] This is especially relevant in industrialized Asian countries, such as Taiwan and South Korea, where "graying" populations increasingly depend on public health services.[16]

Equity and Health Policy

Evaluating the equity effects of a given health care system is not an easy or straightforward task. Indeed, "measuring" equity is inextricably tied to subjective perceptions of relative deprivation and socially constructed meanings and values attached to fairness and appropriateness.[17] Evaluating equity, therefore, requires an appreciation of political context, the articulation and legitimation of different ideas, the nature of the deliberative process, and the strategic choices of relevant policy actors. These factors are explored in detail throughout this book. Nonetheless, health policy scholars provide some important tools and concepts with which we can begin to evaluate, from a more general perspective, how different health care systems promote more or less equitable outcomes.[18]

Health policy is all about who pays what and who gets what. Although there are numerous ways to organize the provision of medical care, ranging from fiscal-based systems to private sector markets with little state intervention, the governments of Taiwan and Korea opted for the social insurance model. An important equity dimension in social or health insurance schemes is the degree to which the programs promote social solidarity. Eligibility for insurance coverage, for instance, is one aspect of social solidarity. Certainly, universal coverage is far more equitable than limited or targeted coverage. The extent of coverage, in turn, determines the size of the common pool. Broader, and ideally universal, coverage promotes greater risk pooling among enrollees. Social solidarity encourages the absorption of risk among different occupational categories, age groups, genders, and so on.[19]

A second dimension of equity in health policy, one related to the concept of social solidarity, is the financing of medical care. Single-pipe financing schemes require that all social insurance enrollees pay premiums (contributions) through a single mechanism into one fund whereas multiple-pipe arrangements require enrollees to pay for health care through decentralized insurance carriers. In general, single-pipe insurance schemes more effectively pool risk among different patients and ensure against risk-averse selection, a feature common to multiple-carrier systems. More extensive financial pooling (i.e., through a single-pipe mechanism) encourages vertical redistribution between income groups so that higher-income households subsidize the cost of medical care for lower-income families. The promotion of horizontal equity, or the assurance that those with the same ability to pay contribute the same amount for medical care, is also more easily achieved under single-pipe financing. Governing authorities can standardize contribution rates for the universe of enrollees or standardize such rates among enrollees from the same income group.[20] One must keep in mind, however, that health care systems in which patients pay additional out-of-pocket user fees, which are often regressive, can undermine or negate the equity-enhancing effects of the single-pipe system. This problem has been difficult to resolve in Korea.

Variations in the provision of medical care benefits also determine the degree to which health policy outcomes are more or less equitable. Selecting which benefits are to be covered under health insurance and which are to be excluded usually involves a contested battle between health care purchasers and medical care providers. Patients tend to have little say in these negotiations and instead rely on third-party purchasers (i.e., insurance carriers, government) to make the best possible arrangements on their behalf. The provision of benefits can be exhaustive, comprising all inpatient and outpatient treatments. In other arrangements, however, the scope of coverage can be minimal. In these cases, uninsured treatments are those for which consumers have to pay directly, often at unregulated market prices. As mentioned earlier, the higher the portion of out-of-pocket payments made by patients, the more regressive the health care system. Moreover, in multiple-carrier systems, the range of insured benefits may not be uniform, for the scope of insured benefits depends on the different carriers' (purchasers') specific programs and is, of course, reflected in the enrollees' contributions. Under these arrangements, patients' medical needs are secondary to their ability to pay, compromising equity in health insurance.[21]

These concepts—social solidarity and risk pooling, financial redistribution, and benefits coverage—are revisited throughout this book. Together they make up an important analytical lens through which to examine the politics of health care reform. For the time being, however, their brief introduction is sufficient to help navigate the story of health politics in Taiwan and South Korea.

Three Phases of Reform

Phase 1:   The origins of limited health insurance in Taiwan and South Korea date back to the authoritarian developmental state period. Though they were welfare laggards by comparative standards, the authoritarian states of South Korea and Taiwan were not opposed to the selective, and thus strategic, implementation of some social protection. In Korea, the 1977 Health Insurance Act mandated that all large enterprises (with more than five hundred employees) provide medical insurance to employees and their dependents. Health coverage for state officials commenced a year later. In 1979, the KMT party-state in Taiwan revised the Labor Insurance Law to expand the scope of medical insurance coverage to firms with five or more employees. Government employees already enjoyed health benefits beginning in the late 1950s. Dependents, however, continued to be excluded.

Despite these efforts at gradual expansion in both places, by 1980 only 24 percent of the Korean population and 17 percent of those living in Taiwan were covered by any form of medical insurance. Publicly funded medical aid programs for low-income households were minimal, and eligibility was arbitrarily decided. Consequently, the provision of medical insurance in authoritarian Taiwan and South Korea targeted the relatively well-to-do and key political allies, leaving those who most required health care protection to seek out care in the private—and typically inflated—medical market. The principles of socioeconomic redistribution and universalism did not factor into these early versions of health care policy.

Phase 2:   In comparison with the piecemeal pattern of social policy development during the predemocratic period, health care policy reform beginning in the late 1980s was comprehensive. Proposals for universal health care were introduced in Taiwan and South Korea shortly after democratic reform was initiated. In 1988 and 1989, Korean president Roh Tae-Woo extended medical insurance coverage to self-employed workers in both rural and urban sectors. The universalization of health care coverage resulted from the addition of new medical insurance funds. By the early 1990s, there were hundreds of such funds in operation throughout Korea's cities, countryside, and business enterprises. In Taiwan, the cabinet-level Council for Economic Planning and Development (CEPD) began to work on an integrated (single-pipe) and universal health insurance system in 1988. After years of planning in the CEPD and in the cabinet-level Department of Health (DOH), the National Health

Insurance (NHI) bill was passed by the legislature in the summer of 1994. The universal, centrally administered, and state-subsidized NHI began operating in the spring of 1995.

In both Taiwan and South Korea, health care reform beginning in the late 1980s resulted in the universalization of medical insurance. Despite the obvious similarity in scope of coverage, however, the specific policy outputs and the policy reform processes differed between the two cases. First, in Taiwan the provision of medical insurance was administratively integrated whereas in Korea health care reform contributed to the further decentralization of health insurance administration. Second, the timing of reform varied between the two cases. The extension of medical insurance coverage in South Korea was implemented over a condensed period of time (1988–89) whereas in Taiwan the planning of the NHI spanned seven years (1988–95). Similarities and differences in the Taiwanese and Korean experiences are explored and explained in this book.

Phase 3:   Both democratic governments initiated a third round of policy reform during the late 1990s. In 1998 and 1999, newly elected Korean president Kim Dae-Jung and his ruling party enacted a series of major health policy reforms. After repeated failures to reform the organization of medical insurance throughout the 1980s, President Kim's regime secured the legislative and bureaucratic support to integrate the entire health insurance system. In an effort to increase social solidarity in the provision and financing of medical insurance, the integration reform consolidated all previously autonomous health insurance funds in a single, centralized, publicly administered fund. In Taiwan, on the other hand, a growing deficit in the NHI system and perceived inefficiencies in the public administration of health insurance prompted the KMT government to initiate an effort in 1998 to privatize and marketize the medical insurance system. This reform trajectory in many ways accorded with global trends in rolling back expensive social policy programs. Many in Taiwan, however, feared that the retrenchment reform would nullify the redistributive effects of the single-carrier scheme implemented in 1995. Consequently, opposition from within the bureaucracy, the legislature, and civil society forced the KMT government to backpedal on its proposed reform. In sum, health care reform during the late 1990s resulted in continued deepening of the welfare state in South Korea and resistance to retrenchment in Taiwan. Issues remain, to be sure. For example, the financial stability of medical insurance in both places is still shaky. In Korea, high copay rates and a relatively restricted list of insured medical care services weaken the redistributive impact of health insurance, despite the integration of funds. In both cases, however, the overall direction of welfare reform was sustained during the 1990s.

The course of health care reform in Taiwan and South Korea can be analytically grouped into three distinct phases (see Table 1). Health care reform trajectories in Taiwan and South Korea moved in tandem and in a similar direction, from limited health insurance schemes before democratic transition to universal and redistributive medical insurance programs during the period of democratization. Nevertheless, there were significant variations within each phase, particularly after the initiation of democratic transition (phases 2 and 3). Therefore, two analytical stories need to be told: a more general one that explains the common trajectory toward progressive welfare reform, and a second one that accounts for variations with respect to, first, the timing of reform and, second, specific health policy outputs. I contend that the introduction of democracy influenced the overall directional change in health care reform whereas the variable pathways of democratization specific to Taiwan and South Korea generated variations in policy and policymaking patterns within this common reform trajectory.

EXPLAINING WELFARE REFORM

Conventional theories of the welfare state, derived from the Anglo-European experience, fall short in providing adequate explanations for the recent social policy achievements in Taiwan and South Korea, most notably in the area of health care. Though the insights they offer are important, these theories need to be analytically situated in and thus modified by the politics of democratic change.

TABLE 1.
Phases of Health Care Reform in Taiwan and South Korea

Country	Phase 1: Authoritarian developmentalism	Phase 2: Democratic breakthrough	Phase 3: Democratic deepening
Korea	Limited health insurance (1977)	Universalization and decentralization (1988–89)	Integration and welfare deepening (1998–2000)
Taiwan	Limited health insurance (1979)	Universalization and integration (1988–95)	Failed privatization and resisting retrenchment (1997–99)

The Conventional Explanations

Structural theorists, including both Marxists[22] and proponents of industrial convergence theory,[23] argue that industrial change alters social structural relations, thus requiring the state to play a more proactive role in social welfare. The introduction of new social policies is a functional response to changing economic conditions. Social structural approaches provide some important insights into the dynamics of social policy reform in Taiwan and South Korea. For instance, new social policy innovations emerged after a long period of sustained industrial transformation. A consequence of industrialization in Taiwan and South Korea was the restructuring of political and economic interests among actors in both places, suggesting that industrial change was a necessary condition for welfare state expansion.

The failure of these structural arguments to identify the precise causal mechanisms linking industrial development to welfare reform, however, limits their ability to explain both the specific timing of and variations in social policy outcomes in Taiwan and South Korea.[24] For instance, welfare expansion in Taiwan and South Korea began during the late 1980s even though both economies had experienced rapid growth since the 1960s. In the case of Korea, the universalization of medical insurance was put into place rapidly between 1988 and 1989 whereas planning for Taiwan's National Health Insurance program was drawn out over seven years, beginning in 1988. The logic of industrialism falls short in providing a full explication of this difference in timing. This book contends that such variations can be best explained through a political lens, more specifically through an understanding of the strategic choices actors made at politically fortuitous opportunities for policy change.

Society-centered approaches to welfare, such as "power resources" or "class mobilization" theories, contend that welfare state development is a function of the balance of class power. Peak labor associations and social democratic (or labor-based) parties mobilize workers and other proponents of social policy reform. They pressure governments to enact or expand the scope of social welfare protection, as was the case in many European welfare states.[25] These political-economic conditions have been absent in Taiwan and South Korea, both historically and in the present period. In the past, the geostrategic position of Taiwan and South Korea during the cold war marginalized domestically what was perceived to be leftist rhetoric from mainstream political discourse. The left was never permitted to exist, and was even thought to be unpatriotic, in authoritarian East Asia. The anti-left legacies of the authoritarian developmental state carried over into the recent democratic era. Socioeconomic issues were not central cleavages in the formal political arena. No labor, left-leaning, or social democratic party exists in Taiwan and South Korea. The largest labor associations, Taiwan's China Federation of Labor and the Federation of Korean Trade Unions, were both sanctioned by the state and perceived to be clients of the ruling party. Simply put, there has been little structural basis on which to mobilize class politics in Taiwan and South Korea.

This is not to say that grassroots, bottom-up political mobilization was nonexistent or inconsequential in democratizing East Asia. Democratic breakthrough in Taiwan and Korea, as in many other late democratizers, was the product of intense societal mobilization. Such mobilization was also instrumental in welfare state deepening in Taiwan and Korea, particularly during the late 1990s. However, the dynamics of political participation in the social policymaking process were ultimately shaped by their specific developmental contexts. Late economic development meant that the working classes in industrial East Asia (and in Latin America) were much more diversified, and thus less unified, than their earlier European counterparts.[26] The absence of any institutionalized left, either in the formal political arena or within civil society, constrained opportunities for welfare state mobilization. Class-based mobilization—or any basis of political mobilization, for that matter—depended on strategic opportunities for political participation, which were in turn constituted by the specific dynamics of democratic change in Taiwan and South Korea.[27]

State-centric theories of welfare development assume the state to be the agent of policy change and therefore the key unit of analysis. The state drives social welfare reform through consensus-building among the executive, the legislative branch, and the bureaucracy. The process of crafting such a consensus is shaped by the different institutional arrangements both within the state apparatus and between the state and society. In other words, social welfare outcomes are determined by state interests, as they are filtered through the decision-making institutions of the state (and society).[28] The statist perspective on East Asian development dates back to the Japanese colonial period.

For instance, according to Huck-Ju Kwon and Yeun-Wen Ku, the Japanese colonial state in both Taiwan and South Korea used social policy as an instrument for creating social dependencies on the state, particularly among those in need of social "relief." There was little concern on the part of the Japanese rulers over socioeconomic redistribution, and not surprisingly, they were outright hostile toward notions of social citizenship. However, the Japanese colonial state, though extractive in its motives, promoted infrastructural development in Taiwan and South Korea, including the modernization of medical sciences and health care more generally. The first modern medical school in Taiwan, and still the most prestigious, was founded by the Japanese authorities.[29] During the postwar period, the developmental states in Taiwan and South Korea were celebrated as the paragon of institutional coherence and state-directed industrialization. These developmental states, however, were primarily interested in maximizing aggregate economic output, which they achieved by minimizing societal participation in industrial and economic policymaking processes.[30] The little social policy reform carried out in this period, particularly in the areas of education and health, was for the purposes of human capital, and thus economic, development.[31]

The state-centric approach is again useful in understanding recent efforts at welfare reform in Taiwan and South Korea. The state was a key actor in determining recent health care reforms in both places. However, where this approach falls short is in explaining why the postwar development states' policy priorities changed, moving away from strictly high-growth objectives toward redistributive social policy (the end of the Japanese era is more easily explained by Japan's defeat in World War II and its subsequent exit from Taiwan and South Korea). In other words, statist explanations have to account for how new political and policy goals are generated in the first place. State-centric explanations for the emerging welfare states in Taiwan and South Korea, I contend, need to be situated in the larger context of democratic change. With democratic change, institutions are reformed, policy networks reworked, and incentives restructured, and thus policy priorities are changed.

Democratization and Social Policymaking

How exactly does democratization matter, then? The study of democracy and economic equality is not new and has been approached from a variety of social science disciplines. Comparative studies have tended to draw from cross-national statistical data, relying on imprecise though quantifiable measures of democracy to deduce relationships between political democracy and socioeconomic equality. In this comparative approach, any elaboration on the precise causal mechanism or causal logic linking democracy and equity is usually absent. As Steve Chan puts it, "The actual policy medium *through which* one attribute (democracy) is supposed to influence another attribute (equality) is often unspecified."[32]

To provide a political explanation for social welfare development in Taiwan and South Korea, therefore, I focus on the impact of democratic change on social policymaking. For example, democratization affects what policy ideas are debated, how social problems are defined, and how decisions are ultimately made. It determines which actors participate in the policy process and how contending interests are represented and contested. Political change often entails a redistribution of power and policy authority. The politics of democratic transition and its potential impact on policymaking processes open up new opportunities for social welfare policy change.

Democratization is a dynamic process. The transition from authoritarian rule to democracy involves a sequence of political (and policy) events. To understand the impact of democratization on policymaking processes, we need therefore to appreciate the temporal reality of political change. The politics of authoritarian breakdown and democratic breakthrough, democratic crafting, and democratic consolidation in the longer term need to be considered sequentially so that their different effects on social policymaking *over time* are not glossed over and are indeed built into the larger explanation. The arguments developed in this book are organized around different stages of political change in Taiwan and South Korea. In reality, these stages are seamless. For our analytical purposes, however, they serve as useful temporal markers. They also coincide nicely with the different phases of health care reform in the two cases.

First, under the authoritarian developmental state, the presidential office in Korea and the KMT party leadership in Taiwan dominated the politics of social policymaking. A shared collective goal among these elite policymakers for rapid economic growth throughout the postwar period ensured vertical coordination and horizontal cooperation within the state apparatus. Redistributive social welfare was understood by these elites to be counterproductive to economic growth. Legislative bodies were in effect rubber stamps and civil society was suppressed, meaning that policymaking networks were small, exclusive, and politically insulated. Social policy reform was thus gradual, piecemeal, and directed from the top down.

Social policy change under the authoritarian states also conformed to a pattern of "crisis and selective compensation." Efforts made toward social policy reform were always in response to a political crisis of legitimacy for the authoritarian regime. Furthermore, social policy compensation tended to target those groups of people who were deemed important to the state, particularly in its interest for political survival. Social policy reform was hardly universal in scope, and it was never intended to promote wealth redistribution. The consequences of this strategy of crisis and selective compensation were highly problematic in that its beneficiaries—civil servants and industrial workers in large firms—were the relatively well-to-do. In this respect, social policy reform not only failed to provide social protection for the vulnerable but also exacerbated preexisting inequities by redistributing benefits back to privileged clients of the authoritarian regime.

Second, the moment of democratic breakthrough was a major turning point in social policy reform, contributing to the universalization of health care. Though the health policymaking process continued to be dominated by the incumbent Roh Tae-Woo regime in Korea and the KMT party in Taiwan, the decision to undertake such a radical reform was, in the first place, a strategic response to the new logic of political competition. These regimes, which had opposed the idea of universal social welfare during the authoritarian developmental state period, were no longer insulated from outside political pressures. They now needed to win support. The implications of this change were not trivial. Anticipating challenges from emerging opposition parties and a revitalized civil society, President Roh and the KMT *preemptively* initiated the universalization of health care during the late 1980s.

In Korea, the Roh regime needed to retain electoral support in the countryside and among workers in the cities. The government thus extended medical insurance benefits to both rural and urban self-employed workers just before and after legislative elections in 1988. The KMT government in Taiwan positioned itself as a catchall party in order to take away political support from the social democratic factions of the opposition Democratic Progressive Party (DPP). It thus began planning for the National Health Insurance program soon after the DPP was formed and one year after martial law was lifted. Democratic breakthrough mattered most in Taiwan and South Korea by redirecting the trajectory of social policy reform toward universalism. In this way, the institutionalization of political competition, specifically the threat of anticipated competition from an emerging opposition, had a tremendous impact on social policy agenda setting.

Third, the dynamics of health care reform during the late 1990s were very different from the patterns of health care policymaking of the late 1980s and even through the early 1990s. There were some similarities, though, particularly in the central role that political competition and the imperatives of maintaining popular support played in shaping policymaking decisions. The Kim Dae-Jung regime in Korea, for instance, responded to societal demands for greater redistribution in health care by legislating the landmark medical insurance integration reform in 1999. In 1998, the KMT government in Taiwan was forced to retract its health insurance privatization reform after it was unable to craft any sort of consensus in favor of the reform within state and society. Ironically, the 1997 Asian financial crisis prompted popular demands for expanding social safety nets rather than scaling them back. Economic insecurity combined with political mobilization in the streets and at the ballot box opened an important window of opportunity for social welfare deepening.

Where this third phase of health care reform differed from earlier patterns was in the degree of inclusiveness in the reform process. Indeed, democratic politics in the late 1990s differed significantly from the way democratic politics had played out earlier. The legalization of associational life, the strengthening of national legislatures, and the opening up of new institutional channels into the state apparatus were functions of democratic reform, though many of these opportunities were not fully realized by policy activists early in the transition process. By the late 1990s, however, previously marginalized actors in Taiwan and South Korea—such as civil society groups, legislators, and professional bureaucrats—emerged as important partners in the policy process. Political learning and adaptation among actors, in addition to the learning of policy expertise over time, facilitated a more contested and thus more representative policymaking process during the late 1990s. In short, welfare deepening in Korea and the politics of resisting retrenchment in Taiwan were the products of substantively democratic policymaking.

Finally, woven into the dynamic politics of democratic change and health policy reform throughout the late 1980s and 1990s was an important ideational shift among dominant actors in Taiwan and South Korea regarding the normative place of social welfare in the democratic developmental state. Ongoing democratic reform in both places involved a discursive process in which new core values and ideas were contested and consequently legitimated in the political mainstream. This sort of contestation was nonexistent during the authoritarian developmental state period, when alternative conceptions of social policy, particularly those that challenged the growth-first developmental ethos of the time, were suppressed. New ideational frameworks were made possible only in democracy. By the 1990s, development was no longer seen as solely about rapid and aggregate economic growth. Rather, new normative

understandings of redistributive social welfare and democratic governance created new expectations for economic growth with equity among
political actors in both Taiwan and South Korea. It was against this
ideational backdrop that the integration reform in Korea and the resistance to retrenchment in Taiwan were legitimated as appropriate and
also politically expedient policy solutions.

LOOKING AHEAD IN THE BOOK

Chapter 2 develops an analytical framework with which we can make better sense of how social policies are made in the context of democratization. By drawing on theories of politics and policy, the inductive
framework offers an analytical structure to help organize the empirical
evidence from Taiwan and South Korea. It also guides the analysis toward
theory building. Here I look at the role of ideas and interests in policymaking, for policy actors, and in network analysis, and the emergence of
political opportunities for policy change. Two important considerations
are built into the analytical framework, which differentiate it from conventional public policy approaches. First, democratization is understood
as a *variable process of change* that entails both similarities and differences
between national experiences.[33] Second, democratic transformation
involves *continual change*. Democratization is not simply a moment of
political rupture, and it must therefore be analyzed as a dynamic process
of change over time.[34]

   Chapters 3 to 6 highlight the empirical details of health care reform
in Taiwan and South Korea, from the authoritarian developmental state
period to the 1990s. Through a detailed exposition of health care reform
processes in different political settings, these chapters point to the relationship between political change and continually changing patterns of
social policymaking. Chapter 3 examines the origins of health insurance
in authoritarian Taiwan and South Korea. Here I contend that the
authoritarian developmental state used social policy for political objectives, not for people's actual welfare needs. Chapter 4 investigates the
processes that led to the universalization of medical insurance after the
moment of democratic breakthrough in Taiwan and South Korea. Chapters 5 and 6 focus on the third phase of health care reform, first in South
Korea and then in Taiwan. Chapter 5 explains how the Kim Dae-Jung
regime in Korea took advantage of certain windows of opportunity to legislate health insurance integration in 1999. Chapter 6 examines the

KMT's failure during the late 1990s to promulgate its marketization and privatization proposal despite strong political, economic, and ideological pressures favoring such a reform.

Chapters 7 and 8 refocus on theory building. In Chapter 7, I look at the processes of ideational change in the context of democratization. Drawing on theories of spatial voting, issue realignment, and social constructionism, I argue that democratic change provided both the ideational space and strategic incentives for political entrepreneurs in Taiwan and South Korea to introduce and, in turn, legitimate new ideas about social policy and social justice more broadly. They mainstreamed the idea of welfare so that by the late 1990s, "development" in Taiwan and South Korea was no longer solely about aggregate economic growth but also about the distributive consequences of such growth. In conclusion, Chapter 8 brings together the empirical evidence to form theoretical arguments about the relationship between democratization and social welfare reform. While recognizing other factors that facilitated social policy change in Taiwan and South Korea, this chapter offers a set of theoretical propositions about how democratic transition contributed to welfare deepening in both cases. The chapter ends by revisiting the globalization thesis, arguing that the politics of democratic breakthrough can be an effective antidote to the economic logic of globalization and the presumed death of the welfare state. I end by arguing that democracy in East Asia has actually strengthened the state.

CHAPTER 2

A DYNAMIC POLICYMAKING FRAMEWORK

This chapter develops a framework of analysis to explore the relationship between democratization and social policymaking, with the aim of drawing out potential causal connections between the processes of political change and specific patterns of health care reform. Ideally, one would like to have a set of hypotheses to test in the context of democratizing Taiwan and South Korea. However, the paucity of theory that looks expressly at the impact of political change on social policy reform prohibits such a deductive framework of analysis.[1] I therefore take a more inductive approach to understanding and explaining the interrelated dynamics of political change and social policy reform. In this way, the arguments developed in this book, and the analytical framework that helps form these arguments, should be of interest to those examining similar questions in other regions of the world.

This is not to say that the ensuing analysis is without theoretical guidance. The analytical framework developed in this chapter incorporates insights from theories of democratization, comparative public policy, and welfare state development. Together this integrative framework sorts out the empirical details of the two cases. Its comparative scope illuminates both similarities and differences in the experiences of Taiwan and South Korea. Its temporal scope helps us make sense of the causal relationships between political change and social policy reform over time. It allows us to explore the politics of social policymaking in authoritarian regimes as well as in the changing (and variable) contexts of democratic transformation in Taiwan and South Korea. Sequencing and chronology are important for distilling causality.

I begin with an elaboration of the different parts of the analytical framework used to illuminate the politics of health care reform in Taiwan and South Korea. I then put the pieces together to formulate what I call a dynamic policymaking framework.

AGENDA SETTING: PROBLEMS AND SOLUTIONS

Policymaking involves, on the one hand, the identification of social, economic, and political problems that need to be addressed and, on the other, the persuasive articulation of solutions that can solve them. John Kingdon offers this observation about problem recognition in the policy agenda-setting process: "There is a difference between a condition and a problem. . . . Conditions become defined as problems when we come to believe that we should do something about them."[2] In other words, problems do not a priori exist; they have to be identified and articulated by political actors. Problems must first move from political irrelevance onto the larger political agenda and then onto more narrowly defined government decision-making agendas. In order for issues to reach the policy agenda, they need to be, in the least, politically salient.

Moving from obscurity to a place on the policy agenda is not at all automatic. Problems gain the attention of policymakers most effectively when available solutions are attached to the identified problems. In the area of health care, for example, problems related to social inequity demand certain solutions whereas perceived problems in systemic efficiency may divert attention to other solutions. Just as policymakers need to be convinced that a problem exists in the first place, solutions need to be convincing in their claims to address the identified problem. Yet solutions to problems are seldom self-evident. Problems and solutions are most effectively linked through the articulation of causal stories. According to Deborah Stone, "policy debate is dominated by the notion that to solve a problem, one must find its root cause or causes."[3] Only through an understanding of the causes of a given problem can we craft remedies that best neutralize that cause or set of causes. Causal stories linking problems and solutions are the stuff of politics. They are the bases of debate, both in the larger political arena and within specific policy communities. Stories reflect actors' ideological positions, material interests in a certain policy area, and ideas about what is right or wrong, acceptable or unacceptable.

The political and policy implications of causal stories are not trivial, particularly those stories that become dominant in any given policy arena. First, the articulation of certain causal stories draws attention to social, political, or economic problems for which attention may have previously been low. Stories set reform agendas. Second, because causal stories necessarily identify the "causers" of certain problems, they direct responsibility to, and demand accountability from, particular political actors or political circumstances. They imply blame. Third, by locating the cause of a given problem, stories can "legitimate and empower particular actors as fixers" of the problem, potentially reconstituting preexisting social, economic, or political institutions.[4] Fourth, the articulation and contestation of causal stories have a funneling effect on policy debates, narrowing the range of feasible alternatives within a given issue area. In these ways, convincing stories, or those that make it from the larger political agenda to the actual decision-making agenda, are the sources of policy change.

Battles fought over contending stories determine how and why policies change (or do not change). The receptivity of powerful political actors to contending causal stories determines how far policy ideas will ultimately travel along the policy process. Policymaking is about persuading others that one's own causal story about problems and solutions is the right one. At a technical level, persuasion and argumentation involve a "complex blend of factual statements and subjective evaluations . . . with mathematical and logical deductions . . . statistical, empirical and analogical inferences, references to expert opinion, estimates of benefits and costs, and caveats and provisos of different kinds."[5] In real-world politics, the persuasiveness of a certain causal story depends also on one's individual skills in the arts of argumentation and an appropriate forum in which to articulate such stories. Power and influence in policymaking are therefore multifaceted and realized within certain political contexts.

This book asks why and how certain causal stories come to be dominant. Specifically, this book is concerned with why and how certain causal stories came to be so dominant in Taiwan and South Korea as to effect real policy change in health care and social welfare more generally. This line of inquiry is especially significant because empirical research shows that existing policies are hard to change.[6] The consideration of new and dominant causal stories is rare. New causal stories, when they do emerge, may do so precisely because they in fact reinforce the policy status quo.

Entrenched interests in past policy decisions and institutional path dependency make the costs of change prohibitively high.[7] Furthermore, evaluating the merits of any new causal story is difficult, given the malleability of evidence in the social world, disparities in actors' abilities to be persuasive, and the inherent difficulties of changing people's minds.[8] Policy networks and the rules that govern how policy stories are contested tend to remain stable and thus resistant to new renditions and stories about problems and solutions.[9]

Although major policy change is rare, it is not impossible. In Taiwan and South Korea, universal and equitable health care evolved from a politically marginalized idea under authoritarian rule (and one that was off the policy agenda) to a salient political issue and ultimately a central issue in health policy debates during democratic transition. In both places, the introduction of universal health care came during the late 1980s and early 1990s after decades of limited and targeted health insurance provision. The implementation of Taiwan's National Health Insurance (NHI) program in 1995 involved the complete restructuring of the pre-existing social insurance scheme. In South Korea, the expansion of medical insurance in 1988 and 1989 under President Roh Tae-Woo resulted in the universalization of health care. During the late 1990s, the Korean government under President Kim Dae-Jung legislated the financial and administration integration of health insurance, a reform proposal that had been discussed for nearly twenty years, though repeatedly dismissed by earlier health care policymakers. At around the same time, efforts by the Kuomintang (KMT) government in Taiwan to privatize and marketize the cash-strapped NHI were rejected. The idea of health insurance integration and a belief in the ability of integrated medical insurance systems to promote socioeconomic redistribution compelled political actors to push for reform in South Korea and to resist the government's retrenchment reform in Taiwan. Why did these new stories about problems and solutions emerge when they did? How did these particular stories become the focal point of health policy reform debates in democratizing Taiwan and South Korea?

INTERESTS AND IDEAS

Interests determine political behavior. Actors behave in ways that maximize their individual or group interests. Their interests are constituted by their location within the larger structures of society, economy, and polity. Class position, social status, and access to the centers of political decision making, for instance, determine individual (and group) interests in political battles and policy debates. Accordingly, interests shape actors' conceptions of problems and solutions and determine which causal stories are more compelling. Profit-maximizing businesses, for instance, may be less likely to recognize problems of poverty if the attached solution is to increase corporate taxation for the purposes of funding new social programs. Legitimate welfare recipients may ignore the problem of welfare fraud if the proposed solution is to scale back social services.

Interest-based arguments, particularly those that focus on material interests, have greatly influenced theories explaining the politics of the welfare state. For instance, industrial transformation and the emergence of modern economies create a new working class, disrupt traditional family roles in social protection, and thus generate a functional interest for the state-sponsored provision of social welfare. Neo-Marxist theories of modern welfare regimes contend that state interests in reproducing labor and quelling worker unrest compelled otherwise unwilling states to promote social welfare. Social democratic or class-politics approaches to the welfare state contend that the size, resources, and mobilization of working-class interests were responsible for the rise of the postwar welfare state in Europe. The institutional context in which class mobilization takes place is important, though institutional variables do not override the underlying interest-based assumption of these theories.[10] That interests, and specifically material or class interests, have figured so centrally in the debate on the welfare state should come as no surprise given that social policy is about conflicts over material distribution and redistribution. In battles over social welfare policy, and health policy more specifically, there are winners, and they come at the expense of losers.[11]

Interests and interest-based arguments offer a compelling rationale as to why policies are so slow to change, if they change at all. The institutionalization of a particular policy entrenches certain interest coalitions in favor of maintaining that policy.[12] The logic of path dependency reasons that institutions, the policies that create them, and the interests invested in them together prevent change. Yet, as alluded to earlier, policies and institutions do change. Economic structural realignments may disrupt the prior interest-based equilibrium. For instance, the changing structure of the labor market and actors' location in the economic division of labor can reconstitute the ways that material interests organize and mobilize around economic, political, and social issues. Political change and actors' relocation in decision-making processes also matter. Changing institutional contexts mediate purely interest-based arguments. Democratic transition, for example, is a major catalyst for institutional reform.

One cannot underestimate the impact of ideas on policymaking processes.[13] Ideational factors do not subsume, nor are they necessarily causally prior to, interest-based arguments. Yet in some instances, ideas can be in tension with prevailing material interests and thus set in motion the dynamics of policy change. Ideational change in Taiwan and South Korea regarding the appropriate place of social welfare and related understandings of democratic governance were instrumental in legitimating new health care reform initiatives. The move from targeted social policy to universal and redistributive conceptions of social welfare was emblematic of, and later reinforced by, such an ideational change.

Max Weber's metaphor of ideas as "switchmen" that alter the course of policymaking provides a different, though not entirely uncomplementary, perspective on purely interest-based explanations of politics. Several scholars have taken to this approach, coming up with their own conceptualizations of ideas and their impact on politics and policy. Judith Goldstein and Robert Keohane define principled beliefs as "consist[ing] of normative ideas that specify criteria for distinguishing right from wrong and just from unjust . . . they translate fundamental doctrines into guidance for contemporary human action."[14] Ideas define the criteria for notions of appropriateness and legitimacy in politics and policymaking. Robert Henry Cox elaborates on this when he writes that there is "cause for policy reform when actors change the conceptual discourse in an area of policy, establishing new grounds for evaluating the legitimacy of policy proposals."[15] Ideas need not supplant the primacy of interests in determining political behavior. Indeed, interests that "fit" with dominant ideas in a given polity stand a better chance of being accepted by decision makers. Ideational consensus within political society may in fact reinforce already dominant interests. Yet ideas can also be in tension with interests, particularly those interests entrenched in specific political, economic, or social arrangements. It is precisely this tension that can lead to political and/or policy change.

In this book, I look at the role of ideas in shaping causal stories in the health care policymaking process. I treat ideas as interpretive frameworks through which actors understand problems and solutions.[16] As argued in the previous section, problems are not conditions stripped of their social meaning. Problems only come to be problems when they are recognized by actors willing and able to articulate them. Problems are not facts, they are *social facts,* such that, according to Michael Howlett and M. Ramesh, "even if the policymakers agree on the existence of a problem, they may not share the same understanding of its causes or ramifications."[17] Causal stories are therefore *portrayals* or *representations* of problems and their appropriate solutions. They are never statements of irrefutable fact. The articulation of new stories, reflective of new ideas about problems and solutions, reshapes the terms of policy debates. Ideas imply what is acceptable, and as a result, what is politically possible, and in strategic terms, what is politically expedient.

Because I am interested in the politics of social welfare, the examination of contested understandings of equity and the appropriate place of equity in social, economic, and political arrangements is central to this book. Equity, fairness, and justice are experiential phenomena, grounded in empirical reality though realized only in their social contexts.[18] Problems of poverty and socioeconomic disparity depend less on statistical accounts of the distribution of wealth and more on the degree to which society is willing to tolerate such a distribution. Equity, socioeconomic justice, and by extension social welfare are therefore legitimated by shared notions of appropriateness.[19] To restate an earlier point, problems of socioeconomic justice, and therefore the appropriate place of social policy in resolving these problems, are not conditions. Objective measures of income distribution, for example, provide only one vantage point for understanding equity. Ideas, I suggest, inform how actors deal with these "facts."

During the period of authoritarian rule in Taiwan and South Korea, state leaders held to very narrow conceptualizations of social, economic, and political development. Economic backwardness was identified as the key problem. Therefore, policies geared toward rapid economic development were deemed the most appropriate solutions. The idea of rapid growth, and indeed, growth at all costs, was dominant among key policy decision makers. Equity was understood not in relational terms but rather in absolute terms. Economic policies were narrowly aimed at the alleviation of poverty and not redistributive justice. In fact, the reach of social policy was limited to political clients of the authoritarian regime, or to those "productive" sectors of society deemed integral to the developmental state's economic project. Redistributive social policy had little standing in that particular conception of development. Policymakers believed that universal social policy was costly, an inefficient use of resources, and a breeding ground for laziness and social apathy. Redistributive social policy was therefore understood to be inimical to economic growth.

The moment of democratic breakthrough prompts a sort of cognitive "unlocking." New actors emerge, and new expectations about development are articulated in the democratizing body politic. Democracy promotes the contestation of ideas and thus new conceptions of socioeconomic equity.[20] Democratic transition was an important turning point in people's understanding of the developmental state in East Asia. New beliefs about the place of social welfare in development and related ideas of legitimate governance emerged from this growing ideational marketplace in Taiwan and South Korea.[21] Problems of economic distribution and social stratification became a part of mainstream political debate, a debate that also increasingly extended beyond the narrow confines of state-level policy networks. Concepts such as "democratic citizenship" and "social rights" were introduced as part of a common and increasingly legitimate political language and discourse.[22] This ideational shift, I argue, created an important backdrop for major social policy innovation in Taiwan and South Korea during the period of democratization.

ACTORS AND NETWORKS

This section examines how causal stories are articulated in political and policy battles. More specifically, I develop a framework for identifying who participates in health care policymaking and for evaluating who matters in the process.

Most often, the bureaucracy, especially those ministries that deal explicitly with health and welfare, is the central actor in health care policymaking. Other branches in the bureaucracy sometimes become involved at certain stages of the policy process. Both the executive and the legislature play critical roles in initiating and deliberating health care reform. Health care policymaking also involves the participation of, or at the least incites responses from, actors outside the formal state apparatus. Policy experts, academics, and researchers who are valued for their specialized knowledge can have a major impact on policy outcomes, as they often shape how actors understand social and scientific problems in the first place.[23] Various societal, nongovernmental groups and movements also have a stake in health policy outcomes. Some groups enjoy a great deal of access to the policymaking process whereas others mobilize on the margins.[24] Though the health policy arena tends to involve fewer actors than other policy areas—largely because of the complexity of the issues and the inability of many actors, both inside and outside the state, to engage the decision-making process—the range of possible actors interested in health care policy can be quite expansive.[25] For the analyst, this situation can appear very messy.

Ever since Peter Katzenstein first used the metaphor *networks* in a 1977 article,[26] similar conceptual frameworks have emerged in the study of politics and policy, including iron triangles,[27] issue networks,[28] advocacy coalitions,[29] policy subsystems,[30] civic networks,[31] and associative networks.[32] Common to each of these unique approaches is the notion that the dynamics of policy change involve patterned interaction within a network of state and society actors who have a stake in a particular policy area. A common stake among actors does not mean, however, that actors hold similar conceptions about problems and their appropriate solutions. Networks are the sites of tremendous conflict for contending causal stories and intense political battles between their articulators.

The network metaphor is a useful heuristic tool for sorting out the many actors involved in any given policy domain. First, it is important to identify who is in the policy network and who is outside it. In other words, network analysis helps us evaluate the inclusiveness or exclusiveness of a given policy network. Second, networks tend to revolve around a core set of decision makers. For instance, the core of the health policy network is often the functional equivalent of the health and welfare ministry. Locating the core and periphery of a given policy network is helpful for explaining the drivers of policy change. Third, network analysis not only tells us who is "in" and who is "out" but also illuminates the spatial distribution of actors inside the network boundaries. It is important to know where the different actors are within a network: where they are located in relation to one another and with respect to the core of the policy network.[33] Fourth, network analysis shows how actors cluster within a given policy network. Actors do not float randomly. Rather, they form alliances, or what Paul Sabatier calls "advocacy coalitions."[34] Identifying these alliances is crucial to understanding the dynamics of policy contestation. Fifth, policy networks are structured by variable institutional arrangements, and participation in policymaking is mediated by these contexts. Internal to the network, institutions constitute the rules of the game by which policy decisions are reached. Externally, these institutions determine the extent to which networks are insulated from or open to outside influence. The institutionalization of political competition—through elections, for instance—expands the scope of possible pressures acting on any given policy network.

As a heuristic tool, network analysis gives us a snapshot of the actors involved in policymaking at a certain moment in time. Comparative network analysis highlights both variations and similarities in how policy networks operate across cases. For example, policymaking among the various East Asian authoritarian developmental states was very similar despite their unique historical and political circumstances. In terms of who was "in," the developmental state in Taiwan and South Korea before the 1980s was very exclusionary. Policymakers were institutionally insulated from outside political pressures, and the number of actors in any policy network was quite small. The core of the policy network was even more exclusive, limited to only a handful of technocratic elites from bureaucratic pilot agencies. The closeness between the authoritarian political leadership and high-ranking bureaucratic officials—or more precisely, the absence of any significant distinction between the ruling party and the state apparatus—meant that the political elite dictated policy outcomes. There were few alliance clusters within these networks. Indeed, vertical coordination through the presidential office in Korea and the KMT leadership in Taiwan ensured little contestation in social policy networks.

Although network analysis provides a snapshot of a specific policy community, policy networks are not static. Networks are dynamic arrangements, and we therefore need to account for change.[35] Generally speaking, democratic transition causes gradual network change. In democratizing Taiwan and South Korea, social policy networks became increasingly less insulated from outside political pressure. The introduction of elections and the institutionalization of political competition during the early stages of democratic transition in Taiwan and South Korea were critical in this regard. The emergence of new actors, relaxed rules for network participation, and strategic political entrepreneurship resulted in more porous health policy networks during the late 1990s. Social policy networks, therefore, only became more inclusive in terms of the number and range of participants over time. Assertive legislators and mobilized social movement groups in Taiwan facilitated a greater societal presence in social policy debates in the latter half of the 1990s. Similarly, in Korea, it was not until the Kim Dae-Jung era of the late 1990s that a maturing civil society outside the state apparatus was able to penetrate elite circles and thus influence health policymaking.

Democratic change over time results in network "boundary shifts."[36] It needs to be stressed, however, that network change resulting from democratic breakthrough is not a one-time occurrence, just as democratic reform in any country is never a fait accompli at the moment of transition. The causal impact of political change on network change is not instantaneous.[37] Expectations that the moment of democratic breakthrough—especially when the ancien régime is able to stay in the democratic game—will automatically result in a radical restructuring of existing policy networks are neither realistic nor substantiated by the experiences of democratizing Taiwan and South Korea. In those cases, the introduction of political competition meant, on the one hand, that social policy networks were no longer insulated from outside political pressures. On the other hand, the internal dynamics of the health care policy network remained unchanged, at least in the short term. After all, the incumbent authoritarian regimes were able to win founding elections in both Taiwan and South Korea. It was not until the mid to late 1990s that the internal composition of health policy networks in both places was significantly altered. In other words, the shape, size, and insularity of these networks during the late 1990s were different from network dynamics that emerged at the moment of democratic breakthrough in the late 1980s, just as they were different from those of the earlier period of authoritarian rule. It is crucial, therefore, to think of network change as a dynamic process, one that mirrors the dynamism inherent to democratization. The reconstitution of policy networks and their linkages to the larger political arena involves a continuous process of change.

OPPORTUNITIES FOR POLICY CHANGE

In order for policies to change, there must be an opportunity for actors to articulate new policy ideas, to mobilize political support, and to participate in the decision-making process. According to Kingdon, policy change—or as he puts it, "when an idea's time has come"—depends on the opening of a fortuitous window of opportunity.[38] John C. Campbell argues that policy change occurs only when "a choice opportunity opens up, in the sense that enough energy becomes available in some situation to overcome inertia, so something new becomes possible."[39] The absence of these opportunities makes innovative policy reform difficult. The example of the authoritarian developmental states in Taiwan and South Korea demonstrates this point.

During the authoritarian period in Taiwan and South Korea, social policy reform, and health care reform more specifically, was piecemeal. There were no major innovations in social policy ideas. Indeed, there were few opportunities for alternative social policy stories to emerge and to rival the authoritarian regimes and their goal of rapid and aggregate economic growth. Socioeconomic equity was understood by policymakers in terms of poverty alleviation, not redistribution, leaving little space for any social policy innovation. Furthermore, political and civil society was demobilized. The crackdown on opposition parties and the outright ban on nongovernmental groups undermined the organizational basis for contending health (and social) policy reform advocates. Even where alternative ideas for health policy reform existed within the state apparatus, actors lacked the policy expertise to articulate in concrete terms the design of new health care systems. In sum, the highly centralized institutions of governance characteristic of authoritarian regimes closed any institutional opportunities for contending policy ideas to emerge.

Even in democratic political systems, opportunities for policy change are few. And if policy change does occur, reform tends to be incremental and conservative in its trajectory. However, I contend that the politics of democratization provides a unique set of opportunities for policy change. According to Sidney Tarrow, "changes in political opportunity structure result from the opening up of access to power, from shifts in ruling alignments, from the availability of influential allies and from cleavages within and among elites."[40]

Exogenous Windows of Opportunity

Exogenous shocks, or events outside a given policy area, can provide opportunities for policy change. Kingdon refers to these external shocks as "focusing events."[41] Exogenous events—such as a terrorist attack, plane crash, financial meltdown, campaign promise, or corporate scandal—spark a "Pearl Harbor" effect whereby an unexpected but catalytic event ignites a burst of policy activity.[42] These sorts of events are, by their nature, unpredictable. Moreover, although they may in the end implicate a certain policy area, their origins are often external to that particular policy community.

In her comparative study of health care reform in Britain, Canada, and the United States, Carolyn Hughes Tuohy argues that the timing of policy change is "determined largely by factors beyond the health care arena in the broader political system."[43] Sabatier elaborates on this point by distinguishing between what he calls "stable parameters" of a policy subsystem and "dynamic system events." For Sabatier, stable parameters include the unchanging distribution of influence among actors, institutional structures, and socioeconomic conditions. Dynamic events, on the other hand, comprise changes to technology and knowledge, reconfigurations in the distribution of resources between actors, and turnovers in government administrations. These sorts of events destabilize prior parameters, thus providing opportunities for significant policy change. Like Tuohy, Sabatier emphasizes that these dynamic events are external and often unrelated to specific policy domains.[44] Exogenous opportunities are the result of fortuitous accidents.

Beginning around the late 1980s, several exogenous opportunities for health policy change opened up in Taiwan and South Korea. Above all, democratic breakthrough—with the legalization of civil society, the introduction of political competition, and the elimination of authoritarian mechanisms for command and control over society—was a significant political shock that offered new possibilities for social policy reform and health care reform more specifically. Administrative turnovers in Taiwan and South Korea were major political events as well. Although the election of new governments in consolidated democracies is quite commonplace, the significance of these turnovers in consolidating democracies is magnified. The election of Kim Dae-Jung to the Korean presidency in 1997 was a key factor in the medical insurance integration legislation. Similarly, the presidential contests in Taiwan between incumbent KMT president Lee Teng-Hui and opposition candidates shaped the course of health care reform during the late 1990s. The election of Chen Shui-Bian to the presidency in 2000 established social policy reform as a key issue in Taiwan's mainstream politics.

The 1997 Asian financial crisis, an event unrelated to health policy, renewed debates about health care and social policy reform more generally in both Taiwan and South Korea. The crisis prompted the Kim Dae-Jung regime to recast labor and business relations, contributing to the strengthening of social welfare policy. Though Taiwan was less hard hit by the Asian financial crisis, policymakers there learned too that social protection made good political sense in an increasingly volatile world economy. The financial crisis was understood in both places to be a consequence of economic globalization, but it was also believed that the proper response on the part of the state should be the broadening of social safety nets. As a window of opportunity for reform, then, political entrepreneurs in both places exploited the 1997 crisis and thus effectively pushed their social policy reform agendas in the direction of deepening rather than retrenchment.

Policy Learning

Opportunities for policy change can also emerge because of factors directly related to a specific policy domain, that is, they can be endogenous to a policy area. In this respect, policy learning facilitates policy change. Policy learning involves actors' cognitive capacities in identifying problems, understanding causal stories, finding solutions, and evaluating policy outcomes. The development of policy expertise, the proliferation of knowledge, and the formation of transnational information linkages between policy actors contribute to this process of learning. New knowledge gained from policy learning is therefore critical to the politics of policy change. Put another way, power and authority in policymaking is dependent, in large part, on actors' stock of expertise.

Policy learning matters in three different ways, all of which were relevant in the processes of health policy change in Taiwan and South Korea. Identifying new problems within a certain policy domain is one way of endogenously creating opportunities for change. In Taiwan, for instance, the universal National Health Insurance (NHI) program experienced a major financial shortfall in 1998. Only three years after the program's implementation, surplus funds for the NHI had dwindled. This new "problem" prompted health care policymakers in Taiwan to consider a range of policy options. After studying the reform experiences of Japan, Germany, the United States, and Singapore, the Department of Health in Taiwan opted to privatize and marketize the NHI program. This reform option, and the problems it sought to address, prompted other health care reform advocates to consider less dramatic alternatives, such as new provider payment schemes, a new expenditure monitoring system, and limited experiments with increasing point-of-delivery user fees. New problems prompted policy learning and thus a spate of new policy innovations.

Second, new solutions to old problems emerge through policy learning. Policies are rarely perfect and thus invite continual learning and tinkering by policymakers. In extreme cases, policy failures demand new policy innovations.[45] Before the recent integration reform efforts in Korea, health insurance was decentrally organized along occupational lines. This meant, in effect, that the redistributive pool within funds was quite small. Moreover, the lack of redistributive mechanisms among funds exacerbated disparities between better-off workers and lower-wage groups. Though this structural arrangement remained intact throughout the 1970s and 1980s, health care policymakers in Korea considered adopting a new solution, learned from the Japanese and German models of health insurance organization. In 1996, the government implemented a redistributive mechanism among medical insurance funds. In Korea, old problems promoted new solutions.

Finally, the emergence of new ideas provides another endogenous source of opportunity for policy change. New understandings about problems and solutions rework the terms of policy debate. The ways in which issues are defined and redefined in a certain policy domain create opportunities for new efforts in policy learning and innovation. Periods of major policy reform are shaped by changes in the "processing of issues."[46] In Taiwan and South Korea, the belief that health policy can promote socioeconomic justice, an idea that emerged into the political mainstream only in the postauthoritarian era, reconfigured how policymakers thought about health care and the purposes of health care policy. New conceptualizations of old social, political, and economic problems, combined with changing normative expectations about what policies should and can do about these problems, together promoted new rounds of policy learning, opening up opportunities for policy change.

Political Learning

Over time, actors learn how to play the political game and, in so doing, learn how to maximize their opportunities to effect policy change. In this respect, institutional reform resulting from democratic transition invites political learning. Political institutions structure the processes of policymaking.[47] If we think of policymaking as a game, institutions are the rules of the game. Formal rules determine how decisions are made. They proscribe and facilitate actors' behavior. Federalist institutions, bicameral legislatures, and presidential systems all have their own explicit rules with respect to policy decision making.[48] Moreover, institutional arrangements vary between cases.

By their very existence, institutions and specific institutional arrangements have what Jack Knight calls a "distributive effect" on the way politics and policymaking play out.[49] Since institutions are the creations of purposive actors, the distributive impact of institutions is an important analytic consideration in the study of policymaking and policy change. The distributive effect of institutions shapes how policies are made. For instance, institutions determine the distribution of formal power in the policy process. The executive veto, the supremacy of the courts, and decision rules in the legislature are all institutionally derived sources of power. Institutions also affect the distribution of information. Policy information—whether expert knowledge about a certain policy area or expertise in forecasting consequences—is, to begin with, already limited in policymaking. Indeed, it is never perfect.[50] Institutional arrangements determine the flow of information among policy actors, resulting in symmetrical or asymmetrical exchanges of information. Since information and the capacity for policy learning are important sources of power in the policy process, the institutional effects on the distribution of information are crucial to understanding the political dynamics of policymaking.

Participation in politics and policymaking is mediated by institutions and changing institutional arrangements endemic to democratic reform. It is important, therefore, to focus on the ways institutions, and changing institutional configurations, constitute the distribution of opportunities with which actors gain entry into or derive advantage from the policy process. We can think of institutions and institutional arrangements as the structural basis of strategic contexts. Although the rules of the game may determine the distribution of formal authority and/or policy information among contending actors, the institutional playing field or strategic context in which actors maneuver has an impact on the degree of influence an actor brings to bear on the policy process. As Tarrow suggests, obstacles to effective political mobilization have less to do with the internal contradictions in the logic of collective action and more to do with the presence or absence of strategic opportunities for concerted action in the first place.

Strategic contexts, and the ability of actors to take advantage of such institutional arrangements, constitute effective power or influence in a given policy arena.[51] It is true that the distribution of influence among actors is rarely uniform. However, this distribution is not determined solely by the distribution of resources or the designation of formal political authority. Rather, policy influence is in part determined by the "goodness of fit" between specific strategic contexts and the ability of actors to exploit these institutional opportunities.[52] We must therefore appreciate actors' capacity to learn and to adapt to these strategic-institutional contexts, particularly during times of democratic change. Some actors learn very quickly and thus swiftly adapt to the new democratic game. For some, political learning takes place over a longer period of time. Some actors never learn.

The processes of learning and adapting involve three considerations on the part of political actors. First, actors must identify a strategic point of entry into the policy process, or what Baumgartner and Jones refer to as "venue shopping." Actors seek out institutional openings through which they can articulate their opinions and participate in policy processes. Second, actors need to organize in such a way as to "fit" with the specific institutional foundations of the policy process. Corporatist structures, for instance, demand that interest groups organize as encompassing peak associations. Actors in fragmented states may choose to penetrate the policy process through decentralized clientelist ties.[53] Institutionalized party systems based on well-entrenched cleavages and party identities might compel actors to forge linkages with particular political parties, taking social policy battles into the legislature. Simply put, strategies for political mobilization and organization need to be tailored to the existing policymaking institutions.

Third, strategic actors have to consider how best to present their respective ideas during policymaking processes. Again, actors need to be aware of the institutional setting in which they are maneuvering. As Baumgartner and Jones note, some ideas "may be well accepted in one venue, but considered inappropriate when raised in another institutional arena."[54] Policy actors need captive audiences if they are to be influential. Moreover, different strategic contexts may lead actors consciously to rework their image to cast a wider appeal. In both Taiwan and South Korea, for instance, labor learned to deradicalize its image, demands, and tactics in order to be heard in the political mainstream. This change came after several frustrating years of being shut out of the policymaking process despite having been a major force in the initial transition to democracy. In short, learning and adaptation are not only about telling the right stories to the right audience but also about portraying the right image.

Because political learning is a process, there is lag time between when democratic reform is introduced and when actors begin to learn and adapt to the democratic game. Expectations that the initiation of democratic transition will immediately result in more participatory political and policymaking processes are therefore unrealistic.[55] The extension of political rights for participation does not automatically translate into what we may ideally conceive as participatory democracy. First, democratic transition is not a one-shot deal, and the processes of democratic crafting are ongoing. The new rules of the game are rarely constructed in toto at the moment of democratic breakthrough. In Taiwan, democratic negotiations spanned the late 1980s to the mid-1990s in a series of constitutional reform meetings.[56] In South Korea, democratic crafting comprised electoral reform, administrative reform, and political party realignment during the same period.[57] The rules of the game changed, at least in the short period after democratic breakthrough, making it difficult for actors to learn and adapt quickly. Second, we must appreciate the fact that political learning takes time. Democratic transition imposes a steep learning curve on political actors. The curve is especially steep for those actors who were previously excluded from the political arena. Learning democracy is not easy.

The Logic of Political Competition

Democratization, above all, is about the institutionalization of political competition. In Taiwan, the formation and legalization of the opposition Democratic Progressive Party (DPP) in 1986, the lifting of martial law in 1987, and the expansion of national-level elections together marked the initiation of democratic transition. Similarly, in South Korea, democratic breakthrough was achieved when incumbent president Roh Tae-Woo announced direct presidential elections for late 1987 followed by full legislative elections in the spring of 1988. In both places, institutionalized competition fundamentally altered the political game and marked authoritarian withdrawal.

Whereas authoritarian states force societal acquiescence and suppress opposition, often through violent means, democracy imposes a political logic of *winning support*. As repressive authoritarian tactics become less tolerated, or better yet illegal, political actors need to reorient their strategies toward capturing popular support. Political competition reworks the exchange relationship between the government and the governed. Political competition thus creates conditions of political uncertainty. Whereas an authoritarian regime enjoys a considerable amount of certainty that opposition movements can be swiftly dealt with and that the demobilization of political society will ensure the regime's political survival, democratic politics is rooted in the assumption of political uncertainty.[58] The degree of uncertainty in any democratic polity is variable, in part reflective of the particular institutions that structure political competition. Yet the mere possibility of defeat or the prospects of electoral victory in democracy alter the ways actors play the political game. Competitive elections promote greater accountability among ruling elites. The chance of losing elections forces governments to be more accountable to the body politic. Accordingly, institutionalized political competition requires that policymakers consider the plurality (and contestation) of ideas, interests, and actors within political society.

Institutionalized political competition provides the forum in which new policy ideas or new causal stories can be heard. Regular elections, for instance, facilitate political debate among actors outside the state apparatus. Policy agenda setting from the outside in or from the bottom up are made possible under conditions of political competition. Indeed, political and policy entrepreneurship is rewarded in democracies. Governments need to find issues and constituents with which to win popular support. Actors outside the formal institutions of government similarly need to be entrepreneurial, selling their ideas and exchanging their political support for a more meaningful voice in policy matters.

Governments and aspirants to government must be responsive to the demands, policy ideas, and initiatives of actors from within both the state and society. During the late 1990s in Taiwan, the KMT government was forced to backpedal on its health insurance retrenchment reform primarily because of the lack of widespread political support for the multiple-carrier proposal. Given its fear of losing political support, particularly with legislative and presidential elections scheduled shortly thereafter, the KMT was compelled to respond accordingly. In South Korea, President Kim Dae-Jung ran on an election platform that, in response to demands made by increasingly powerful civic groups, promised to integrate the medical insurance system in order to promote greater socioeconomic redistribution.

In addition to what we might call the response imperative, the institutionalization of competition entails a *preemptive* logic to political strategy and policy reform. The iterated electoral game is a strategic one.[59] Even in the absence of any real impending electoral threat, democratic governments may choose strategically to preempt societal demands through policy reform, thus ensuring against the potential future loss of political support. This preemptive logic was clearly at play during the early stages of democratic transition in Taiwan and South Korea. By all measures, the nascent opposition parties were not significant challengers to the incumbent regimes in either place shortly after democratic breakthrough. Nonetheless, both ruling governments decided to initiate health care reform in order to win away bases of political support from the opposition while maintaining the support of their preexisting constituencies. In this respect, then, the preemptive logic inherent to political competition influenced the processes of setting the social policy agenda in Taiwan and South Korea and ultimately policy reform.

Thus far, I have presented a generalized understanding of political competition. The introduction of democratic competition creates a new strategic field for political actors. From this strategic context, opportunities for policy change may emerge as a result of political responsiveness or strategic preemption. This generalized conceptualization, however, underemphasizes the important variations in competitive contexts. Giuseppe Di Palma, in his work on democratic crafting, reminds us that "democracies differ, at times substantially, in the way they try to balance wins and losses, in the instrumentalities they choose to guarantee political equality, in how they regulate competitive access to government."[60] Different competitive contexts demand different strategic adaptations on the part of contending actors. Although the general logic of political competition holds true in a broad sense, variations in the degree of competition and the basis of political contestation are significant in shaping political strategies and ultimately the course of policy change.

The degree of competitivenes in a democratizing polity is determined, in part, by the way democratic breakthrough is achieved in the first place.[61] Democratic transition in Taiwan was managed by the KMT regime whereas in Korea, democratic breakthrough resulted from an intense confrontation between state and society, resulting in a much higher degree of competition from the start. The timing of founding elections also affects the degree of competitiveness in emerging democracies. The fact that electoral competition was phased in gradually in Taiwan meant that electoral challenges to the incumbent KMT were considerably less pronounced than those faced by the Roh Tae-Woo regime in Korea, where founding elections were held right away. Finally, electoral systems matter. Resistance by the KMT to reform Taiwan's unique multimember district electoral system, a scheme that disadvantages smaller parties, at first limited opportunities for alternative parties to challenge the ruling regime.[62] In contrast, electoral reform in Korea, before the 1988 legislative elections, helped new opposition parties gain votes, increasing their share of seats in the National Assembly.[63]

Variations in the degree of competitiveness had a significant impact on how health care reform was initiated during the early stages of democratic transition in Taiwan and South Korea. Though the logic of political competition compelled both regimes to preempt universal health care reform, the higher degree of competition in the Korean case forced the Roh regime to implement quick-fix reforms. In Taiwan, the KMT was afforded the time and political latitude to plan a more transformative health care reform policy. This contrast is developed more fully in Chapter 4.

Understanding the basis of political competition illuminates the salient issues and cleavages around which political entrepreneurs mobilize for the purposes of winning political support. In most cases of democratic transition, the initial political cleavage is one that divides prodemocracy activists and hard-line conservatives who resist political change. However, this cleavage is usually short-lived. Soon after the moment of democratic breakthrough, new cleavages emerge that in turn reconstitute the bases of competition. In Taiwan, ethnic identity and national self-determination became the most divisive political cleavage in electoral politics. In Korea, regionalism, reinforced by charismatic leaders, came to dominate political competition. For proponents of social welfare reform in Taiwan and Korea, then, the absence of socioeconomic cleavages at first suggested dim prospects for the emergence of new social policy agendas.

Theorists of democratization, however, understand political cleavages and the basis of political competition to be much more dynamic in the context of democratic transition and consolidation. In particular, democratization and the introduction of political competition promote the ongoing construction of new and politically salient cleavages.[64] In contrast to the median voter theorem, which states that strategic political actors (i.e., parties) in stable polities will necessarily converge on the median voters' preferences,[65] the highly charged politics of democratic transition promotes the diversification of issue structures and the multiplication of political cleavages, thus forming entirely new, and continually shifting, bases of political competition.[66] Knowing the cleavages inherited from the predemocratic period provides only a surface analysis. What is needed, therefore, is a deeper investigation into the ways strategic actors adapt to competitive contexts and in turn articulate new salient cleavages and attract new bases of political competition. As I argue in Chapters 5, 6, and 7, socioeconomic cleavages emerged in Taiwan and South Korea, though well after the moment of democratic breakthrough and only after political entrepreneurs strategically constructed these new bases of political competition for the purposes of electoral gain.

TOWARD A DYNAMIC POLICYMAKING FRAMEWORK

By their nature, inductive frameworks do not directly give us answers; they merely pose the right guiding questions. From an empirical standpoint, the framework developed in this chapter helps sort out the details of health policy reform over a long period of time in Taiwan and South Korea. At a theoretical level, this framework of analysis illuminates the ways democratic transition, or political change more generally, influences social policy change. It sheds explanatory light on the relationship between the larger sweep of social, economic, and political change on the one hand and the microlevel politics of health care policymaking on the other. The analytical framework is hardly elegant, but that is by design. Given the theoretical and empirical challenges of this book, the framework's complexity and exhaustiveness are precisely its strengths. Indeed, the theoretical questions posed here demand a more inductive approach, one that draws insights from theories of democratization, comparative public policymaking, and welfare state development. This book looks to understand and explain social policy change. It is not explicitly about hypothesis testing.

The analytical framework developed in this chapter affords comparative analyses across national experiences. The framework illuminates important similarities between Taiwan and South Korea, in terms of both political change and social policy reform. Yet it also draws out significant differences between the two cases, highlighting how variable pathways of political change differently affect how social policy reform is carried out. As an inductive, conceptually driven, comparative framework of analysis, the arguments developed in this book should help drive other comparative research agendas that focus on the implications of democratic change. It should also inform studies of reform in policy domains outside health care.

Explaining Policy Change

In this chapter, I break down the processes of policy change and examine the myriad ways that political change restructures the politics of policymaking. At its core, the politics of policy change involves the contestation of causal stories, conceptualized as coherent though contending interpretations of problems and their solutions. These stories are the bases of politics and policy in that they represent the range of competing interests in a given policy area. Going beyond solely interest-based explanations of policy innovation and change, however, I also argue that ideas or interpretive frames shape how actors perceive problems and devise solutions. Evaluating the efficacy of a proposed policy solution, therefore, incorporates a criterion of appropriateness. Both interests and ideas reflect the social, economic, and political contexts in which policy battles are fought.

I furthermore point to the multitude of actors potentially involved in health care policymaking. As a heuristic tool, the concept of policy networks helps us organize our empirical analysis of what can otherwise be a messy picture. Network analysis provides a way of examining who is involved in health policymaking, where actors are located within the health policy network, who are their allies, and the linkages between actors on the inside and those in more peripheral positions. Although health policy networks tend to be rather exclusionary, given the complexity of health care policy, an exploration of policy networks over time allows us to chart change, particularly network change resulting from democratic reform. Policy networks are thus understood to be a dynamic concept.

Finally, I develop in this chapter four different windows of opportunity for policy change. First, exogenous events, often unrelated to any specific policy domain, can trigger the process of policy innovation and change. Learning about new solutions, recognizing new problems, and responding to new ideas are a second, though endogenous, source of opportunities for reform. Effective participation in policymaking requires information and expertise, thus placing a premium on effective policy learning by actors. Third, political learning and adaptation to new strategic-institutional contexts resulting from political change is very much a part of the democratization project. Changes that result from democratic breakthrough and continual democratic reform provide savvy or astute learners with new political opportunities to penetrate once closed policy processes. Fourth, the institutionalization of political competition opens up new opportunities for policy change. Regular political competition creates an arena in which policy ideas can be floated. Actors rework their political strategies to fit the democratic game and thus the new imperatives of winning support, overcoming political uncertainty, and promoting accountability. This in turn leads to a new logic of policy reform based on "constituent responsiveness" and "preemptive reform."

Stages of Political Change

The sheer complexity of this analytical framework implies that the explanations generated in this book regarding health care reform and welfare state development in democratizing Taiwan and South Korea go beyond the simple teleology of the democratic class struggle. Political change—whether the transition from authoritarianism to democracy or the deepening of democracy from the moment of breakthrough to consolidation—is not instantaneous. The process of democratic transformation is continuous, evolving over much longer periods of time than we might intuitively expect. This is not an idiosyncratic disclaimer for the specific cases of Taiwan and South Korea, insofar as the conceptual distinctions between *democratic breakthrough, transition,* and *democratic consolidation* are meaningful from a cross-national perspective.[67]

The extension of political citizenship and the de jure right to participate in political decision making do not guarantee the de facto practice of a more participatory democracy, for several reasons. For one, "the rules of the game" in new democracies "require a prolonged process of habituation and institutionalization to become robust and fully effective."[68] Crafting the rules of the game and then adapting to these new rules take time. Opportunities for political inclusion, particularly in previously exclusive policy networks, require adaptive strategies that can be learned only over time. The institutionalization of political competition does not necessarily mean that there are even legitimate contenders, at least just after the introduction of democracy. Political learning is not instantaneous. In this respect, chronology and the sequencing of political events are crucial to understanding the dynamics of health care reform spanning the authoritarian period through the late 1990s in Taiwan and South Korea. Causal connections between democratic reform and social policy change can be distilled only through a temporally sensitive framework of analysis.

Because democratization is a continual process of change, different aspects of this analytical framework carry more explanatory weight at different times. In this book, I focus on three policy reform episodes. The first episode, explored in Chapter 3, captures the dynamics of health care policymaking in the authoritarian developmental state context. The following two reform periods occur after the moment of democratic breakthrough (Chapters 4 to 6). The introduction of political competition, or the institutionalization of procedural democracy during the late 1980s and early 1990s, compelled the transitioning regimes in Taiwan and South Korea to preemptively initiate universal health care reform. It was not until the late 1990s, roughly a decade after the moment of democratic breakthrough, that new actors emerged onto the policymaking scene, effectively penetrating previously closed policy networks and expanding the scope of policymaking participation.

◇◇◇◇◇◇◇◇◇◇◇◇◇◇◇◇◇◇◇◇◇◇◇◇◇◇◇◇◇◇◇ ◆ ◇◇◇◇◇◇◇◇◇◇◇◇◇◇◇◇◇◇◇◇◇◇◇◇◇◇◇◇◇◇◇

CHAPTER 3

AUTHORITARIANISM AND THE ORIGINS OF SOCIAL INSURANCE

The origins of health insurance in Taiwan and South Korea date back to the authoritarian developmental state. Then, however, the scope of coverage was far from universal. In 1980, only 17 percent of the population in Taiwan benefited from some form of medical insurance. That figure was only slightly higher in South Korea, at 24 percent. Furthermore, the pattern of health care reform was piecemeal and gradual throughout the predemocratic period. Coverage was limited to select portions of the employed population, excluding dependents and the aged. This occupational, or "productivist," bias reinforced the postwar economic project of the East Asian developmental state. The idea of welfare and the redistributive principles of social policy were negated by the larger imperatives of rapid and aggregate economic growth, the authoritarian developmental state's first priority.

The specific patterns of health care policymaking in Taiwan and South Korea reflected more general patterns of policymaking in the authoritarian developmental state, centering on a highly trained bureaucratic apparatus. The pilot agencies within the bureaucracy were the Economic Planning Board (EPB) in Korea, formed in 1961, and the Council on U.S. Aid (CUSA) in Taiwan, the predecessor to the supraministerial Council for Economic Planning and Development (CEPD). These elite corps of technocrats ensured both vertical coordination and horizontal cooperation among the various ministries, thus keeping in line other powerful branches of the bureaucracy such as those in charge of industry, finance, defense, and social welfare. In this way, the East Asian developmental state was the epitome of internal institutional coherence. The authoritarian state also effectively demobilized civil society in Taiwan and South Korea. Social movement groups were banned under martial law. Labor and capital were both organized by the state and co-opted into the state's top-down sphere of influence. Policymaking under authoritarianism was therefore centralized and politically insulated. Indeed, health care reform in authoritarian Taiwan and South Korea was a statist project.

The dominance of the state over society provided a degree of autonomy for bureaucratic policymakers in Taiwan and South Korea. Nevertheless, state officials were, in the end, agents of the principal political elites.[1] South Korean president Park Chung-Hee established his own corps of policy planners in the Presidential Secretariat, often referred to as the Blue House. In Taiwan, the Kuomintang's (KMT) political leadership similarly directed policymaking. Party cells penetrated every branch of the government. In this respect, then, social policymaking was not immune from politics, or more specifically, the political objectives of the authoritarian regimes. In authoritarian Taiwan and South Korea, the course of health care reform—and social policy change more generally—reflected a political pattern of "crisis and selective compensation." Social policy was a political instrument used by the state to weather times of political crisis.

The consequences of this authoritarian political logic were significant. First, social policy change was not intended to benefit those who needed social protection. Second, selective compensation actually had an intensely regressive effect. Those without social insurance were forced to pay unregulated and thus inflated prices for health care. Third, the developmental state's high-growth economic project and the political requisites of authoritarian survival undermined the principles of universal and redistributive social welfare. Because the authoritarian state was not institutionally accountable to a universally empowered electorate, for instance, it could afford to pursue strategies of selective compensation. Universal social welfare was therefore never a political necessity.

ORIGINS OF HEALTH INSURANCE IN KOREA

In the summer of 1962, President Park Chung-Hee issued a memorandum to the Supreme Council for National Reconstruction (SCNR) requesting that the Committee on Social Security (CSS), which was a part of the Ministry of Health and Social Affairs (MHSA), begin work on new social policy reform projects.[2] Under severe time constraints, the CSS immediately started planning a mandatory and universal health insurance program.[3] A year later, the first Health Insurance Act was passed, but the program fell far short of what the CSS originally envisioned. Due to the lack of time, and thus the need for easy structural reform, the CSS was forced to adopt a multiple-carrier scheme organized within companies.[4] Administration of health insurance was to be carried out by firms themselves. The 1963 program was also limited in its coverage, as medical insurance benefits were extended only to those who were employed in large firms, essentially the labor aristocracy. As one CSS member lamented, "I regret very much that the [1963] health insurance program did not cover the poor who needed it most."[5] The most significant compromise to the CSS proposal came when the SCNR unilaterally amended the bill to make participation in the medical insurance program voluntary, minimizing the government's fiscal burden. More important, the state feared the political backlash from big business allies, who would have been required under a nonvoluntary program to pay a 50 percent insurance premium.

The voluntary program's implementation was delayed until 1965, and not surprisingly, only two firms joined the scheme. After the Industrial Accident Insurance (IAI) program was implemented in 1963, state authorities felt that a separate medical insurance scheme was redundant, and consequently, the voluntary health insurance program was scrapped.[6] Throughout the rest of the decade and into the early 1970s, President Park and his corps of policymakers turned their attention to promoting rapid economic growth. Health policy was no longer a priority.

Though pension schemes had been selectively implemented beginning in the early 1960s, Park announced in January 1973 that the government was planning a new pension program that would cover workers in firms with thirty or more employees.[7] The plan was abandoned during the 1974 OPEC price spikes, when government resources were diverted to managing the economy, thus taking away the start-up subsidies required by the new program. The reform effort of 1973 should not be interpreted as a genuine attempt at social policy innovation, however. It was later revealed that its motivation was to quickly raise much-needed capital for the heavy industrial drive planned by President Park. Health insurance (as opposed to pensions) was a less attractive policy option because it would require the quick turnover of revenue for the short-term financing of medical care. Simply put, health insurance was less useful in terms of generating investment capital for the state.[8] Again, social policy initiatives were subsumed under the high-growth imperatives of the developmental state.

In the spring of 1976, President Park announced that a new health insurance program was to be implemented in the following year. The program would first extend coverage to lower-income groups and gradually expand thereafter. On unveiling the Fourth Five-Year Plan that summer, Park reiterated, "Health insurance for those with some amount of income can be delayed. For those with low incomes, a gradual and practical program should be developed."[9] On December 22, 1976, the second Health Insurance Act was passed, and on July 1, 1977, a compulsory, though severely limited, medical insurance program began operation. In the following year, a second health insurance scheme was created for government employees.

Given the government's aborted attempts to institutionalize health insurance in the 1960s and pensions in the early 1970s, why was the state willing to implement mandatory, though limited, medical insurance during the mid-1970s? One explanation is that U.S. pressure on the Park regime compelled the president to institutionalize the new reforms.[10] Others suggest that North Korean criticisms about the lack of public health provision in South Korea prompted Park to act. Korean sociologist Chan-Ung Park contends that Park's strategic motivation in launching health insurance in 1977 was driven by domestic factors, such as the state's failure to implement the 1974 pension program. Increased media attention on severe inequities in the health care system drew criticisms of Park's leadership and, indeed, his promise for development. The extension of health insurance was to gain much-needed political legitimacy for Park, especially in the wake of the highly repressive 1972 Yushin Constitution.[11]

As before, the policy process that resulted in the 1976 Health Insurance Act was insulated from outside influence. President Park designated the Ministry of Health and Social Affairs to be the primary actor in designing the new health insurance program. The Committee on Social Security, which had been so instrumental in introducing the idea of universal health insurance during the early 1960s, was marginalized. The principal drafters of the 1976 bill were members of the MHSA's Bureau of Social Insurance (BSI); none were from the more progressive CSS. According to Myongsei Sohn and his colleagues, the president and the Blue House secretariat were not central to the policy process. However, the minister of health and social affairs, Hyun-Hwak Shin, kept Park and his advisers abreast of the ministry's activities, and thus Park was never far from the center of policymaking action.[12]

Few societal groups participated in the policymaking process. The Korean Medical Association (KMA) was the only nonstate actor that had any access to the core of the policy network, and even then, doctors' participation was limited to negotiating the details of the pricing mechanism. Societal input from consumers was minimal. Representatives on the financing side of the health insurance scheme, including the Federation of Korean Industries, the Korean Employers Federation, the Federation of Korean Trade Unions, and the Urban Industrial Mission (an independent workers' movement), remained on the periphery of the policy network.[13]

Although the MHSA began serious work on health insurance reform only in early 1976, President Park demanded that the program be implemented by the summer of 1977. Policymakers were again working under tremendous time constraints, which meant little room (or time) for policy innovation. The lack of outside input and alternative policy ideas undermined creative policymaking. Because BSI officials from the ministry had little experience with health insurance policy, the chief drafters of the 1976 bill were forced to refer to earlier models, most notably the failed 1963 voluntary medical insurance proposal. The new scheme was therefore based on the multiple health insurance society system. The fee-for-service provider payment scheme was copied verbatim from the Japanese model.[14] The president and the MHSA rejected alternative policy ideas; both were in favor of the ready-made multiple-carrier system.

The 1976 Health Insurance Act made it mandatory for all firms with five hundred or more employees to establish an enterprise-level health insurance society (HIS). The program was far from universal in reach. Each HIS was to be a self-governing, de facto autonomous insurance carrier. In terms of financing, the employer and employee each paid half the contribution rate, which ranged from 3 to 8 percent of the employee's monthly income. Insurance societies set their own premiums according to enrollees' utilization rates. Health insurance covered only basic outpatient and inpatient services, and treatments that fell outside the coverage plan were paid entirely out-of-pocket by the patient. In addition, insurance enrollees were subject to a copay levy equaling 40 percent of the total cost for outpatient services and 30 percent for inpatient treatment.[15] Government subsidization in the health insurance system was negligible.

On July 1, 1977, 486 health insurance societies began operating.[16] Six months later, the government employees' (and private schoolteachers') health insurance program commenced, operated by a single carrier, the Korean Medical Insurance Corporation (KMIC). Though the rate of coverage increased steadily through the late 1970s, less than 21 percent of those employed (excluding dependents) benefited from medical insurance by 1980. This extent of coverage was a vast improvement over the 9 percent coverage rate in 1977 but was still well short of universal.[17]

The 1976 Health Insurance Act essentially locked in the structure of health insurance organization. Before 1998, more than twenty years later, every effort at health insurance reform involved only the gradual addition of new health insurance societies. In short, the 1976 act was a watershed policy event for its lasting structural legacy in health care policymaking.

ORIGINS OF HEALTH INSURANCE IN TAIWAN

The idea of limited social insurance in Taiwan originated during the civil war period while the KMT was still on the mainland. Certain groups, such as state and military personnel, received social insurance benefits in exchange for political loyalty to the KMT.[18] In 1950, after the KMT had relocated to the island of Taiwan, the provincial government established the first labor insurance (LI) scheme, covering workers employed in firms with at least twenty employees. By 1953, the LI program had been extended to small enterprises (ten-plus workers) and fishermen and on a voluntary basis to those working in firms with fewer than ten employees. The Military Servicemen Insurance Program was also legislated into law in 1953. The KMT decided in 1958 to formally legislate in the central government the Labor Insurance Act and the Government Employees' Insurance Act. The overarching administrative and financial responsibilities for social insurance were subsequently moved from provincial jurisdictions to the central government. Two ministries in the cabinet carried out the collection of insurance funds and the administration of the separate schemes. The government employees' insurance (GEI) scheme was managed by the Ministry of Examination (or Examination Yuan). The labor insurance program was under the administrative aegis of the Ministry of the Interior but directly managed by the Bureau of Labor Insurance. Unlike in Korea, where health insurance was decentralized into hundreds of different insurance societies, in Taiwan the system was organized along two principal administrative and financial units.

Social insurance in Taiwan provided an integrated benefits package. Labor insurance, for instance, entailed a set of "bundled benefits," including those for work-related injury, old age, disability, death, maternity, and most significantly, medical care. By the 1970s, over half the total benefits expenditure from the LI program went to cover the costs of health care. According to Tung-Liang Chiang, 64 percent of one's total LI premium was spent on medical care coverage.[19] Because patients in Taiwan did not have to pay an additional out-of-pocket copay levy, as was the case in Korea, insured medical care benefits were paid for entirely from the social insurance funds.

As in the Korean system, however, there were different financing arrangements between the two major social insurance schemes. Monthly contribution rates ranged from 7 percent of monthly earnings for those enrolled in the LI program to 9 percent in the GEI program after 1977. Whereas in the Korean health insurance system the employer and employee split the premium contribution burden evenly, Taiwan's LI program stipulated that employers contribute 80 percent of the monthly premium. For self-employed workers enrolled in the voluntary LI scheme, 70 percent of the monthly contribution was paid by the enrollee and the remaining 30 percent was subsidized by the government.[20] In the GEI scheme, government employees paid 35 percent of the monthly contribution and the balance was covered by the state.[21]

Between 1952 and 1980, the percentage of the population covered under the labor insurance scheme increased from 2 to 14.3 percent. Including beneficiaries of the government employees' insurance program, the total insured portion of the population was about 17 percent in 1980, a significant improvement though still very short of universal.[22] By and large, health insurance provisions benefited only those who were employed. Dependents such as children (under fifteen, even if employed) and the elderly (over age sixty) were excluded, despite the fact that both groups were far and away the most frequent users of medical care.[23] It was not until 1982 that dependents of GEI enrollees received social insurance benefits, and even then these dependent beneficiaries represented only a small portion of the population.

There were furthermore significant disparities in the distribution of benefits between those covered by the LI scheme and the civil servants who benefited from the GEI program. On retirement, workers in the LI scheme who claimed their old-age benefits (a lump-sum cash payment) were forced to forfeit their medical care coverage. In other words, LI enrollees had to choose between the two benefits. Government employees did not have to make such a choice because in 1965 the KMT government expanded health insurance coverage for all retired government employees. Civil servants thus enjoyed both old-age benefits and continued medical care coverage after retirement. Not surprisingly, the take-up rate for old-age benefits among GEI enrollees was nearly double that among LI enrollees in the late 1960s. Moreover, old-age benefits paid out under the GEI program were considerably more generous—double, in terms of cash value, in the 1970s—than those offered by the LI scheme.[24]

The KMT regime faced a series of international and domestic political setbacks during the 1970s, prompting a new wave of social policy reform. After mainland China gained international recognition and Taiwan was expelled from the United Nations in 1971, the KMT announced an important resolution called the "Measures to Protect Workers' Interests and Improve Workers' Livelihood."[25] Non-KMT candidates increasingly challenged the political establishment after the introduction of supplementary elections for the central Legislative Yuan and the National Assembly beginning in 1972. Though parties were banned, the KMT lost an unprecedented number of seats to independent candidates in municipal and provincial elections in 1977.[26] A wave of anti-KMT protests in Chung-Li in 1977 and in Kaohsiung in 1979 exacerbated the ruling party's legitimacy crisis. Diplomatic rapprochement between the United States and China in 1978 undermined the KMT's claim to be the legitimate government of China. In this critical period, President Chiang Ching-Kuo formed a new social welfare task force.

Numerous voices and social policy reform proposals immediately surfaced within the state apparatus. The supraministerial Council for Economic Planning and Development (CEPD), formed in early 1978, proposed that the government radically restructure old-age benefits into a separate full-fledged pension program. The Ministry of Economic Affairs (MEA), however, opposed the CEPD's vision because of concerns about the impact of any major social welfare reform on the international competitiveness of Taiwan's industrial export economy. The MEA's view resonated more with KMT party leaders. As one KMT member put it, "Social security has been approached as a partnership in which the government and the individual share responsibility. No huge and unwieldy bureaucracy needs to be created."[27]

In the end, the Executive Yuan (cabinet) announced in May 1978 that it intended to revise, though not structurally reform, the labor insurance system. The main objective in the reform effort was to adjust eligibility requirements and benefits in the LI program, bringing them more into line with the government employees' insurance scheme. As in Park Chung-Hee's Korea, reform was carried out through regulatory tinkering rather than any major structural change. Consensus among the KMT leadership, the cabinet, and the KMT-dominated legislature ensured that the labor insurance revisions were easily passed in early 1979. Similar to the Korean experience, societal input was not a factor in determining the reform policy outcome.

The revised law allowed workers from smaller firms (five-plus employees) to enroll in the LI scheme. The minimum age requirement for enrollees, which was previously fifteen years of age, was also lifted. As a result, the number of workers enrolled in the LI program increased from 2.3 million in 1979 to 4.15 million in 1985.[28] Eligibility requirements for old-age benefits were relaxed as well, so that workers no longer had to be sixty years of age and with fifteen years of insurance enrollment to qualify for benefits. Under the revised law, any worker of retirement age who had been insured for at least one year could claim old-age benefits. Finally, self-employed workers saw their share of the monthly contribution decrease from 70 percent of the total premium to 60 percent, with the government subsidizing the balance.

The 1979 revisions failed to address one key discrepancy between the LI and GEI schemes: the immediate cancellation of medical insurance coverage for retired workers claiming old-age benefits under LI. It should come as no surprise, then, that in spite of the relaxed eligibility requirements for old-age benefits, the take-up rate for these benefits did not change significantly after the 1979 revisions.[29] The state opposed the simultaneous provision of health care coverage and old-age benefits in the LI scheme, fearing that such a reform would drain the financial resources of the LI program. Indeed, beginning in the 1960s, the government employees' insurance scheme recorded a deficit, which increased exponentially throughout the 1980s.[30] By maintaining this disparity between schemes, the KMT party-state clearly signaled its commitment to absorbing extra costs for the GEI program and its unwillingness to do the same for workers enrolled in the revised labor insurance scheme.

IMPLICATIONS OF EARLY HEALTH INSURANCE REFORM

After two aborted attempts at social insurance reform in Korea (the 1963 Health Insurance Act and the 1973 pension reform), the Park regime finally implemented a limited medical insurance program in 1977. In Taiwan, social insurance was first devised in the 1950s and gradually expanded in the late 1970s. What effect did these reforms have on health care provision in Taiwan and South Korea?

Coverage

Health care reform in the period before democratic transition did not result in the universal extension of medical insurance; in fact, far from it. In 1980, one year after medical insurance in Korea had been expanded to include medium-sized firms (three hundred or more employees), approximately 24 percent of the population was covered by some form of health insurance. The employees' insurance program was expanded again in 1981 to workers in firms with at least one hundred employees. That same year, the government initiated a pilot program of health insurance coverage for self-employed workers in five rural districts and one city. The scope of coverage then increased to 30 percent of the population. Even after the EIS program was further extended to small firms (sixteen-plus employees) in 1983, only 39 percent of the population enjoyed some form of medical insurance.[31] Because almost half the working population in Korea was technically self-employed, most Koreans were excluded from the existing insurance schemes.

The expansion of health insurance coverage in Taiwan throughout the 1980s was similarly gradual and short of universal. In 1980, only 17 percent of the population benefited from any medical insurance scheme. The new eligibility requirements written into the 1979 labor insurance law revisions slowly increased the scope of medical insurance coverage. In 1985, the government also introduced a pilot program for farmers' insurance (FI) in forty-one townships. About 7 percent of the agricultural labor force (or about 0.5 percent of the entire population) enrolled in the pilot FI scheme during its first year of operation.[32] By the end of 1985, health insurance coverage island-wide was still only about 25 percent of the population. That number increased to 37.5 percent in 1988 because of the sixfold increase in the number of farmers enrolled in the FI program and the gradual enrollment expansion in the existing LI program. The continued exclusion of dependents, however, meant that island-wide coverage rate still remained short of universal even by the early 1990s.

Structural Organization

The organization of social insurance in Taiwan more closely approximated an integrated system with fewer insurance carriers. Before the introduction of farmers' insurance in the mid-1980s, the two main administrative bodies in charge of social insurance were the Bureau of Labor Insurance of the Ministry of the Interior (for labor insurance) and the Central Trust Bureau of the Examination Yuan (for government employees' insurance). Though monthly contributions were collected by various insurance units, such as trade or occupational unions, premiums and enrollee membership were consolidated into one of the two insurance schemes.[33] The Korean system, on the other hand, was organized along the lines of the Japanese cooperative or the German sickness fund system of medical insurance. Funds were collected by decentralized units (i.e., at the firm level). Unlike in Taiwan, funds were not pooled between individual insurance societies. There were more than six hundred separate employee insurance societies in 1980, each with its own membership and administrative apparatus in control of its own funds. The organization of health insurance in Korea was much more decentralized than in Taiwan, both administratively and financially.

Social Solidarity

Social solidarity in health care, or the degree to which a program promotes pooling among wage categories and health risk groups, is reflected in the structural organization of a given health care system. In Korea, social solidarity was severely compromised, in part because of its nonuniversal enrollment and also because of the decentralized structure of its medical insurance schemes. Because funds were collected and retained at the enterprise level, the uneven distribution of risk was perpetuated. Workers in occupationally higher-risk sectors or firms were pooled separately from workers in lower-risk occupational categories. In terms of financial pooling and redistribution, higher wage earners by and large enjoyed both lower premium rates and greater financial stability in their respective insurance funds. Low wage earners, on the other hand, were forced to pay higher premium rates in order to receive the same medical care. The fact that the Korean system failed to institutionalize any interfund subsidization mechanism before the 1990s minimized the effects of financial redistribution or vertical equity. Moreover, many important and often expensive services were not covered by the Korean medical insurance program and thus were paid for directly out-of-pocket, severely undermining the progressivity of the system. In 1980, Koreans paid 84 percent of the nation's total health care bill directly out-of-pocket while health insurance accounted only for the remaining 16 percent.

Taiwan's system, based on the labor insurance and government employees' insurance schemes, fared better in terms of financial redistribution and risk pooling. Nonetheless, the overall pooling effect in Taiwan, as in

Korea, was compromised by the nonuniversal coverage of medical insurance. Those without insurance were forced to pay inflated, unregulated prices for medical treatment.

Medical Care Providers

In both places, the delivery of medical care was (and continues to be) dominated by private sector providers. During the 1960s, the share of public hospitals in the total number of such medical facilities decreased in Taiwan and South Korea. The overall proportion of beds in public sector providers declined precipitously during that same period. By the 1970s, approximately two-thirds of all hospital beds in both Taiwan and South Korea were in private facilities.[34] Because of this shift in the public-private share of medical care institutions, private sector providers enjoyed tremendous leverage in negotiating payment and compensation schemes.

Prices for medical services rendered under the health insurance programs were negotiated into fee-for-service (FFS) schedules. State interests were to keep prices as low as possible in order to avoid spiraling health care costs. However, powerful medical providers in Taiwan and South Korea successfully pushed for multiple-pricing mechanisms as a way of increasing their incomes. In Korea, providers demanded that the range of insured services regulated by the fee schedule be limited. Prices for services that fell outside this range, or uninsured benefits, were drastically raised in order to compensate for, and in reality augment, incomes that were perceived to be squeezed by the FFS schedule. In Taiwan, large private sector hospitals argued that a uniform fee schedule for all medical care providers did not reflect the different quality of treatment patients received at the various types of medical facilities. Thus, hospitals reserved the right to negotiate a separate fee schedule, resulting also in a two-tiered payment system. Furthermore, in a collective effort to recoup income lost to the larger hospitals, primary care physicians tended to "overdoctor" their patients. Clinic-based physicians in Taiwan also raised prices on medical treatments for uninsured patients, as in Korea, essentially adding another tier in the pricing of medical care.[35] In sum, the combination of FFS payment schemes and the dominance of private sector providers resulted in multitiered pricing mechanisms in Taiwan and South Korea, arrangements that most adversely affected those who were excluded from medical insurance coverage.

AUTHORITARIANISM AND SOCIAL WELFARE

This overview of the origins and implications of early efforts at health insurance reform in Taiwan and South Korea reveals some common patterns. Health care reform was gradual. The scope of the reforms was not universal, and in fact, health care policies selectively targeted beneficiaries based on the political interests of the state. Finally, efforts to implement limited health insurance were initiated by the authoritarian states rather than from within society. This is not to say, however, that health policy change in Taiwan and South Korea progressed in identical ways. As discussed earlier, there were significant variations between the two experiences in terms of the timing of policy change, the institutional or organizational bases of reform, and the targeted beneficiaries of health policy reform.

Understanding Equity and Development

As outlined in Chapter 2, ideas shape debates about "relevant" problems and their "appropriate" solutions. In the immediate postwar period, Taiwan and South Korea faced extreme economic stagflation. Economic recovery, therefore, was the highest priority. Uncontested leadership in the policy process meant that the political elite could narrowly construe policy ideas and initiatives. Out of this political economic context emerged a consensus among policymakers around those policies that promoted *rapid* and *aggregate* economic growth. Distributive concerns were secondary, and redistributive social policy ideas were nonexistent.

In an effort to legitimate the authoritarian state in South Korea, particularly in the face of resurgent social and political mobilization throughout the 1950s and early 1960s, state leaders there crafted a new national identity based on fervent anticommunism and a moralistic anti-Japanese economic nationalism.[36] "Catching up with Japan" in economic development was the basis of political legitimacy. Economic nationalism justified the authoritarian developmental state and its growth-first economic policies.[37] Slogans such as "self-reliance" came to dominate popular discourse. Ideas or actions thought to be inimical to the goal of rapid economic growth were considered unpatriotic and anti-Korean.[38] Growth at all costs for the collective good of the nation remained the official developmental ethos in Korea until the late 1970s.

The understanding of development among state policymakers in Taiwan was slightly different though still anchored in the promotion of rapid and aggregate economic growth. The main difference was that in Taiwan, the distributive consequences of economic growth were of some political concern for the KMT leadership. Ethnic tensions between the Chinese mainlanders who arrived with the KMT during the late 1940s, a minority group on the island, and the Taiwanese inhabitants meant that political stability was critical to the ruling regime. Extreme inequality was understood to be a potential source of political crisis. Still, concerns surrounding distributive outcomes were not so much about proactively reducing socioeconomic inequalities as they were about ensuring that disparities did not translate into political threats for the ruling party. Rapid growth was therefore seen as the best solution to this political problem.

Before democratic transition, both regimes similarly dismissed redistributive imperatives in their understandings of development. Redistributive social policies and the idea of social welfare were demonized and portrayed as communist. Health insurance benefited those who were in relatively less need of social protection. Equity was narrowly understood to be the alleviation of poverty. In 1962, Park Chung-Hee himself wrote: "Economic equality in this context means not so much the communal ownership of property or its equal distribution, but the guarantee of the minimum right to survival and subsistence. It means, in other words, that employment opportunities should be equally provided, lowest individual income should be increased uniformly to the minimum level, and the people's minimum living standard should be guaranteed."[39] Poverty alleviation was defined in terms of basic needs (such as employment and food) rather than in relational or relative understandings of equity.[40] Economic policymakers in Taiwan held similar ideas about equity.[41]

This minimalist conceptualization of equity was not entirely based on ideological predispositions or geostrategic conflicts with the communist regimes of North Korea and China. Policymakers in both authoritarian developmental states actually *believed* that aggregate economic growth would trickle down and raise the absolute fortunes of society's have-nots.[42] Rapid economic growth, therefore, was imperative. Most important, government intervention in redistribution, and social welfare more broadly, was understood to be counterproductive to rapid growth. As Yeun-Wen Ku describes in the case of Taiwan, although "the state's high degree of autonomy over the domestic market and society meant that the state did have the option of pursuing universal welfare measures, it chose not to . . . welfare was sacrificed in return for faster economic growth."[43]

The authoritarian regimes understood similar causal stories about equity and the means through which to achieve these minimalist goals: rapid economic growth. The idea of substantive redistributive policy was not even in the realm of possibility given the way the objectives and processes of development were defined and understood by the ruling elite.

Political Crisis

Authoritarian welfare state expansion adhered to a political logic. Others have explored nonpolitical explanations regarding welfare development in authoritarian East Asia, such as economic growth, industrial development, and transnational learning.[44] Although these factors were important in facilitating limited health care reform, they fail to capture the political motivations for the gradualist and strategically selective approach to welfare state development in the first place. In his important work on democracy and public policy in Japan, Kent Calder argues that political crises compelled the otherwise conservative Liberal Democratic Party (LDP) regime in Japan to implement significant social welfare policies: "the principal engine of domestic, non-industrial policy innovation in Japan, particularly in its re-distributive dimensions, is crisis, rather than the routine lobbying of corporate interest groups (either business federation or labor unions) or even the strategic planning of the state."[45] Calder argues, for instance, that the legislation of national health insurance in 1958 and the program's implementation in 1961 corresponded with the period in which the LDP was trying to consolidate its authority in Japan.

The political logic of Calder's argument—the incidence of crisis and subsequent compensation—has also been explored in nondemocratic contexts. Peter Flora and Jens Alber argue that social security was first introduced by authoritarian or monarchical regimes in western Europe that used social welfare policy as a tool for modern state building.[46] In his work on the origins of social security development in Brazil, James Malloy writes, "Authoritarian elites have perceived paternalistic social policies as a means of diminishing social conflict and buying social peace . . . such types of reforms can well be perceived by administrative technocratic elites as a means of controlling social discontent by giving with one hand (social insurance benefits) what is effectively taken by the other (increasingly regressive distributions of income)."[47] In the East Asian developmental state context, Yeun-Wen Ku notes that capitalist imperatives imposed by the global economic system forced the KMT regime in Taiwan to sacrifice social welfare reform except during international or domestic political crises.[48] Huck-Ju Kwon similarly argues that "the political and institutional logic of social policy in Korea has been primarily determined by the politics of legitimation. . . . Those in power attempt to prove their legitimacy by the use of political measures such as social policy."[49] In all these interpretations of social welfare reform in authoritarian East Asia, and beyond for that matter, social policy is an effective political instrument. In the specific cases of Taiwan and South Korea, social policy was used sparingly though strategically. Historical patterns of social policy reform in Taiwan and South Korea demonstrate that the implementation of new social welfare policies or the expansion of preexisting programs occurred during or just after times of acute political crisis.

The KMT faced two periods of political crisis. The first was during the 1950s when the outsider regime was trying to consolidate its authority and legitimacy in Taiwan. Not surprisingly, the party-state first implemented limited social insurance programs for military veterans, civil servants, and workers employed primarily in public sector firms. Fostering loyalty to the state was crucial for the KMT. The second major period of crisis for the regime came during the 1970s, when it confronted intense political challenges both domestically and internationally. Diplomatic setbacks in 1971 and again in 1978, an economic downturn in aggregate growth over the course of that decade, and the rise of non-KMT candidates in supplementary elections together began to challenge the KMT's uncontested hegemony and the party's legitimacy on the island. More specifically, opposition mobilization around an emerging ethnic Taiwanese consciousness prompted the KMT to rethink its domestic policy agenda. The ruling party was thus forced to make some limited overtures in social welfare reform, such as reforming the labor insurance law in 1979.

The 1970s likewise brought political crises to the Park Chung-Hee regime in South Korea. Park's forceful imposition of the highly repressive Yushin Constitution in 1972 diminished the legitimacy of his regime. The labor, state, and business pact of the growth-at-all-costs 1960s also began to wane. Economic nationalism was increasingly questioned as the sole source of political legitimacy. The *minjung* movement, comprising intellectuals and workers, challenged the developmental ethos of the authoritarian state. This movement arose in response to Park's new heavy industrialization drive, initiated in the early 1970s.[50] Park thus turned to social policy reform as a way of rejuvenating both his political and economic regimes. In light of his government's failed attempt to create a national pension program in 1973, Park made health insurance reform a priority in 1976, placing severe time constraints on health policy planners. He needed reform fast.

Social policy reform in the authoritarian developmental states was therefore reactive to moments of political crisis.[51] Policymaking was hurried and consequently involved little structural change. Piecemeal reform in both Taiwan and South Korea required only the extension of coverage and tinkering with benefits. After 1976, health insurance reform in Korea entailed a gradual expansion in the number of health insurance funds. Medical insurance reform in Taiwan followed a similar additive pattern. The urgency for quick responses during times of crisis inhibited social policy learning and innovation. Moreover, authoritarian policymaking practices prevented consensus building in the development of new social policy, as societal input was nonexistent. Indeed, initiatives in social policy reform did not address the actual welfare needs of the larger population but rather fulfilled the political needs of the authoritarian regimes.

Selective Compensation

Although the logic of political crisis helps explain the timing of social policy change, the theory of crisis and compensation developed by Calder is less helpful in explaining the limited scope of social policy reform in authoritarian Taiwan and South Korea. Calder's Japan was democratic whereas the developmental states of Taiwan and South Korea were authoritarian.

The logic of crisis and compensation plays out differently in democratic and authoritarian contexts. Political crisis in Japan resulted in the creation of new national social welfare programs based on the principle of universal entitlement. In authoritarian Taiwan and South Korea, however, compensation never was universal in scope and in fact was strategically selective in its beneficiaries. The absence of meaningful democratic institutions in Taiwan and Korea precluded the need for the state to offer solutions that were broadly encompassing. In other words, there were no political incentives or payoffs to extend universal social policy benefits in the absence of any political threat of universal proportions against the authoritarian regime. In fact, powerful economic reasons militated against what was thought be to be expensive social welfare reform.

Consequently, the distributive effect of health care reform in Taiwan and South Korea was far from progressive, benefiting those who were in relatively less need of social protection. In Korea, limited coverage in medical insurance favored government officials, those who were employed in large conglomerate firms, and their dependents. The relative labor aristocracy, who were already better off than the majority of workers in terms of wages and working conditions, benefited even more disproportionately through the selective targeting of social welfare benefits. Though this structural bias exacerbated socioeconomic disparities, selective compensation guaranteed political support from the most economically productive sectors of Korean society. This support was particularly important for Park as he tried to legitimate his aggressive industrialization plan for the 1970s. Social insurance benefits in Taiwan were extended only to those who were employed. Dependents of workers and those who were unemployed continued to be excluded. Like the Korean medical insurance system, social welfare in Taiwan was skewed to benefit the "productive" sectors of the economy, revealing a similar occupational bias. Social insurance, furthermore, disproportionately favored the public service sector, notably government employees and their families. For the authoritarian KMT, it was important that government officials remained loyal to the ruling party and to the developmental state more generally.

CONCLUSION

In the absence of democracy, there were no political incentives for the authoritarian state to promote universal social welfare. Therefore, the extension of social welfare benefits in Taiwan and South Korea privileged those distributional coalitions or sectors that were politically and economically vital to sustaining the authoritarian states and their developmental regimes. The uneven distribution of social welfare benefits was a strategy aimed at gaining selective support for the regimes, not legitimacy in the universal, democratic sense. Furthermore, policymakers believed that policies aimed at promoting redistribution from higher to lower income groups were inimical to rapid economic growth. Problems of equity were understood only in terms of poverty alleviation, not socioeconomic redistribution. This belief system was unchallenged, as the health policy network was closed off to actors and interests outside the state apparatus. In sum, social policy reform was motivated by the political economic interests of the authoritarian elites and their allies rather than by the welfare of the vulnerable.

The next chapter looks at the impact of democratic breakthrough on the politics of health care reform. Interestingly, the internal dynamics of preexisting health care policy networks in Taiwan and South Korea were not significantly altered even after the introduction of democratic reform. Where democratic breakthrough mattered was in the processes of agenda setting and in sparking a politically motivated shift to universalism in health care policy. The logic of state responsiveness was necessarily different in democratic settings than under authoritarian rule. In a democracy, the state needs to address social policy demands made by a universally mobilized citizenry. Thus, in contrast with the political logic of authoritarianism and selective welfare, democratic politics require universal solutions.

CHAPTER 4

DEMOCRATIC BREAKTHROUGH
AND UNIVERSAL HEALTH CARE

Democratic transition in South Korea began on June 29, 1987, when Roh Tae-Woo, the chosen successor to authoritarian president Chun Doo-Hwan, announced direct presidential elections for later that year. He then unveiled his constitutional reform plan, guaranteeing new freedoms for the press, political parties, and opposition dissidents.[1] In Taiwan, the breakdown of authoritarian rule was initiated with the "illegal" formation of the opposition Democratic Progressive Party (DPP) in late 1986 and the lifting of martial law in 1987. Elections were then gradually expanded, and for the first time, opposition party candidates could freely compete in electoral competition.[2]

Universal health care was implemented in South Korea and Taiwan after democratic breakthrough, and indeed, these watershed events were very much intertwined. In both cases, the institutionalization of political competition—the legalization of associational life, introduction of elections, and formation of opposition parties—created conditions of increasing political uncertainty for the incumbent regimes. The political logic of democratic transition thus made universal health care a winning political strategy. From the perspective of the ruling elites, political competition forced the incumbent regimes to adapt to a new strategic context. For citizens, this moment of political opening provided an important opportunity to influence the social policy agenda. Though the health policy decision-making process in Taiwan and South Korea continued to be dominated by incumbent state elites, it was the interaction of these elites and newly enfranchised citizens that pushed the agenda-setting process in the direction of universal health care.

CONVERGENCE AND DIVERGENCE IN HEALTH CARE REFORM

In Korea, employee-based health insurance schemes gradually increased throughout the 1980s, but it was not until after democratic transition had begun that the Roh Tae-Woo government expanded health care coverage to the self-employed, who constituted about half of all workers in Korea.[3] In January 1988, just after the founding presidential elections and a few months before the first national assembly elections, 138 rural self-employed insurance societies (SEIS) were formed, covering 1.7 million previously uninsured farming and fishing households, or approximately 6.7 million people. In early 1989, the Roh Tae-Woo government created an additional 117 urban SEIS, providing coverage for 12.6 million self-employed workers and previously uninsured individuals. After this second expansion, close to 100 percent of all Koreans benefited from some form of medical care coverage.

In Taiwan, the National Health Insurance program was implemented in March 1995. Though the Kuomintang government first announced its intention to create a universal health insurance system in 1986, it was in 1988, just after the lifting of martial law and the formation of the DPP, that the ruling regime began planning its health care reform. Throughout the 1980s, the KMT government gradually extended health insurance coverage to farmers on a trial basis. However, the proportion of the total population benefiting from medical insurance was still below 50 percent by the late 1980s. After the promulgation of the NHI in 1995, health care coverage reached 97 percent of the island's population.

Despite obvious similarities in the Taiwan and Korean experiences in health care reform—specifically, the initiation of reform after the moment of democratic breakthrough and the universal reach of both health care programs—differences between the two countries' experiences were nonetheless significant. In terms of structural organization, for instance, the universal health insurance systems were very different (see Figure 4.1). The Korean scheme, which more closely approximated the German and Japanese models, maintained a large number of decentralized health insurance societies (HIS), 420 by the early 1990s.[4] In this respect, then, the universalization of health care in Korea resulted from

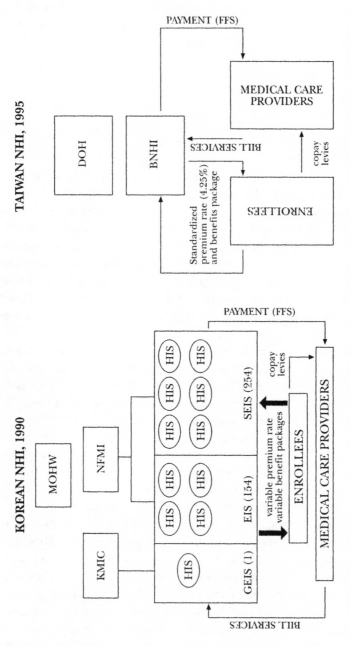

Figure 4.1. Universal health insurance systems in South Korea and Taiwan. BNHI: Bureau of National Health Insurance. DOH: Department of Health. HIS: health insurance society (GEIS: government employees' insurance societies; SEIS: self-employed insurance societies). KMIC: Korean Medical Insurance Corporation. MOHW: Ministry of Health and Welfare. NFMI: National Federation of Medical Insurance.

an increase in the number of HIS without any substantive structural reform. Since each HIS was financially and de facto autonomous, "additive" reform in Korea (i.e., adding new insurance societies) had a limited impact on risk pooling and socioeconomic redistribution. In contrast, the course of health policy change in Taiwan was "transformative." During the late 1980s, there were twelve health insurance schemes in Taiwan operating under the administrative aegis of three social insurance programs: labor insurance, farmers' insurance, and government employees' (and private schoolteachers') insurance. Unlike Korea's decentralization plan, health care reform in Taiwan resulted in both the universalization and structural integration of medical insurance under a single-pipe mechanism administered by the central Bureau of National Health Insurance (BNHI).

The pacing and timing of reform highlight a second point of divergence between the two cases. In South Korea, the extension of medical insurance to rural and urban self-employed workers was carried out in a compressed period of time, between 1988 and 1989, almost immediately after the moment of democratic breakthrough. In Taiwan, on the other hand, planning for the NHI program began in 1988 but spanned seven years until the program's eventual implementation in 1995. The longer planning period in Taiwan facilitated the KMT's more structurally ambitious reform.

These variations in the substantive scope of reform and in the pacing and timing of policy change, I contend, reflected divergent patterns of health care policymaking. In South Korea, health care policy change was a product of reactive decision making whereas in Taiwan, the universalization and integration of medical insurance was shaped by a pattern of purposive planning. In this chapter, I argue that these different policymaking patterns, and therefore different reform outcomes, can be best explained when the two cases are analytically situated in their unique pathways of democratic transition. In one sense, democratic reform in Taiwan and South Korea similarly launched new trajectories of universal health care reform. Nevertheless, the politics of democratic breakthrough in South Korea and Taiwan were different in many ways, leading to important variations in policymaking processes and policy outcomes.

DEMOCRATIZATION AND FRAGMENTATION IN KOREA

In South Korea, mobilization around the issue of socioeconomic disparity was a major part of the politics of democratic breakthrough. By the late 1970s, economic growth had begun to slow. Moreover, despite aggregate wage increases since the 1960s and the overall alleviation of poverty through economic growth,[5] the distribution of economic benefits was increasingly skewed in terms of industrial structure and income. Large firms (chaebols) were systematically favored by the developmental state in the allocation of market share and investment capital.[6] Between the 1960s and 1980s, the distribution of income worsened,[7] and by the late 1980s, the degree of socioeconomic inequality was staggering.[8] Jang-Jip Choi argues that Korea's social structure was "reconstituted in pyramidal form" as a result of rapid economic growth.[9]

Korean industrialization thus fomented a social consciousness that demanded not only economic justice but also political reform. As the business elite became more enmeshed in the top echelons of political power, the economic have-nots and even the middle classes were further marginalized from the formal political arena. Increasing inequality was synonymous with increasing political alienation. The *minjung* movement of the 1970s popularized the notion that Korea's political and economic futures were intertwined, inseparable, and needed to be resolved in tandem. The grassroots movement framed its demands in a language of moral nationalism and around a new national identity based on the selfless hard work and triumphs of the ordinary person. The *minjung* activists saw themselves as the true patriotic vanguard. They demonized the Park regime as the protector of the privileged Korean elite. In sum, the bottom-up democratic impulse in Korea was articulated as both a political and socioeconomic critique of the authoritarian developmental state.[10]

Military leader Chun Doo-Hwan assumed the presidency in 1980 after Park's assassination and quickly imposed martial law. In response to intensified *minjung* and worker protests in 1980, Chun attempted to appeal to moderate forces, reasoning that political instability threatened economic recovery. Middle-class allies in the *minjung*-democracy movement, increasingly wary of the *minjung* movement's grassroots radicalism and more generally concerned about Korea's economic slowdown, sided with Chun's authoritarian approach to economic reform. Chun promised to eliminate corruption, break the collusion between the state and big business, and regain control over the chaebols.[11] Though his reforms were successful in stimulating economic growth in the early 1980s, his efforts to rein in the chaebols proved ineffective.[12] Speculative trading and buying among the rich, fueled by low interest rates (aimed at stimulating productive economic activity), exacerbated disparities between the haves and the have-nots. Furthermore, despite its rhetorical commitment to promoting a social safety net, the Chun regime fell short in addressing the issue of welfare reform. The regime's failed efforts at leveling the social and economic playing fields revitalized and strengthened the *minjung* movement, which by then had gone underground but had not disappeared.

Intensified confrontations between the ruling Democratic Justice Party (DJP) and the *minjung*-democracy alliance sparked democratic breakthrough in Korea. The United Minjung Movement for Democracy was organized one month before the 1985 National Assembly elections.[13] Popular dissident leaders Kim Young-Sam and Kim Dae-Jung joined forces to form the New Korea Democratic Party (NKDP). The unified opposition party unexpectedly won 29 percent of the popular vote, but the ruling DJP gained only 35 percent. The results were surprising since the electoral system was institutionally gerrymandered to favor the ruling party.[14] Moreover, the state's suppression of the press, opposition politicians, and civil society more generally was supposed to guarantee little competition for the ruling party.[15] The poor showing by the DJP led President Chun to break off promised negotiations for constitutional reform in 1986. Rather than initiate democratic reform, as the opposition movements hoped, Chun reverted to authoritarian repression.

The strong showing by the NKDP in 1985 and the resolve demonstrated by opposition leaders to cooperate to delegitimate the authoritarian regime and install presidential elections strengthened the commitment of prodemocracy activists. Most important, the rebirth of the *minjung*-democracy movement, in conjunction with the formation of the new opposition party, lured middle-class activists back into the opposition camp.[16] Thousands of protests and demonstrations launched by middle-class, working-class, church-based, student, and intellectual activists erupted in the spring of 1987. In an unexpected move, Chun's handpicked successor to lead the ruling Democratic Justice Party, Roh Tae-Woo, capitulated on several of the opposition's demands in June of that year: direct presidential elections were held in December 1987, National Assembly elections took place in the spring of 1988, and a new constitution was promulgated shortly thereafter.

In sum, a highly mobilized opposition movement based on what seemed to be a social democratic political agenda, at least in rhetoric, forced democratic breakthrough in Korea, apparently setting a fortuitous stage for social policy reform in the late 1980s.[17] Intuitively, we should expect that the immediacy of founding elections for both the legislative and executive branches would provide political windows of opportunity through which *minjung*-democracy leaders could push for major socioe-conomic change. However, democratization is a dynamic process. Unpre-dictable twists and turns in the course of democratic transformation can deflect even the most rational expectations.

Elections for the presidency and the National Assembly shortly after the moment of democratic breakthrough had a tremendous impact on the course of democratic transition in Korea. Unlike in Taiwan, where full elections for the legislature and direct elections for the president were delayed until the early 1990s, immediate founding elections in Korea hastened the fragmentation of Korean politics and exacerbated an already looming crisis of governance. For instance, the marriage of polit-ical convenience forged in 1985 between opposition leaders Kim Young-Sam and Kim Dae-Jung dissolved just two years later. Kim Young-Sam founded the Reunification Democratic Party (RDP), and Kim Dae-Jung formed the Party for Peace and Democracy (PPD). These charismatic leaders shaped political party identities,[18] and regional antagonisms rein-forced the enmity between the two Kims and their followers.[19] Though expectations were high that the political party system might develop into one that reflected the socioeconomic cleavages articulated so forcefully by the *minjung*-democracy movement, this anticipated partisan realign-ment was derailed because of the personal rivalry between the two Kims and competition between their regional support bases.

Mirroring political developments within the opposition leadership, the once formidable cross-class alliance of prodemocracy grassroots movements also collapsed soon after democratic breakthrough. After the summer of 1987, Korean civil society quickly split into "radical" and "moderate" camps.[20] Middle-class activists gravitated toward the political center, distancing themselves from their former grassroots allies. The middle class had much more to gain politically and economically by play-ing the electoral game and by ensuring economic stability. Labor groups and student organizations were increasingly pushed to the political mar-gins, perceived as too radical in their ideology and tactics.[21] By the end of the 1980s, opposition forces were unable to articulate a unified reform agenda.

The incumbent regime itself also faced serious challenges in consoli-dating its authority in the posttransition political order. Roh Tae-Woo gambled correctly that the rivalry between the two Kims would split the opposition vote in the December 1987 presidential elections. He won the founding presidential elections, though with just over one-third of the vote. With such a weak mandate, Roh was unable to launch any significant policy reforms on his own. The inability and unwillingness of opposition leaders to cooperate on substantive policy matters further hamstrung Roh's ability to govern.[22] The crisis of governance worsened after the 1988 National Assembly elections when the three major parties split the popular vote, leaving few prospects for effective coalition building in the legislature.[23] In this fragmented political context, it is clear why Roh chose to pursue additive health care reform: it was the reform path of least resistance and largest political gain.

ADDITIVE HEALTH CARE REFORM IN KOREA

The idea for universalizing health insurance was not new to Korean health care policymakers. In the early 1980s, the Chun Doo-Hwan regime created the Joint Commission for Medical Insurance, laying the groundwork for health insurance expansion. Between 1981 and 1982, the Chun government launched a pilot program of regional medical insurance for self-employed workers. At around the same time, key officials in the Ministry of Health and Social Affairs (MHSA) implemented a "partial consolidation" reform in which smaller, employee-based health insurance societies were integrated with larger ones in order to promote risk and financial pooling within funds.[24] Subsequently, MHSA officials began to discuss the merits of integrating all the insurance funds. Blue House officials scrapped this idea in 1982, however, because of opposition from business interests. Later, after the ruling party's election debacle in the 1985 assembly elections, President Chun renewed his promise to initiate significant welfare reform, notably with the universalization of health insurance.[25] In a 1986 joint conference between the MHSA and ruling party officials, state leaders again revisited the idea of expanding medical insurance to self-employed workers but, as before, to no avail.

Though many of these health policy proposals were not implemented under the Chun Doo-Hwan regime, primarily owing to big business opposition, they left an important legacy: President Roh inherited a corps of experienced policymakers and numerous reform ideas when he took power in late 1987. Yet few of these policy options were politically viable or strategically attractive. Roh's relatively poor showing in the founding presidential elections and the opposition parties' anticipated gains in the upcoming 1988 legislative elections left the ruling regime on shaky political ground. Roh anticipated that the opposition parties would be competitive in 1988. Thus, for health care reform to win political support for

Roh in the short term, the reform needed to benefit many but would also have to be quick and relatively simple. Health insurance integration was not, in this respect, a politically viable option, for the logistics of such a reform would need to be worked out over a longer period of time. Also, any structural reform of the existing HIS system required legislative approval, and it was almost certain that the opposition parties would gain enough votes in the 1988 assembly elections to threaten the ruling party's majority in the legislature. It was a gamble not worth taking.

Roh recognized, however, that these political circumstances could nonetheless be turned into a strategic advantage. He decided to expand the number of health insurance societies to include self-employed workers. Additive health policy reform was attractive to the weakened regime for three reasons. First, the lack of ideological rigidity in the political party system allowed the ruling party to use welfare populism to gain votes. The inability of the opposition parties to craft a distinctly social democratic identity gave the ruling party the opportunity to co-opt such social policy ideas into its own agenda.[26] Second, fragmented political conditions and the immediacy of founding legislative elections created a frenzied political atmosphere conducive to the doling out of political pork in exchange for electoral support, especially in rural areas. Furthermore, the most strategically useful type of political pork was one in which distributive gains could be felt immediately by numerous beneficiaries. The extension of health insurance benefits was ideal in this respect. Third, the simple expansion of health insurance coverage to self-employed workers did not require legislative approval and could be implemented through executive order. Additive reform was thus the product of rapid and reactive decision making, a consequence of the ruling party's instinct for political survival in the face of immediate elections and a fragmented political arena. President Roh preemptively initiated universal health care reform as a strategic, short-term political solution for shoring up the ruling party's electoral support, particularly in the countryside.

Rural Expansion

Health insurance cards were distributed to farmers in late December 1987, though premium contributions were deferred until later. Roh reasoned that this concession would win his party popularity in the countryside for the upcoming National Assembly elections. However, his plan nearly backfired. After premiums were assessed in early January, the rate was set so high—about 80 percent of the contribution rate was to be borne by the insured—that farmers mobilized in protest. It seemed grossly unjust to farmers that employee-based insurance schemes provided a 50 percent premium subsidy for enrolled workers (employers paid half the premium) whereas self-employed workers were expected to pay over three-quarters of the premium.[27] In March 1988, one month before the founding legislative elections, organized demonstrations for reforming the rural self-employed insurance program reached a peak. Farmers' associations forged links with politically savvy activist groups held over from the mid-1980s *minjung* movement. Progressive social organizations of rural-based medical professionals also joined the reform alliance.[28] Farmers demanded that the government finance 50 percent of the contribution for rural health insurance. In early April, the government conceded to the farmers' demands. The fact that founding National Assembly elections were to take place later that month was no coincidence.

Farmers represented a critical base of electoral support for the ruling party. First, the electoral reforms of 1987, wherein double-member electoral districts were reduced to single-seat constituencies, took away second-place votes in rural districts, making rural popularity even more crucial in legislative campaigning.[29] The resizing of electoral districts also gave rural areas a disproportionate weight in terms of seat distribution. Second, the farmers' movement had shown itself to be a highly mobilized and organized sector of civil society throughout the 1980s.[30] Grassroots leadership provided by national civil society groups and professional medical-based social movements (such as Physicians for Humanism) broadened the appeal of the farmers' movement by cross-cutting, and thus mitigating, traditionally salient cleavages such as regionalism. Third, farmers' attention was singularly dominated by the issue of health insurance reform in the period immediately before the 1988 assembly elections. This focus on a single issue unified the movement, again cross-cutting potentially fragmentary electoral divisions. Finally, regionalism, the single most important electoral cleavage in Korean democracy, was less salient in rural politics, making farming and fishing households a more "winnable" constituency for the contending parties.[31] The net gain from doling out political pork in exchange for electoral support was thus higher in rural voting districts.

Urban Expansion

Health insurance for urban self-employed workers was extended on January 1, 1989. The reasons for this expansion of welfare were less clear-cut than in the case of farmers. Self-employed workers were not organized, certainly not to the degree of the industrial trade unions. Given the saliency of regional cleavages among urban voters, workers were also less likely to vote as a bloc. Indeed, it is unclear why the Roh government decided to go ahead with the implementation of urban self-employed health insurance. However, when viewed in terms of the logic of political competition and the strategic imperative for preemptive social policy reform, this second phase of expansion makes more sense.

The results of the April 1988 assembly elections were hardly decisive. The ruling party was unable to gain a majority, winning only 125 of the 299 assembly seats, a large portion of which were from rural districts. The opposition parties led by Kim Young-Sam and Kim Dae-Jung together controlled 129 seats, mainly from the cities. In a rare instance of cooperation, both opposition parties pushed for the complete universalization of health insurance, which required the expansion of medical insurance to the urban self-employed. The ruling party, finding itself needing to win more political allies, co-opted the opposition's policy agenda. Grassroots movements in the cities further compelled the ruling regime to respond to demands for reform.[32] In the months before and after the 1988 assembly elections, the government offered more welfare concessions. During this period of welfare extension, self-employed workers expected that they too were entitled to a piece of the expanding welfare pie.[33] In this respect, the inclusion of the urban self-employed in the health insurance system may not have won the government any more support, though it certainly prevented any loss of support in urban voting districts for the already precarious ruling party. Simply put, competitive uncertainty compelled the Roh regime to initiate social policy reform preemptively.

Health Insurance and Clientelism

The extension of regional health insurance to self-employed workers, and thus the expansion in the number of health insurance societies, indirectly helped President Roh consolidate political support among local political elites. Though the regional self-employed insurance societies functioned as quasi-autonomous bodies, the president in effect appointed their directors. These appointees gained important sources of authority; access to funds (i.e., enrollees' contributions), for instance, gave them an endless supply of resources with which to establish individual fiefdoms in their respective jurisdictions. In exchange, Roh obtained these local elites' political loyalties. In other words, the expansion of health insurance laid the foundations of a center-local patronage system for the Roh regime. Most director positions were thus filled by political appointees close to the ruling party and the ancien régime. The overwhelming majority of new appointees were formerly employed by the military, the ruling party, or the civil service.[34]

This form of clientelism was particularly evident in the regional medical insurance programs for self-employed workers. By 1990, the expansion of regional SEIS provided the regime with more than two hundred fifty new patronage positions. Appointees selected to direct the regional health insurance societies provided central state actors important channels through which to penetrate local political networks, especially important because local elites were best able to mobilize district voters at election time.[35] It is not surprising, then, that the ruling party leadership drew the boundaries of the regional self-employed health insurance societies to closely approximate those of the electoral districts.

MANAGED DEMOCRATIC TRANSITION IN TAIWAN

The promulgation of universal health care in South Korea and Taiwan were similar in that the reform processes were initiated in the immediate postdemocratic breakthrough period. Taiwan's health policy reform experience, however, spanned a much longer period of time. With the integration of medical insurance under one carrier, reform in Taiwan also entailed a structural transformation, unlike in Korea. Understanding the dynamics of health care reform in democratizing Taiwan requires an appreciation of the central role played by the ruling Kuomintang party in managing the dual processes of democratic transition and welfare reform.

The Adaptive KMT

The politics of ethnic identity underpinned democratic change in Taiwan. Identity conflict in Taiwan was (and still is) driven by contending ideas of what constitutes a distinctive "Taiwanese" identity from a "mainlander" Chinese ethnicity. The early construction or experience of Taiwanese identity was a reaction to severe KMT repression, such as the 1947 "er-er-bah" incident and the period of "White Terror" during the 1950s. Efforts by the KMT to propagandize "Chinese" history and the importance of reunification with the mainland further accentuated this outsider/insider divide.[36] Taiwan was derecognized by the international community during the 1970s, first with the loss of its seat in the United Nations in 1971 and then with the normalization of relations between the United States and China in January 1979. These setbacks in international relations allowed opposition forces to tie the diplomatic future of Taiwan (and the Taiwanese) to democratic reform on the island. Support for democracy and the redistribution of political power to reflect the ethnic makeup of the island was de facto support for Taiwan's self-determination.[37] Grassroots mobilization erupted across the island, and the opposition *tangwai* movement gained momentum in the midst of the KMT's crisis of authority.[38]

In response, the KMT set out to reestablish its authority on the island, no longer as an outsider émigré regime but as a legitimate Taiwanese regime. President Chiang Ching-Kuo recognized that the KMT had to remodel itself as a ruling party of the Taiwanese and for the Taiwanese.[39] It was because of this change in strategy that the KMT was able to retain the authority to manage the course of democratic transition in Taiwan. The KMT was extraordinarily effective in political learning and in adapting to new political circumstances.[40]

Beginning in the late 1970s, the KMT leadership initiated a controlled process of political liberalization. To trump the ethnicity card played by the opposition, the KMT strategically promoted the gradual "Taiwanization" of the party-state.[41] Ethnic Taiwanese were recruited into positions of prominence in the party leadership, in the central government, and at local levels.[42] In 1980 the ruling party allowed non-KMT candidates to contest elections for supplemental seats in the legislature.[43] The expansion of central-level elections showcased the KMT's willingness to play by increasingly democratic rules of the game. The ruling party's strategy paid off, at least in the early 1980s, when the KMT consistently gained over 80 percent of the popular vote in supplemental elections.

In terms of elite-level negotiations, President Chiang strategically engaged the moderate leadership of the *tangwai* while continuing to consolidate a reformist faction within the KMT.[44] Moderate *tangwai* leaders reciprocated, negotiating an ordered transition with the ruling party and reining in the more radical factions within the opposition. Strategic efforts by the ruling party facilitated a negotiated democratic transition in Taiwan with the KMT at the helm, in contrast with the confrontational politics of democratic breakthrough in Korea.

Democratic transition in Taiwan was initiated between 1986 and 1987. In September 1986, just months before scheduled legislative elections, *tangwai* leaders announced the founding of the Democratic Progressive

Party (DPP). The KMT's response was conciliatory. In fact, President Chiang oversaw the speedy passage of the new Civil Organizations Law in late 1986 and the lifting of martial law in 1987. Chiang was an astute politician who recognized that the legitimacy pact between the authoritarian KMT regime and Taiwanese society had run its course. The moderate party leadership also realized that meaningful political change was needed if the KMT was to continue legitimately to hold onto power. As Bruce Dickson reasons, "KMT leaders decided refusing to adapt to the changed environment was a greater threat than setting and enforcing the terms and pace of political change."[45] Democratic breakthrough was therefore not an admission of defeat by the KMT but rather a strategic move led by Chiang to reinvent and then reinvigorate the KMT's dominance in Taiwan's democratic politics.

Consolidating KMT Dominance

As argued earlier, the immediacy of founding presidential and assembly elections in South Korea sharpened personal rivalries among political elites and weakened the ruling regime. In contrast, the gradual introduction of elections in Taiwan contributed to the KMT's continued dominance in political and policy arenas. In supplemental elections in 1986 and 1989, KMT candidates won 80 and 71 percent of the contested seats and 69 and 61 percent of the popular vote, respectively.[46] Lee Teng-Hui, Chiang Ching-Kuo's successor, assumed the presidency after National Assembly delegates selected him in early 1990. Even with the formation of an official opposition party in 1986 and the expansion of electoral competition throughout the late 1980s, full elections for central government bodies were not held until 1991 and 1992, and direct elections for the president did not occur until 1996.

Despite the KMT's seemingly dominant position during the early stages of democratization, it was not an entirely smooth transition for the ruling party. Internal party politics initially threatened the KMT leadership's efforts to consolidate its authority over the island. President Lee Teng-Hui personified the indigenization of politics demanded by Taiwanese nationalists, but he drew heavy criticism from the hard-line mainlander ("nonmainstream") faction of the KMT.[47] Lee was thus forced to play off the KMT's moderate ("mainstream") and conservative factions and the opposition party to solidify his own power base in the ruling party. In June 1990, he convened the National Affairs Conference (NAC), where political elites from the ruling and opposition parties drew up a blueprint for constitutional reform. Moderate factions from both parties forged a consensus on several important reform measures, including the forced retirement of life-tenured parliamentarians, direct elections for the governor and for the mayors of Taipei and Kaohsiung, and fully contested elections for the National Assembly and Legislative Yuan in 1991 and 1992, respectively. For Lee, the outcomes of the NAC silenced his hard-line opponents within the ruling party.[48] Though factional tensions would later reemerge in internal KMT politics, Lee was nonetheless relatively successful in strengthening his mainstream faction and securing his personal leadership over the ruling party in the early stages of democratic transition.

The consolidation of the KMT's dominance in Taiwan's democratic transition was also facilitated by the inability of the opposition Democratic Progressive Party to balance its own contending factions. For instance, tactical differences between the moderate Formosa and radical New Tide factions of the DPP persisted after the party's formation in 1986.[49] The moderate faction pursued reform from within the existing constitutional order whereas the more radical New Tide faction believed "street politics" and grassroots mobilization would hasten political reform. New Tide activists were also much more adamant about pushing for Taiwan's national self-determination and independence. Moderates in the party remained politically pragmatic about the independence issue, opting only to endorse "self-determination" in the party's charter rather than any outright claims for independence. Thus, it was unclear what the DPP stood for during the late 1980s. Such factionalism constrained the development of a competitive opposition party that could challenge the KMT in the immediate posttransition era.[50] Nevertheless, for the KMT, the mere threat of political competition by the DPP compelled it to rethink its overall policy strategy.

TRANSFORMATIVE HEALTH CARE REFORM IN TAIWAN

Health care reform in Taiwan, as in Korea, was in large part motivated by political factors rooted in the logic of political competition. In early 1986, just ten months before year-end legislative elections, Premier Yu Kuo-Hwa publicly announced the KMT's intention to implement a universal health insurance program by 2000. In 1989, another election year, Premier Yu announced that the start date for the new medical insurance scheme had been pushed up to 1995. Popular opinion in Taiwan overwhelmingly favored extending medical insurance coverage to the entire population.[51] The May 20th Incident of 1988, when farmers were suppressed by KMT authorities, galvanized the farmers' movement, which in turn pressured the ruling regime to offer more social welfare concessions.[52] The incident also focused citizens' attention on the paucity of meaningful social policy in Taiwan more generally. Thus, the KMT, like the DJP in Korea, was forced to co-opt the opposition's reform agendas, particularly those expounded by the New Tide faction of the DPP. Though the immediate challenges to KMT rule were not as severe as those faced by the DJP in South Korea, the opening up of political space for democratic mobilization in Taiwan nonetheless reoriented the KMT's strategic thinking. The ruling party now needed to win popular support, or at least not lose what support it enjoyed. As in the Korean experience, it was the logic of political competition that set the health care reform agenda in Taiwan on a universalist trajectory.

Health care reform in Taiwan was also partly motivated by the need to solve public administration problems. Those without any medical insurance coverage had found ways to enroll illegally in the various preexisting programs, making fraudulent claims of employment by a firm or self-employment. By 1993, the number of people claiming health insurance benefits amounted to 120 percent of the employed population![53] Moreover, the preexisting social insurance programs were, or were soon to be, operating at a loss. Perpetual underreporting of income on the part of employers and irrational premium rate setting contributed to revenue shortfalls.[54] The fact that each social insurance program—labor insurance, farmers' insurance, and government employees' insurance—was administered by a different ministerial branch of the government inhibited efficient decision making and effective monitoring of premium collection. The universalization reform effort would therefore rebuild the health insurance system in its entirety.

Executive Policymaking

The initial planning of the National Health Insurance reform was done by a special task force under the Council for Economic Planning and Development, the supra-advisory body for the cabinet (Executive Yuan). The Health Insurance Research and Planning Task Force, a small network of public health scholars, was formed in 1988. The task force was granted considerable latitude in its design of the NHI program. Though the ruling party maintained close communication through a quasi-supervisory body, the Health Insurance Research and Planning Supervisory Small Group, members of the task force were generally unencumbered by party dictates.[55]

Three principles guided the task force's planning effort: redistributive equity, systemic efficiency, and cost containment.[56] In its 1990 report to the Executive Yuan, the task force outlined a four-point framework for reform. The first recommendation, in contrast to the Korean reform pattern, was the integration of the health insurance system. In the late 1980s, there were twelve different health insurance programs.[57] These schemes were to be integrated into a single, publicly managed health insurance fund. This single-pipe system, the task force contended, would maximize the redistributive impact of social insurance by expanding the common pool of resources and spreading the costs of medical care more equitably.[58]

Second, the preexisting provider payment system, based on a fee-for-service (FFS) scheme, needed to be replaced. The FFS payment system lacked any mechanism with which to discourage overdoctoring, especially among primary care clinicians. Furthermore, the differential fees paid to care providers allowed large hospitals to use their de facto cartel power to squeeze higher prices from the government (see Chapter 3). The net effect, of course, was a rapid and continual increase in aggregate health care expenditures. The task force argued that some supply-side cost containment measures were therefore necessary, and it drafted a proposal for a global budget system whereby the insurance carrier or third-party purchaser (the Bureau of National Health Insurance), along with provider representatives, would set and adhere to an annual budget.[59]

Third, the task force deliberated at length about the financing scheme for the new health insurance program. Though the idea of extracting funds from general tax revenues was considered, in the end the task force decided to maintain the preexisting payroll contribution scheme.[60] It recommended, however, that the proportion of contributions be readjusted so that employers and employees each paid 50 percent of the premium. Under the preexisting labor insurance system, for instance, employers were required to pay 80 percent and employees 20 percent. To cover workers' dependents, the task force proposed that both the employers and employees pay a fixed rate, calculated from the national average number of dependents per household.[61]

Fourth, to curtail the overutilization of medical facilities and the rise in aggregate health care expenditures, the task force considered demand-side cost containment mechanisms. They argued that the implementation of a copayment or user fee system would discourage patients from making wasteful (and costly) visits to the doctor. The task force proposed a 10 percent copay levy for inpatient services and 20 percent copay fee for outpatient treatment, calculated from the total cost of the care received.[62] In addition, the task force sought to institutionalize a referral system based on differential copay rates for each level of medical provider. Patients would therefore pay a higher copay rate (of 40 percent) if they went to a large hospital without a primary care physician's referral slip.

In June 1990, the Council for Economic Planning and Development officially endorsed the task force's health care reform proposal. The challenge of turning ideas into policy was then given to the Department of Health (DOH) of the Executive Yuan. In the DOH, the Health Insurance Reform Small Group (*xiao zu*) was established and placed under the supervision of the deputy minister of health. The group was divided into four policy divisions—financing, provider payment, medical care delivery, and legal affairs—each headed by an outside academic expert. The DOH small group worked with cabinet members throughout the early 1990s to finalize the reform bill.

The DOH small group had the task of developing a politically viable and administratively tenable legislative proposal. Whereas the original task force approached health care reform as an academic problem, the DOH came at the policymaking process from a more political administrative perspective.[63] It turned out, however, that the legislative proposal prepared by the DOH mirrored closely the broad principles outlined by the task force. In his analysis of what he calls "technical rationalists" (CEPD task force) and "state interests" (DOH small group), Kuo-Min Lin shows that the two camps' ideas about health insurance reform were in fact quite similar.[64] The equitable financing and delivery systems outlined by the CEPD task force, for example, were important for the KMT regime as it tried to trump the opposition DPP by initiating an equitable medical insurance reform. Furthermore, the integrated system strengthened the state's capacity in financial management and administrative coordination and afforded the state greater leverage vis-à-vis the medical professional associations. Consequently, the DOH small group and the Executive Yuan made few revisions to the original task force's proposal.

In the end, only two changes were made, and they did not implicate the overall structure of the integration reform. First, the DOH small group lowered the CEPD's proposed individual burden in monthly contributions from 50 percent to 40 percent of the total premium, with the employer paying the balance. Second, the Executive Yuan decided that both enrollees and their dependents should pay for health insurance coverage, recommending a premium levy for each household member.[65]

The bulk of the policymaking work on the National Health Insurance reform bill was conducted within elite circles. The ruling party's main role in the initial planning stages was to insulate, as best it could, the CEPD task force and the DOH small group from particularistic societal demands. At the same time, the task force and the DOH made great efforts to keep the general public informed about the planning for the NHI, in part to gain political points by highlighting the regime's commitment to social policy reform. However, elite networks remained closed off in terms of public input in the actual decision-making process. Outside participation in the reform process occurred only after the Executive Yuan's bill (drafted by the DOH) was submitted to the legislature in October 1993.

Five members of the Legislative Yuan submitted their own reform bills in 1993.[66] In July 1994, just weeks before the legislature was to vote on the NHI bill, the Committee for Action on Labor Legislation (CALL), an independent labor organization, submitted its own NHI proposal through opposition legislator Lin Rui-Ch'ing.[67] The content of the various members' bills ranged from slight modifications to the government's proposal to systematic overhauls. These proposals were by and large individual legislator's efforts and not the result of advocacy coalition building in the legislature or in society more generally. To be sure, the relative newness and complexity of the reform proposal highlighted the dearth of social policy expertise within the legislature. Perhaps most important, the reform proposal offered by the government was, for the most part, well planned. It was politically difficult for vote-seeking legislators to argue against the government's claim to have created a more equitable and efficient system.

Legislators thus bickered over numbers. They debated the premium rate for health insurance contributions, in the end agreeing on 4.25 percent.[68] A second controversy centered on the proportional breakdown of premiums. After much deliberation, a compromise formula of 30:10:60 (employee/government/employer) was adopted by the legislature.[69] Third, the government's proposed differential copay scheme was challenged, and legislators finally agreed on a new copay scheme based on the following differentials: 20 percent (clinic), 30 percent (district hospitals), 40 percent (regional hospitals), and 50 percent (large medical centers).[70] Nongovernmental organizations played a sideline role in these debates. For the most part, societal input reflected particularistic interests. Labor organizations pushed for a lower premium rate. Primary care physicians pressured legislators to increase the copayment rate for outpatient visits to large hospitals as a way of encouraging patients to seek care first from clinical doctors.

Aside from these adjustments, the NHI bill that had been approved by the executive in late 1993 remained virtually unchanged. The structural aspects of the reform were not compromised, and the bill was eventually passed in a rushed session of the Legislative Yuan in July 1994. Politically, it was crucial for the ruling party to implement the bill as scheduled, given several upcoming elections: gubernatorial elections in late 1994, Legislative Yuan elections in 1995, and founding presidential elections in early 1996. Even President Lee Teng-Hui made personal appeals to the Legislative Yuan to work around the clock to ensure the bill's passage.[71] The KMT had promised health care reform, and in the context of democratic competition, it had to deliver. The NHI began operation as scheduled in March 1995.

Explaining Executive Politics

In both Taiwan and South Korea, universal health care reform was initiated in response to political pressure, in anticipation of political competition, and thus under conditions of greater political uncertainty for the incumbent regimes. However, the contrast in policymaking styles between the KMT government in Taiwan and the Roh Tae-Woo regime in Korea was significant, reflective of two pathways of democratic breakthrough. President Roh was forced to react quickly to electoral challenges at the outset. He thus pursued an easier, additive reform path. The KMT regime in Taiwan, on the other hand, was afforded the political latitude to control and lead from the top down a transformative health care reform process even within the constraints of democracy. Several factors account for executive dominance in Taiwan.

First, the KMT exerted tremendous party discipline over its legislative rank and file. Before the 1989 legislative elections, the KMT leadership enjoyed exclusive authority over the nomination and appointment of its electoral candidates. When the KMT experimented with a primary nomination system during the 1989 and 1992 legislative elections, decisions were still nonbinding and ultimately left to the discretion of the party leadership.[72] A KMT legislator's political future, in terms of both reelection and promotion to key posts, was dependent on the party leadership's evaluation of her or his performance, often measured by party loyalty.[73]

Moreover, the lack of policy expertise among KMT legislators, a reflection of the complexity of health care reform, combined with the gains in popularity won by the reform proposal, left ruling party legislators with little opportunity or even incentive to challenge the party leadership. KMT party discipline and the party's sizable majority in the Legislative Yuan (63 percent of the seats between 1992 and 1995) ensured that the executive's proposal was effectively translated into policy.

Second, the opposition DPP was unable to mount a serious challenge to the executive's reform bill, partly because of the party's minority position in the Legislative Yuan. Internal factionalism exacerbated problems of effective mobilization. The party was divided on economic issues.[74] One DPP party member explained that the opposition party was founded on "political principles" such as democratic institution building, the expansion of elections, and political self-determination, not social welfare. Indeed, the opposition *tangwai* movement of the predemocratic period, the precursor to the DPP, did not articulate a consensus platform on social policy reform.[75] The DPP, therefore, was in no position during the early 1990s to offer a tenable and cohesive alternative to the government's NHI proposal.

Third, civil society in Taiwan immediately after democratic breakthrough was highly fragmented. Though the legalization of civic associations was promulgated in democratic Taiwan, civil society actors were not a political counterweight to the governing regime during the early stages of democratic reform. New societal groups were organized along particularistic lines in the early 1990s, undermining intergroup cooperation. Furthermore, conflicts over competing interests, leadership personalities, tactics, and political party affiliations inhibited effective collective action, especially in forming alternative policy coalitions. For example, the medical profession was deeply divided between clinic physicians and those employed in large hospitals.[76] Within the labor movement, enduring conflicts between the Committee for Action on Labor Legislation, the Taiwan Labor Front, and the state-sanctioned China Federation of Labor took away opportunities to forge any working-class, let alone cross-class, coalitions that could rival the dominance of the relatively coherent KMT state apparatus.[77]

Finally, the asymmetry of policy information and expertise between state policymakers and societal or legislative actors limited direct bottom-up participation in policy decision making. Because the KMT party-state was so effective in insulating the planning process, societal groups and legislators were limited in their access to important policy information and data. Policy learning was constrained. The Taiwan Labor Front, for instance, offered some principled critiques of the government's reform package, but the task of turning these principles into alternative policy proposals was beyond its expertise.[78] Legislators from both the ruling and opposition parties similarly lacked the requisite policy skills to challenge the KMT's proposed reform. The relative lateness in which societal groups or legislators were able to engage the policy debate in the first place also inhibited their ability to organize and present well-designed policy alternatives. Ku Yu-Ling, one of the principal drafters of the proposal of the grassroots Committee for Action on Labor Legislation, recounts: "We were at a disadvantage from the start. We had heard that the government was planning on implementing a national health insurance program, but we were uninformed about the details. We really had to start from the very basics to even begin to understand the government's proposal. How were we supposed to know what a 'global budget' was?"[79] These societal-based actors eventually gained expertise in health care policy. It was only over time, however, that they narrowed the information gap between state and society and thus were able to penetrate the policymaking process.

CONCLUSION

The institutionalization of universal health care in democratizing Taiwan and South Korea was a significant departure from the piecemeal and selective reform efforts of the authoritarian states in the two places. The universalization of health care in democratizing Taiwan and South Korea represented a significant shift in social welfare reform. Social policy was no longer used instrumentally for retaining the political support of select distributional coalitions or for the productivist purposes of human capital development. Universal health care in both places provided for those who needed social protection.

The fact that these monumental reform efforts were initiated shortly after the moment of democratic breakthrough in Taiwan and South Korea was no coincidence. The introduction of democratic reform created conditions under which universal social protection was made a political priority. Specifically, democratic breakthrough influenced the health care policy agenda-setting process. Political competition, or anticipated competition, altered the strategies of the ruling elite, whose political survival was no longer guaranteed. Making procedural democracy work, in this respect, was crucial in setting a new and universal trajectory in social policy reform.

Strategic Policymaking

Several aspects of the empirical account offered in this chapter may nonetheless sit at odds with our expectations of the impact of democratic change on social policymaking. For one, universal health care reform in Taiwan and South Korea was initiated by the incumbent regimes that had made the transition from the earlier authoritarian period. Policy decision making continued to be dominated by the state. There seemed to be little direct societal or legislative participation in the policymaking process. To be sure, democratic transition, at least at the beginning, did not force a significant restructuring of policy networks, which remained exclusive and elitist. Expectations that democratic change automatically brings about participatory policymaking, therefore, seem to have fallen short.

Nevertheless, the fact remains that major health policy reforms in Taiwan and South Korea were initiated by socially conservative political regimes that had previously eschewed the idea of universal health care. The dramatic policy turnarounds of Roh Tae-Woo and the Democratic Justice Party (DJP) in Korea and the KMT in Taiwan need to be accounted for. In this chapter, I have argued that the politics of democratic breakthrough—specifically, the legalization of associational life, the right to participate in political affairs, the formation of opposition parties, and the institutionalization of elections—compelled the DJP and the KMT to initiate universal health care reform. Though democratic breakthrough may not have immediately resulted in participatory policymaking, it fostered a much more participatory polity, which in turn reset the health care reform agenda.

Three factors in particular influenced the health policy agenda-setting process. First, the strategic imperatives of democratic competition, or more accurately, anticipated competition, compelled the KMT and the DJP to initiate health care reform preemptively as a way of winning political support. Political pressure from mobilizing groups and the electorate more generally affected the strategic calculations of the incumbent ruling parties. The mere threat of political competition reordered social policy priorities and altered the direction of health policy reform. Second, ideological flexibility in terms of left-right politics and the lack of entrenched party programs built around these socioeconomic cleavages in Taiwan and South Korea provided the previously conservative ruling parties the opportunity to turn to social policy as a winnable issue. In Taiwan, ethnic conflict underpinned the politics of democratic transition, allowing the KMT to exploit social policy cleavages to boost its popularity. In Korea, the inability of emerging opposition forces to craft any sort of social democratic identity permitted the DJP to co-opt these reform ideas. In both places, universal health care presented itself as a winning strategy.

Finally, democratic change and the universal extension of the right to political participation (i.e., enfranchisement) altered the logic of crisis and compensation introduced in Chapter 3. The authoritarian developmental state selectively compensated social policy beneficiaries, who, ironically, tended to be those who least needed social protection. The democratizing state in Taiwan and South Korea, on the other hand, could no longer pursue such a narrow strategy. Universal inclusion of citizens in the political process, even in the most minimalist sense such as through the right to vote, demanded compensation similarly universal in scope. Social welfare exclusivity ran the risk of political mobilization on the part of excluded groups, a risk the regimes could no longer afford in the context of democracy. Thus although the logic of crisis and compensation work similarly in authoritarian and democratic contexts—political crisis leads to social policy reform—the scope of compensation in democracies is necessarily broader, and in Taiwan and South Korea was universally encompassing.

Variable Transitions

This chapter has also demonstrated how the politics of democratic transition and patterns of democratic breakthrough differ between cases. I have argued that variations in the politics of democratic transition affected the specific health care reform experiences of Taiwan and South Korea differently. Variations were evident in the timing of health care policy reform, the patterns of policy decision making, and actual health policy outcomes.

Democratic breakthrough in Korea quickly led to the fragmentation of politics. Specifically, the intense confrontation between state and society, the preexisting enmity between opposition leaders, and the tenuous foundation of the *minjung*-democracy alliance contributed to this political fragmentation. The immediacy of founding elections, for both the presidency and the National Assembly, created a highly charged, extremely competitive, and fractious political arena. It was in this context that incumbent president Roh Tae-Woo, whose hold on power was then precarious at best, was put in a position of reactive decision making. His regime sought to gain short-term popularity and legitimacy through the universal extension of medical insurance. Needing a quick and easy solution, Roh pursued what I call additive reform, which was the most politically viable option under the circumstances.

Whereas great competitive uncertainty characterized the Korean political system in the short period after democratic breakthrough, the central role played by the KMT party in setting the course of democratic reform in Taiwan ensured that the incumbent party continued to enjoy significant (though short of absolute) policy authority. Because democratic breakthrough in Taiwan was an elite-driven process, the KMT was able to maintain its presence in both the legislature and the Executive Yuan. The prospect of future challenges—or anticipated competition—to the regime compelled the KMT to initiate universal health care reform, but the specific political context of the late 1980s, and even into the early 1990s, allowed the ruling party to direct a reform process of purposive planning over a longer period of time. The urgency and time constraints for reform were less pressing for the KMT than for the Roh regime in Korea. Health care reform in Taiwan was therefore much more transformative in scope, and the KMT was thus able to portray itself not only as a democratic reformer and the engine of economic growth but also as a promoter of socioeconomic justice. The NHI was designed to reduce political uncertainty for the KMT precisely when the party was forced to play a new political game of institutionalized uncertainty.

CHAPTER 5

COALITION BUILDING IN KOREA

During the late 1990s, the Korean government legislated a series of health policy reforms that administratively and financially integrated the medical insurance system. Despite having debated the integration idea for nearly twenty years, it was not until after the election of Kim Dae-Jung in 1997 that the state was able to legislate this structurally ambitious reform plan. To be sure, health insurance integration was central to Kim's election campaign. President Kim skillfully assembled a coalition for reform, and for the first time, societal actors were key partners in the reform process, from agenda setting through the final decision-making stages. Kim also restructured the bureaucracy, installing reform-minded officials in central positions in the Ministry of Health and Welfare (MOHW). Lastly, he engineered a legislative coalition in favor of the integration reform within the National Assembly, using his institutionally derived powers as party leader and his personal authority as president to ensure consensus among his legislative rank and file. It was Kim's ability to balance the democratic imperatives of wider societal inclusion in the policy process, on the one hand, with the marshaling of political authority within a network of reformers, on the other, that facilitated this landmark social policy legislation.

THE IMPETUS FOR REFORM

The universalization of health insurance during the late 1980s was an important first step in the development of a more comprehensive welfare

state in Korea (Chapter 4). Approximately 13 percent of those covered
under the new self-employed medical insurance program were over the
age of fifty-five, and 32 percent were nineteen or younger.[1] The government's cofinancing of the self-employed insurance program marked a
radical shift in the burgeoning welfare state, changing its role from
strictly regulatory to more provisionary. However, the simple expansion
of medical insurance coverage, or additive reform, was less than successful in maximizing the redistributive impact of social insurance.

High levels of out-of-pocket payments made the program inherently
regressive.[2] In addition, the narrow scope of benefits covered by the
program exacerbated the regressive nature of the system. Uninsured
treatments, which accounted for 25 to 33 percent of all inpatient and outpatient medical care expenses between 1983 and 1989, fell outside the
state-regulated fee schedule.[3] In other words, private sector medical care
providers enjoyed free reign in setting "market" prices for uninsured treatments. Out-of-pocket payments (both copay levies and payments for uninsured medical care treatment) accounted for 59.7 percent of all health
care financing in 1990. Meanwhile, funding from medical insurance contributions and government financing made up only 23.1 and 17.3 percent
of the total bill, respectively.[4] In terms of redistribution across income
groups, 1996 figures for the government employees' insurance program
indicate that the bottom-income quintile, which represented 10.4 percent
of the national income, paid 14 percent of all out-of-pocket fees. The top
quintile made up 33 percent of national income, though these patients
accounted for only 24 percent of all direct fees.[5]

Structural decentralization in the organization of Korean medical
insurance undermined the principle of social solidarity and in fact worsened built-in disparities among the various health insurance societies
(HIS). In the early 1990s, there were more than four hundred of these
societies, organized in three categories: employee insurance societies
(EIS), self-employed insurance societies (SEIS), and the single government employees' insurance (GEI) program. The addition of insurance
societies during the late 1980s, rather than the enlargement or consolidation of preexisting funds, meant that the size of the social insurance
pool for redistribution was reduced quite drastically. The only exception
was the GEI program, which comprised 4.6 million enrollees in 1990;
most insurance societies' membership ranged from under 50,000 to just
over 100,000 enrollees in 1990. Rural SEIS enrollment rates were lowest,
with an average of approximately 45,000 members for each insurance
fund.[6] Furthermore, unlike in the Japanese and German sickness fund

schemes, there were no mechanisms for interfund or inter-HIS subsidization in Korea.[7] In terms of risk pooling, then, low-risk occupational groups such as public civil servants were exclusive members of a large and relatively healthy pool. Higher-risk industrial and/or rural workers, on the other hand, were grouped together in smaller insurance societies.

The disparities and structural inequities between health insurance societies are illuminated further when one considers the relationship between medical insurance financing and benefits across occupational categories. Because each HIS functioned as a quasi-autonomous body, individual insurance societies set their own premium contribution rates. In 1993, self-employed workers paid on average 13,652 Won per month whereas government employees paid 12,816 Won. Industrial employees paid the least, at 10,738 Won per month.[8] Although self-employed workers paid the most, they were the least frequent users of medical services.[9] For example, in 1993, members of self-employed insurance societies (SEIS) averaged 3.656 claims per person (both inpatient and outpatient claims) whereas industrial workers averaged 3.987 claims and government employees averaged 4.463.[10] In terms of the cash value of medical benefits, self-employed workers consistently paid the most in premium contributions yet received the lowest value of medical benefits (see Table 5.1). Government employees, on the other hand, paid the least in annual insurance contributions but received the highest value in benefits. Proponents of health insurance integration thus argued that the decentralized system of medical insurance organization in Korea limited both risk and financial pooling among health insurance societies, an arrangement that exacerbated disparities among types of funds.

In order to promote greater equity in health care, the government initiated a series of major reforms in the late 1990s. The reform effort, carried out in two stages, integrated the formerly decentralized and disparate health insurance societies into a single, publicly administered

TABLE 5.1.
Benefits versus Contributions in South Korean Health Insurance Societies, 1998

	Government employees' insurance	Employee insurance	Regional self-employed insurance
Yearly contribution per person (in Won)	127,002	137,412	138,345
Yearly benefits per person (in Won)	186,180	153,372	144,514
Ratio of benefits to contributions	1.47	1.12	1.04

Source: *1998 Medical Insurance Statistical Yearbook* (Seoul: National Federatio of Medical Insurance, 1999), 380–85.

insurance carrier. The first reform measure, the 1997 Medical Insurance Act, required that the 227 regional self-employed insurance societies be unified into one fund and then integrated into the government employees' insurance society. This single fund was managed by a new parastatal organization, the National Health Insurance Corporation (NHIC). By the end of 1998, the Korean health insurance program was organized as a dual system comprising the NHIC and the National Federation of Medical Insurance (NFMI) (see Figure 5.1). The latter was the umbrella organization for the 145 enterprise-based employee insurance societies (EIS). In January 1999, the Kim Dae-Jung government passed a second and more radical reform bill that required all health insurance societies, including the 145 EIS, to be integrated into a single financial and administrative unit. The NFMI was to be disbanded on July 1, 2000, and all its member insurance societies integrated into the NHIC. The second reform thus ended up looking a lot like the NHI scheme in Taiwan.

OBSTACLES TO INTEGRATION

The idea for health insurance integration in Korea was not a new one. Debate surrounding the integration reform actually began in the early 1980s. However, the absence of any major bottom-up social forces in favor of the integration reform, along with the lack of political will among key decision makers and the state's close relationship with big business, obstructed earlier efforts at structural reform.

A Contest of Elites, 1980–1982

As of 1980, there were more than six hundred HIS covering approximately 20 percent of the workforce.[11] These small insurance societies limited the risk-pooling and redistributive effects of social insurance, exacerbating financial disparities between funds. It was in this context that the idea of health insurance consolidation was first introduced. In early 1980, the Ministry of Health and Social Affairs (MHSA) merged several small insurance societies. This consolidation reform introduced new ideas about the equity-enhancing effects of insurance integration.[12] The ministry's Advisory Committee, made up primarily of members of the progressive Committee for Social Security (CSS), began to explore the idea of comprehensive health insurance integration. Minister Chun Myung-Kee worked closely with his Advisory Committee, and in September 1980,

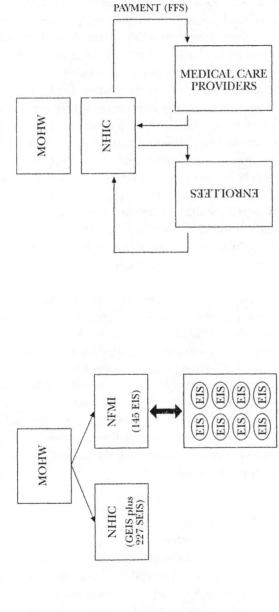

REFORM #1: DUAL STRUCTURE (October 1998)   **REFORM #2: INTEGRATED STRUCTURE** (1999)

Figure 5.1. Health care legislation in South Korea, 1998–1999. EIS: employee insurance societies. MOHW: Ministry of Health and Welfare. NFMI: National Federation of Medical Insurance. NHIC: National Health Insurance Corporation.

he publicly announced the MHSA's intention to integrate the entire medical insurance system.

Opposition to the reform quickly mobilized. The media, a conservative voice in Korean politics, were the first to critique the reform proposal. Business organizations, longtime allies of the Korean developmental state, were quick to follow. Funds collected by the enterprise-based insurance societies provided companies with important sources of capital that could be reinvested back into enterprise coffers. Big business was therefore opposed to any reform that would take those revenues away. Furthermore, the National Association of Medical Insurance Societies (NAMIS), the umbrella organization representing all employee insurance societies (and backed by big business), argued that the existing decentralized system provided enterprise-level mechanisms with which to manage labor-employer relations more effectively.[13] These relations, already tenuous, would be aggravated if medical insurance funds were integrated, leading to further political instability.[14] Both the NAMIS and the Federation of Korean Industries (FKI) vehemently lobbied Chun Doo-Hwan's advisers in the Blue House. President Chun consequently rejected the MHSA's proposal in 1982.

Political imperatives left Chun with little choice. The proponents of health insurance integration comprised only a small group of bureaucratic elites within the MHSA. There was hardly any societal support for integration in the early 1980s, making it politically costly for Chun to endorse such a radical change. Furthermore, Chun needed to forge a cooperative relationship with big business, particularly if he wanted to stabilize and rebuild the national economy.[15] Thus, whereas reform-oriented bureaucratic elites offered a theoretical and intellectual argument for integrating health insurance, conservative forces laid out a more convincing political incentive for maintaining a separated system. For President Chun, the choice was simple.

The 1989 Veto

After 1982, proponents of health insurance integration in the MHSA were dismissed or demoted, and the ministry was restaffed with bureaucrats who were either opposed to or neutral about the integration reform. Integration was off the government's agenda. It was not until the late 1980s that the idea reemerged on the national policy agenda, largely because of the rise of nationwide farmers' movements around the issue of health insurance expansion in early 1988 (see Chapter 4). The grassroots

National Committee for Medical Insurance Integration (NCMII) was formed in June 1988, just after the spring legislative elections.

The NCMII comprised forty-eight social movement groups, including urban poor organizations, farmers' associations, medical professional social movements, and church-based organizations. The new coalition revitalized the activities of those bureaucrats-in-exile who had been pushed out of the MHSA in the early 1980s.[16] In late 1988, the NCMII proposed an integration reform bill to the Health and Social Affairs Committee of the National Assembly. Legislative support for the bill came from the two major opposition parties, Kim Young-Sam's Reunification Democratic Party (RDP) and Kim Dae-Jung's Party for Peace and Democracy (PPD). Some defectors from the ruling Democratic Justice Party (DJP)[17] and Kim Jong-Pil's conservative New Democratic Republican Party (NDRP) also supported the reform legislation,[18] despite opposition from the MHSA and the ruling party leadership. With a slim majority, the integration bill passed in the National Assembly in early 1989.

Bottom-up societal mobilization and patchwork coalition building in the legislature nearly succeeded in seeing the integration reform through. However, President Roh Tae-Woo vetoed the legislation in March 1989. The government's position at the time was that the integration of health insurance funds violated private property laws. Officials argued that once an enrollee paid his or her monthly contribution, those funds and any surpluses accrued from them were the private property of the insurance society held in trust for the enrollee. The government therefore had no legal claim to those funds.[19]

According to others, however, Roh vetoed the bill because of political considerations.[20] Kim Jong-Dae, then a high-ranking bureaucrat in the Ministry of Health and Social Affairs and a proponent of maintaining the decentralized system, convinced Roh that the integration of medical insurance would politicize social welfare and that the government should avoid political battles over issues such as premium rate adjustments.[21] Second, the reform bill enjoyed little ministerial support, particularly in the revamped MHSA, and thus prospects for any concerted cooperation between the bureaucracy and the National Assembly were slim. Third, the National Federation of Medical Insurance (NFMI)[22] and influential business federations lobbied the Blue House, and Roh himself, in opposition to the reform. Like his predecessor, Chun Doo-Hwan, Roh could not afford to alienate business, especially given his party's precarious base of support during the late 1980s.

Finally, one must not overestimate the influence of the grassroots health care reform alliance. It was hardly an encompassing movement. The independent labor movement, for instance, did not play an integral role; workers were already eligible for health insurance and were less sympathetic than other groups to the 1988 farmers' movement. To be sure, labor's activities during the late 1980s tended to reflect its particularistic interests, such as workplace conditions and wages, rather than social policy broadly defined. In this respect, then, bottom-up mobilization without the participation of workers made it politically easier for Roh to reject the integration reform in favor of his business allies. Roh's decision to veto was about ensuring his short-term political survival.

Conservative Statism in the 1990s

Korea's young democracy took a conservative turn in 1990, when three of the four main parties merged to form the Democratic Liberal Party (DLP). The DLP brought together Roh Tae-Woo's DJP, Kim Jong-Pil's NDRP, and Kim Young-Sam's RDP. President Roh sought to create a dominant party in order to break the crisis of governance and legislative deadlock that resulted from the close 1988 assembly elections.[23] The coalition controlled three-quarters of the National Assembly's seats. The merger of these unlikely political bedfellows was, according to some, a "marriage of convenience."[24] To opposition leader Kim Dae-Jung and his grassroots followers, the 1990 merger was a "coup d'état against democracy."[25]

The conservative coalition marginalized progressive social forces from the political and policymaking arenas, and civil society again receded to the political sidelines. The crackdown on labor mobilization, which began in late 1989 and continued through the early 1990s, decimated the independent labor movement. The high courts ruled against workers throughout the early 1990s, upholding the government's prohibition of third-party intervention in labor-management bargaining.[26] The ruling coalition repeatedly rejected new labor law reform proposals from the Ministry of Labor.[27] The newly formed DLP also amended the Sixth Five-Year Plan, scaling back proposed welfare initiatives in favor of high growth.[28] Given the powerful influence of the chaebols and the institutional (and strategic) persistence of these patron-client ties, the state remained cozy with business. Though Kim Young-Sam was not in favor of the conservative position taken by the ruling party in areas of social and labor policy, he remained silent. He was biding his time until he could take control of the DLP, which he did in 1992.

With a slim victory over Kim Dae-Jung in the 1992 presidential elections, Kim Young-Sam immediately pursued a new populist agenda, hoping to shake the conservative legacy of the DLP. In 1993, Kim's government initiated several reforms, including the passage of the "real-name" transaction law in order to flatten the growing disparities in wealth, the institutionalization of local government autonomy, and several anticorruption measures.[29] In terms of progressive social policy reform, however, Kim's regime failed to meet popular expectations.[30] Political pressure from the conservative faction of the ruling party, an important legacy of the 1990 conservative coalition, forced Kim to backpedal on the pace of labor reform.[31] For example, the December 1996 railroading of new restrictive labor laws through an eleventh-hour session of the National Assembly drew the ire and criticism of civil society movements and even some of Kim's political allies.[32] Because of Kim's inability to break the collusion between big business and the state, the concentration of commercial and financial privileges remained skewed in favor of the chaebols. To make matters worse for Kim, allegations of corruption involving his family delegitimated his crusade against state-business collusion.

Conservative statism persisted into the Kim Young-Sam era, preventing the promotion of innovative social policy ideas. Centralized control by the ruling party leadership over the bureaucracy, including the Ministry of Health and Welfare (MOHW), ensured that progressive voices for integration reform were effectively silenced throughout the early to mid-1990s.[33] With democratization, many anticipated that the authoritarian-era bureaucracy would become increasingly porous, pluralist, and administratively decentralized.[34] Yet despite some administrative reforms made during the Kim Young-Sam period, the symbolic effect of those changes far outweighed their practical significance in the policymaking process in general, and for social policy more specifically.[35] Bureaucratic reform was planned from the top down, involving only the Blue House and a few select ministries. Couched in the rhetoric of globalization and the need for a leaner and more efficient bureaucracy, administrative reforms in 1994 resulted in the merging of the Economic Planning Board (EPB) and the Ministry of Finance, forming the "super" Ministry of Finance and Economy (MOFE). The MOFE enjoyed even greater policy authority than the EPB had under Park Chung-Hee. The number of bureaucrats also increased.[36]

Administrative reform did not devolve authority away from the ruling party, as was anticipated. Instead, the reforms further centralized the bureaucratic hierarchy, making it easier for the Blue House and the president to manage and coordinate the activities of the MOFE and the line ministries. The Ministry of Health and Welfare, for instance, remained conservative in its position on health care reform. The alliance between the state and business, combined with the dominant position of the MOFE backed by the powerful Blue House, limited the policy options of the MOHW.[37]

In sum, although the idea of health insurance integration was first introduced in Korea during the early 1980s and reintroduced in the late 1980s, various obstacles stood in the way of turning the idea into policy. The legacies of the authoritarian developmental state, and in particular the resiliency of the state-business alliance, undermined integration reform throughout the 1980s. Politically, the state took a conservative turn in the early 1990s. The formation of the Democratic Liberal Party in 1990 recentralized political authority and thus further silenced proponents of integration reform in the legislature, the bureaucracy, and civil society.

COALITION BUILDING FOR INTEGRATION

Ironically, some health policy initiatives made during the Kim Young-Sam administration set the stage for complete integration during the late 1990s. In 1994, the first of two Health Care Reform Committees recommended that thirty-nine of the smallest SEIS be merged, thereby increasing the size of insurance pools among vulnerable workers.[38] That year, a second Health Care Reform Committee considered two new reform initiatives for self-employed workers' medical insurance.[39] First, in order to strengthen the self-employed insurance societies, the committee implemented an interfund subsidization program.[40] Second, the reform committee proposed to consolidate the 227 regional SEIS into sixteen larger funds.[41] Though the second consolidation reform proposal did not become official policy, it was in this policy context that the ideas of consolidation, interfund transfers, and social solidarity were legitimated as tenable policy alternatives.

During the last months of the Kim Young-Sam regime in 1997, ruling party legislator Hwang Seong-Gun introduced a partial integration reform bill, the 1997 Medical Insurance Act, which would consolidate all 227 regional self-employed insurance societies into a unified fund. This fund was to be integrated into the government employees' insurance carrier, the renamed National Health Insurance Corporation (NHIC).

Because Hwang represented a rural electoral district, he had been a long-time supporter of consolidating regional self-employed insurance societies. Others have pointed out that because Hwang himself was a former chairman of the government employees' insurance carrier (the precursor to the NHIC), he was predisposed to the idea of a publicly administered and financially integrated insurance system.[42] Most important, the enterprise-based employee insurance societies and their business allies—the perennial opponents of integration—were not at all implicated in Hwang's reform proposal.

Legislative coalition building was needed first. Kim Young-Sam's New Korea Party (formerly the DLP) controlled only 139 of the 299 assembly seats (46.5 percent) and thus required the support of nonruling party legislators for the partial integration bill to pass. Hwang Seong-Gun crossed party lines and enlisted the support of opposition party members, most notably Lee Seung-Jae, a legislator from Kim Dae-Jung's National Congress for New Politics (NCNP). With little opposition from corporate interests, the patchwork coalition of ruling and opposition legislators approved the Medical Insurance Act in November 1997. The National Health Insurance Corporation began operation as scheduled on October 1, 1998.

The election of Kim Dae-Jung to the presidency in December 1997 was instrumental in deepening health policy reform. First, Kim promised to integrate the health insurance system, a demand made by civil society groups during the presidential election campaign. Second, the 1997 financial crisis provided a window of opportunity for Kim to tackle issues relating to economic and social policy reform. Ironically, Kim benefited from the 1997 financial crisis, which gave him a broad base of support from both blue- and white-collar workers to lead corporate restructuring and social policy reform.

President Kim brokered the Tripartite Commission in early 1998, bringing together representatives from labor (including both the independent Korean Confederation of Trade Unions and the state-sanctioned Federation of Korean Trade Unions), business, and government.[43] Participants negotiated a series of policy trade-offs, announcing in early February one hundred reform proposals. With respect to the social policy agenda, the unions accepted the legalization of corporate layoffs in exchange for reforming the social security system. Promises were made for a universal pension program and the immediate integration of health insurance. Thereafter, ruling party officials, MOHW bureaucrats, and key National Assembly politicians worked together, introducing the integration reform bill to the legislature in August 1998. The proposal was immediately referred to the Health and Welfare Committee (HWC) of the assembly.

NCNP legislators were forced by the ruling party leadership to support the integration bill. The renamed opposition Grand National Party (GNP, formerly the ruling New Korea Party), however, did not impose an official party line. In fact, GNP members in the Health and Welfare Committee of the legislature had mixed opinions about the reform bill. Some were opposed to integration whereas others, such as prominent legislators Hwang Seong-Gun and Kim Hong-Shin, fully supported the proposal. Opponents of the reform idea nonetheless remained relatively quiet. They knew that if they voted down the integration bill, they ran the risk of alienating the GNP's electoral support among workers, farmers, and middle-class civic groups. Electoral considerations shaped legislators' policy positions. The fact that many nongovernmental organizations closely monitored and publicized legislative activities further compelled opposition legislators reluctantly to support the reform idea.[44] After nearly four months of deliberations, the Health and Welfare Committee endorsed the proposal and introduced a new draft bill to the floor of the legislature in early December 1998. The National Assembly passed the integration bill in January 1999.

Thus far, I have recounted the general story of Korean health care reform through the late 1990s. Over the course of the 1980s, attempts by the bureaucracy and the legislature failed to integrate the medical insurance system. Yet during the late 1990s, the structural reform was officially legislated. The next sections examine the key actors and their strategic maneuvering throughout this process of coalition building for health policy change. Specifically, I focus on the interrelated dynamics of societal mobilization, elite policymaking, and legislative consensus building.

SOCIETAL MOBILIZATION

According to elite survey data collected in 2000, 126 out of 132 legislator and bureaucrat respondents in Korea, or 96 percent of respondents, indicated that they perceived societal group influence in the policy process to be on the rise. Only 2 of the 132 respondents felt that such influence was on the decline. Increasing influence among societal groups corresponded with increased contact between these groups and state-level policymakers, a relatively recent development in Korea's young democracy. Put another way, societal actors found new institutional channels through which to gain direct access to the policy process. For instance, 54 percent of Ministry of Health and Welfare officials surveyed (n = 13) claimed to meet with societal group leaders at least once a month, and 79 percent of Korean legislators (n = 84) indicated that they meet with these groups monthly. Furthermore, policymaking officials have become very proactive in forging links with societal group leaders: 43 percent of legislators (n = 86) and 30 percent of bureaucrats (n = 43) indicated that they themselves initiate contact with societal group leaders.

Bottom-up societal initiatives were critical in shaping the politics of health care reform in the mid to late 1990s. In 1994, eighty social movement groups joined together to form the National Solidarity Alliance for the Integration of Health Insurance and the Expansion of Health Insurance Benefits, the precursor to the Health Solidarity Coalition.[45] The coalition's top priority was the structural integration of medical insurance. It also developed strong links with the then opposition party, Kim Dae-Jung's National Congress for New Politics (NCNP). In fact, Health Solidarity leaders drafted a new health insurance integration proposal for the NCNP in 1996. Opposition legislator Lee Seung-Jae, himself a product of the late 1980s health policy reform movement, introduced the integration reform bill to the National Assembly that November. Despite having 71 signatories, all from the NCNP, the bill was quickly defeated in the legislature. This episode, however, cemented ties between the Health Solidarity Coalition and the NCNP. Their relationship persisted well into the late 1990s, and Health Solidarity was a key ally in the reform coalition assembled by President Kim Dae-Jung.

Popular Support

The Health Solidarity Coalition enjoyed broad-based societal support. It mobilized a cross-class alliance of social activist movements. One of the lead partners in Health Solidarity, for instance, was the independent labor movement. Recall that during the late 1980s, social movements concerned about health care reform were unable or unwilling to ally with workers. Yet as one Health Solidarity member explained in 2000:

> We knew that labor was an absolutely critical ally in the 1990s if we wanted this integration policy to pass. After 1987, the voice of the labor unions increased, though their overall influence did not. In the early 1990s, however, we conducted some studies and decided that the most important ally

was the labor movement. Our movement's increasing influence, combined with the mobilization ability of the labor movement, would complement each other well in terms of a strategy for getting our voices heard in the policy process.[46]

Health Solidarity leaders specifically targeted the Korean Confederation of Trade Unions (KCTU).[47] Described as "more of a social cause group," the KCTU was recruited into the Health Solidarity Coalition, both for its ability to mobilize its rank and file and for its progressive orientation.[48] The KCTU was concerned about the status of self-employed workers (both rural and urban) and sought to redress the structural inequities of the existing decentralized medical insurance system. The KCTU had already formed a tacit solidarity pact with farmers by the early 1990s, leading to increased cooperation between workers and farmers in health insurance reform.[49] Though the Federation of Korean Trade Unions (FKTU) initially supported the integration reform when the idea was first seriously discussed at the Tripartite Commission in early 1998, the FKTU was not a part of the Health Solidarity Coalition. The FKTU and its historical relationship with the authoritarian state made Health Solidarity leaders suspicious of the federation's direct participation in the health care reform coalition. Its tacit support, however, was welcomed.

In addition to reaching out to more "radical" groups in civil society, the Health Solidarity Coalition enlisted the leadership of moderate civic groups. Reformers formed an alliance with the Citizens' Coalition for Economic Justice (CCEJ) and the People's Solidarity for Participatory Democracy (PSPD). The CCEJ, founded in 1989, and the PSPD, formed in 1994, are considered the new generation of posttransition social movement coalitions. They have incorporated middle-class activists, members of the professional class, academic experts, and politically marginalized socioeconomic groups into their ranks. These movements transcend particularistic interests and appeal broadly to the general public. According to one observer of Korean civil society, these new broad-based activist groups "reject the class-based and confrontational strategies of the past in favor of a nonviolent, peaceful and lawful movement style and specific policy alternatives."[50] They focus on quality-of-life issues such as social welfare, social and political rights, corruption, and the environment. Public opinion survey data show that these civic organizations are considered to be more trustworthy and thus more effective than government representatives of citizens in public policy debates. One scholar concludes that the civic groups "have come to acquire moral, social and political hegemony over the traditional interest associations."[51] The legitimacy and broad-based political support of groups such as the CCEJ and the PSPD increased Health Solidarity's political leverage.

The Health Solidarity Coalition leadership effectively mobilized its constituent members and fostered cooperation among a wide range of social activist groups. Coalition leaders drew on a dense network of personal ties within civil society that dated back to the *minjung* and democracy movements of the 1970s and 1980s. The various incarnations of health care reform alliances—from the farmers' movement of the late 1980s to the rejuvenated coalition of 1996—strengthened this network of like-minded reformers.[52] Moreover, the single-issue focus of the coalition facilitated cooperation among otherwise antagonistic social activist groups. Health Solidarity was a coalition of societal groups that sought the integration of health insurance and nothing more.[53] It was not, as many outside observers might have speculated, a leftist or class-based movement that saw itself as a political vanguard. In sum, both the single-issue agenda and cross-class composition of the Health Solidarity Coalition effectively crosscut and mitigated fragmentary "left-right" and "moderate-radical" cleavages within civil society.

Expert Activism

The knowledge gap between elite policymakers and societal groups was narrowed through continual policy learning, which in turn raised the policymaking profile of social movement actors. Health Solidarity was not only a political movement; it was (and continues to be) a policy movement made up of what I call expert-activists. During the integration reform process, Health Solidarity comprised a sophisticated corps of policy experts who were capable of providing tenable policy alternatives. For example, Yang Bong-Min, a professor at the School of Public Health at Seoul National University (SNU) and a longtime advocate of the integration reform, was also a standing member of the CCEJ's central policy research committee. Kim Yong-Ik, one of Health Solidarity's leaders dating back to the 1980s, is a professor of medicine at SNU. One of the earliest bureaucratic proponents of the integration reform, Cha Heung-Bong, maintained close ties with social movement leaders after he was dismissed from the Ministry of Health and Social Affairs in the early 1980s.

Because of their gains in policy expertise, social movement leaders enjoyed unprecedented access to key decision-making bodies of the state during the late 1990s. Policy learning paid off for civil society groups that had previously been shut out of the policy process. Indeed, expert-activists from Health Solidarity served on important government commit-tees in the Kim Dae-Jung regime. This involvement not only provided a downward transmission of important policy information but also culti-vated important political connections between Health Solidarity and state-level policymakers. In 1998, both Kim Yong-Ik and Yang Bong-Min served on the MOHW's Executive Integration Committee, the principal body in charge of implementing the integration reform. Cha Heung-Bong (later appointed minister of health and welfare), CCEJ secretary-general Yoo Jong-Sung, and the KCTU's Young-Gu Huh also participated on the Executive Integration Committee. Unlike in the past, societal actors were able to enter the inner core of the health policy network dur-ing the late 1990s. Indeed, Health Solidarity was not simply an army of grassroots protesters. It was an organization of well-informed and highly connected policy experts who articulated broad-based societal concerns about health care reform and who effectively engaged elite policymakers throughout the late 1990s.

MAKING ELITE CONSENSUS

As the failed efforts at integration under President Roh Tae-Woo teach us, grassroots mobilization, though critical for policy change, is not suffi-cient. A consensus for reform among policy elites is also required. To that end, President Kim Dae-Jung rebuilt the state apparatus. Kim's "consoli-dation of executive power" reinforced the dominant position of the pres-idential Blue House over the state bureaucracy. The newly formed Budget and Planning Bureau (BPB) sat above the Ministry of Finance and Economy and was directly accountable to the presidential office. The regional background and political loyalty of candidates for ranking min-isterial positions were key criteria in the staffing of Kim's new bureau-cracy.[54] Bureaucratic initiatives were thus shaped by the president's agenda. Ironically, despite President Kim's popular appeal and demo-cratic credentials, his administrative reforms further centralized policy-making authority within his corps of allies.

These general trends in bureaucratic reorganization also implicated the Ministry of Health and Welfare, especially given the attention that social policy reform received during Kim's election campaign. The MOHW charted a new reform agenda in health policy and planning. The first order of business for the Kim regime was to marginalize the MOHW opponents to the integration reform. The most notorious casualty of the MOHW shuffle was Kim Jong-Dae, a twenty-seven-year veteran in the ministry. Kim, a staunch critic of the integration reform and one of the advisers who had counseled both Chun Doo-Hwan and Roh Tae-Woo about rejecting the integration reform in 1982 and again in 1989, was ranked as high as the number three official in the ministry (director of policy and planning) before his demotion in early 1999. He was excused from the MOHW later that summer.[55] Despite a new leadership in the MOHW, some of the officials I spoke to stated off the record that they were still personally skeptical of the integration reform although publicly they had to endorse the idea.

The MOHW was the central node throughout the policy reform process. Lee Sang-Yong was appointed director of the MOHW's health insurance division, the most important ministry position in the reform process. Within this division, there was a general consensus in favor of the integration reform, as almost all the ranking bureaucrats were loyal to Lee.[56] Lee and his corps of officials coordinated the activities of both the ministry and the National Health Insurance Corporation, the new administrative body governing the integrated insurance funds.[57] The Executive Integration Committee was similarly accountable to Lee and the MOHW. External research support came from the Korean Institute of Health and Social Affairs (KIHASA), the unofficial think tank of the MOHW and the Kim Dae-Jung administration more generally.[58] The president of the KIHASA served as the chairman of the Executive Integration Committee. The MOHW also benefited from President Kim's personal patronage, as the presidential office firmly supported the integration reform agenda. The Blue House secretary for labor affairs and social welfare, Kim Yoo-Bae, was the principal conduit between the president and the MOHW. He provided important political backing for the ministry.

The integration of medical insurance in the late 1990s was the product of a tightly knit network of actors: ruling party officials, politicians, and MOHW bureaucrats. Before his inauguration in late 1997, President-elect Kim assembled his transition team, bringing together party officials and representatives from the various ministries in a coordinated effort to establish new policy proposals. The subcommittee in charge of social policy included MOHW bureaucrats, ranking members of the party, and key ruling party legislators. The party's central figure in the area of social policy was Lee Sang-Yi, who later became the director of the party's health policy committee. Beginning in early 1998, Lee Sang-Yi worked with MOHW officials to set the broad parameters of the integration reform plan. Lee Seung-Jae, a prominent NCNP legislator who had proposed the integration reform bill to the National Assembly in 1996, was also enlisted to help with the drafting of a new integration proposal. In the ensuing months, Lee Sang-Yi, Lee Seung-Jae, and Lee Sang-Yong of the MOHW (the "three Lees") worked on the integration bill. The ministry presented the final bill to the National Assembly in late summer 1998. Though the bill was formally proposed by the ministry, it was ultimately a product of the "three Lees."[59]

CRAFTING LEGISLATIVE CONSENT

The election of Kim Dae-Jung to the presidency meant that his National Congress for New Politics (NCNP) party was technically the ruling party. However, President Kim inherited a National Assembly in which his "ruling party" did not enjoy a legislative majority. In fact, after the 1996 National Assembly elections, the NCNP controlled only 79 seats, or 26 percent, of the legislature. Kim was thus forced to form a legislative alliance with the conservative United Liberal Democratic (ULD) party, gaining its 50 seats. Even then, the NCNP-ULD coalition was still far short of a working majority. In the first few months of his tenure, Kim worked hard to woo legislators from the opposition Grand National Party. Several members of the former ruling GNP recognized that the political tides were changing and joined Kim's shaky alliance. By the fall of 1998, Kim had patched together a razor-thin majority, controlling 153 seats in the 299-member National Assembly.[60] With such a slim majority, and one built on Kim's odd alliance with Kim Jong-Pil's conservative ULD party, how was President Kim able to amass the requisite support to pass the integration reform?

Committee Politics

After the integration reform bill was introduced to the National Assembly, the proposal was immediately tabled to the legislature's Health and Welfare Committee. Generally speaking, most legislative decisions in Korea are de facto made in committee. Because the National Assembly deals with hundreds of bills per session, legislators have little time to assimilate thoroughly all the bills that are introduced. In addition, legislators are understaffed, often having only two or three permanent staff members, even fewer of whom offer any expertise in major policy areas.

It is a common perception among government officials that legislators have very little understanding of the bills that are introduced and debated in the legislature. In fact, 93 percent of bureaucrats (n = 44) and 70 percent of legislators (n = 88) surveyed disagreed with the statement, "After policy proposals have been introduced into the National Assembly, legislators completely comprehend the policy's content." Consequently, members of the legislature rely heavily on the outcomes of committee deliberations to inform their votes on the floor. This pattern is not uncommon in most democracies.

Also not uncommon is the fact that partisan politics tend to determine committee decisions, in Korea and elsewhere. Park Chan-Wook's survey study, which examines legislators' opinions about the National Assembly, found that 55 percent of respondents agreed that partisanship affects the decisions of legislative committees.[61] One of the few exceptions to this generalized view of committee politics, according to Park, is the Health and Welfare Committee. Park describes the HWC as a "pure policy committee." According to his survey data, every member of the HWC indicated that "specialized policymaking" was the committee's single most important objective. Only 17 percent felt that partisan considerations factored into committee decisions.[62] Indeed, the HWC is thought to be its own policy community. Most of its members are considered experts in the area of social policy, especially when compared with their colleagues in the legislature. Unlike members of other legislative committees, most of the HWC's members remain on the committee for both half-terms (two years each), spanning the entire duration of their four-year tenure in the National Assembly.[63] The policy expertise demonstrated by the HWC has earned the committee considerable authority; 92 percent of its decisions are adopted in the National Assembly.[64]

This view of the HWC, however, is only somewhat accurate in the case of committee deliberations about health insurance integration during the late 1990s. For one, partisan politics mattered among ruling party members. Eight of the sixteen members of the HWC during the 1998–2000 session were from the ruling NCNP-ULD coalition, and they had no choice but to support the integration reform proposal.[65] The other eight members were from the opposition party, the GNP. No such consensus existed here, for the GNP did not have an official party line.[66] Nonetheless, opponents to the reform idea remained relatively quiet during committee discussions for fear of alienating key electoral constituents. It was not surprising, then, that in December 1998 the bill was reintroduced on the floor of the legislature with the Health and Welfare

Committee's stamp of approval. The integration reform proposal was swiftly passed in the National Assembly one month later.

Party Bossism

With rare exceptions, Korean legislators are not policy oriented. They are elected not for their policy ideas but for their affiliations with certain party leaders. As argued in the previous chapter, Korea's democratic transition did not produce programmatic parties. Consequently, the dictates of the "party boss," rather than any overarching principles or political programs, are the most important determinants of legislator behavior. As David Steinberg comments, parties "remain the weakest link in the democratic process, standing for nothing aside from the *ex cathedra* pronouncements of their leaders."[67] This lack of autonomy vis-à-vis party leaders undermines incentives for National Assembly lawmakers to be politically innovative. With respect to the integration reform, Kim Dae-Jung, as both president and party leader, imposed strict party discipline on ruling party legislators throughout the legislative process.

Korean legislators are not considered very influential policymakers, especially when compared with their counterparts in democratizing Taiwan. According to my survey data, legislators are perceived to wield the greatest influence in Taiwan's policy process (n = 110), ranking even higher than the president (second) and bureaucrats (fourth). As discussed in Chapter 6, Taiwan's multiple-member district electoral system affords legislators greater institutional autonomy in the party and the legislature than in Korea (n = 132), where legislators are ranked a distant third, behind the president (first) and bureaucrats (second). Whereas 68 percent of elite respondents in Taiwan (n = 109) perceived legislators' influence to be increasing, only 34 percent of bureaucrats and legislators in Korea (n = 131) felt that National Assembly members' influence on the policy process was on the rise. In fact, 43 percent of respondents in Korea perceived legislators' influence to be declining.

Institutionally, the candidate nomination system within Korean political parties is highly centralized. The party boss himself selects electoral candidates. One former ruling party legislator laments: "The most important consideration for a congressman is not the interests of his district but rather pleasing the party boss. It is a total lie if a National Assembly member claims that he is working for his electorate's interests. His only interest is staying with the party line in order to get nominated by the party boss for the next election."[68] In other words, the political fate of a legislator lies in the hands of the party leadership, not in his or her legislative performance, policy expertise, or constituent representation. For instance, there exists no primary system or mechanism whereby party members collectively nominate electoral candidates. Party funds for running election campaigns are distributed at the discretion of the party leadership. Furthermore, the 1988 electoral reform gave party leaders even more leverage in the nomination process.[69] The single-member district system increased competition among candidates to win the nomination of the party leadership. Fewer proportional representation seats up for grabs (a result of the 1988 reform) also tightened competition among potential candidates from within the same party to be placed high on the party list.[70] Despite efforts from the new "386" generation of legislators to democratize political parties through the implementation of, for instance, a primary system for candidate nominations, these reformers remain skeptical that any significant change will come soon.[71] In sum, the nomination process within political parties strengthens the leadership's hand in internal party politics, ensuring loyalty to party bosses and thus party discipline in the National Assembly.[72] This situation hastened the legislative passage of the integration reform bill in 1999, even though President Kim's ruling coalition controlled only a slim majority in the National Assembly.

INTEGRATION THREATENED

Though the integration reform was formally legislated in January 1999, the implementation process soon stalled. Opposition to the integration reform quickly emerged. Opponents to the reform effort agreed in principle with the aims of integration, but their concerns about the details of the 1999 policy stymied the government's attempts to swiftly integrate the finances of the enterprise-based employees' insurance societies.

Opponents of the reform by and large conceded that, at least theoretically, the consolidation of health insurance funds should promote greater socioeconomic equity. In this regard, they believed in the same causal stories as the proponents of the integration reform. However, these opponents also contended that the legacies of the preexisting decentralized medical insurance system would undermine the intended equity effects of the integration reform. Self-employed workers, who make up approximately 45–50 percent of the entire labor force, tend to underreport their incomes to the national tax authorities. Ok-Ryun

Moon and Soonman Kwon found that only 22 percent of urban self-employed workers' incomes and 57 percent of rural self-employed incomes are actually reported.[73] As a result, self-employed workers have paid less than their correct, and therefore fair, share of the premium burden. Critics of the integration reform also pointed out that the lack of income transparency was particularly egregious because many of those classified as self-employed workers were high-income professionals such as doctors, lawyers, and business entrepreneurs.[74] Integration, therefore, would not promote equity but would instead widen disparities between employed and self-employed workers.

Though the Federation of Korean Trade Unions was initially allied with the independent labor movement during the Tripartite Commission negotiations in early 1998, it changed its position less than a year later. Chung Kil-Oh, of the FKTU, explained, "The FKTU agrees in principle with what the integration reform is trying to do, so long as it better and more fairly re-distributes income; but not the integrated system the government has proposed."[75] The FKTU's allies in this policy battle, ironically, were the Federation of Korean Industries (FKI) and the Korean Employers' Federation (KEF). Because employers share the premium burden with employees, the integration of the enterprise-based and self-employed insurance funds would, in effect, mean that firms would have to subsidize the cost of health care for self-employed workers. Furthermore, both employers and the FKTU opposed merging firms' or insurance societies' accumulated reserve funds on legal grounds,[76] and they challenged the integration reform in the high courts, claiming that the forced consolidation of funds violated private property laws.[77]

Again, it is important to note that the opponents of the integration reform refrained from attacking the idea's principles of equity. Given the reform's widespread appeal among civic groups and other important electoral constituencies, criticizing its equity effect was politically counterproductive. Rather, opponents reframed their arguments by drawing attention to other policy areas that required fixing before the equity benefits of integration could be fully realized. Critics pointed, for instance, at the government's inability to enforce transparent income reporting as an obstacle to medical insurance integration. Their concerns were not entirely ignored by the Kim Dae-Jung regime. In early 1998, the government introduced a new premium-levying formula for self-employed workers based on extra-income holdings.[78] In early 1999, President Kim ordered the formation of a tax reform task force made up of academic experts and government officials. Though the task force spent a year working on various proposals, it made little progress in drafting comprehensive reforms. Some observers claim that big business obstructed any serious attempts at reform; others suggest that tax reform was not a high priority for President Kim all along and that the task force was mainly for show.[79]

According to opponents of integration, reform of the taxation and income-reporting systems needed to be implemented first, and only then should health insurance be integrated. Proponents of integration reform contended that integrating health insurance first would force the hand of the government, compelling it to initiate the much-needed taxation reform. The debate became one about the pacing and sequencing of policy reform, not about the principles of socioeconomic equity.

In July 1999, the FKTU initiated a campaign among its union ranks to oppose the integration reform, demanding that the government delay the program's implementation. Cha Heung-Bong, the newly appointed minister of health and welfare, brought an amendment to the National Assembly to postpone the financial integration of the employee-based and self-employed insurance societies until January 1, 2002. Administrative integration, however, was to go ahead as scheduled in early 2000.[80] Opposition GNP lawmakers in the National Assembly did not oppose the amendment, believing that the government's plans would eventually self-destruct. After a three-month petition campaign, the FKTU presented five million signatures to the government in September 1999. In response, the MOHW proposed a second amendment to delay the administrative integration of the different health insurance societies from January 1, 2000, to July 1, 2000. GNP legislators opposed this second amendment, arguing that the ruling party and the MOHW were simply stalling for time.[81] Despite GNP efforts to filibuster and delay passage, the ruling coalition pushed the amendment through the National Assembly in October 1999. Administrative integration of the health insurance societies thus commenced July 1, 2000, and complete financial integration was scheduled to begin January 1, 2002. The governing party, however, was forced to assure opponents of the integration reform that it would work to resolve the income-reporting problem.

CONCLUSION

The election of Kim Dae-Jung to the presidency opened a fortuitous window of opportunity for proponents of the integration reform. Ironically, so too did the 1997 financial crisis. These key events provided Kim with the opportunities to build a coalition, from the top down and from the bottom up, for medical insurance integration. First, the emergence of the Health Solidarity Coalition demonstrated a broad societal consensus around the integration idea. With the blending of grassroots activism and expert activism, societal actors gained not only political legitimacy in the eyes of official policymakers but also significant authority and expertise in the area of health care policy. Second, the reworking of elite policy networks facilitated the integration reform. New political appointments in the Ministry of Health and Welfare and in the presidential Blue House gave the ruling party leadership tremendous influence within a tight network of allied policy actors. Third, the exercise of party discipline during legislative proceedings facilitated the passage of the integration reform bill in the National Assembly.

The integration reform agenda was therefore established through the interaction of societal initiatives, on the one hand, and the government's responsiveness to these demands, on the other. Furthermore, the actual decision-making process and the scope of the health care policy network were extended to new actors such as Health Solidarity, MOHW bureaucrats, and key legislators. This pattern of policymaking was unprecedented in Korean social welfare politics. The integration reform process, when understood in this way, was the epitome of advocacy coalition building and substantive democratic policymaking. The significance of this process cannot be overstated when one considers this reform episode in the longer-term development of Korea's still young democracy.

Nevertheless, health care reform under Kim Dae-Jung, though technically democratic, involved a very centralized policymaking process. The role played by Kim Dae-Jung in promulgating the integration reform, in terms of both his institutionally derived authority and his personal leadership, lent itself to a style of policymaking that could be characterized as "forcing consensus."[82] This too was not insignificant.

Indeed, the politics of forced consensus threatened the implementation of the integration policy. The failure of reformers to address and resolve thorny policy legacies at the outset, most notably low levels of income reporting, posed potentially detrimental challenges to the state's goal of promoting greater socioeconomic redistribution. In fact, the opposition party successfully passed an amendment in the Health and Welfare Committee of the National Assembly in late 2001, postponing financial integration again to 2003. Luckily for proponents of the integration reform idea, the 2002 presidential election of Roh Moo-Hyun, the left-of-center candidate and successor to Kim Dae-Jung, strengthened the government's mandate to see the integration reform through. Opposition to the integration reform gradually waned, in part because of President Roh's populist support base and in part because of the opposition movement's inability to sustain mobilization over the long term. Financial integration was completed in July 2003. The reform was simply too popular, and the government could not backpedal on its promises.

Despite this victory for the Kim Dae-Jung government and the new Roh administration, policymakers in Korea learned an important lesson: the concentration of authority in democratic politics also means the concentration of political accountability.[83] Policymakers learned that efficient policymaking does not necessarily make for effective policy reform and that institutionalized accountability in democratic politics places an even higher premium on consensus building among all contending actors. In short, the politics of forcing consensus even within the rules of the democratic game makes for shaky coalitions.

CHAPTER **6**

RESISTING RETRENCHMENT IN TAIWAN

In an effort to increase the systemic efficiency of the National Health Insurance program and, more important, to shift the financial burden of the increasingly cash-strapped NHI away from the state, the Kuomintang proposed to privatize and marketize medical insurance in 1997. The proposal came only two years after the universal program was introduced. This reform, had it been implemented, would have undone the structural integration and public administration of the NHI scheme. In many respects, the KMT's efforts to revamp the health care system were in line with global trends in welfare state retrenchment. However, the ruling party was unable to craft a consensus among lawmakers in favor of the proposed reform. Legislators, bureaucrats, and civil society actors together resisted retrenchment.

This counterintuitive policy "non-event" is significant for several reasons. First, although the course of health care reform during the late 1990s in Taiwan did not deepen the nascent welfare state per se (as was the case in Korea), resisting retrenchment prevented the reversal of the health care reform trajectory established earlier in the democratic period. Redistributive social welfare was maintained as a policy priority. Second, the politics of resisting retrenchment highlights a new pattern of policymaking in Taiwan which featured new actors, new institutional settings, and a more inclusive policy process. In short, unlike in the past, when the KMT was at the helm of the policy process, the new politics of policy decision making demanded broader notions of consensus building.

FINANCIAL CRISIS IN THE NHI

The 1995 NHI program was very successful in promoting socioeconomic equity. Public satisfaction with the NHI continually hovered around 70 percent. In my own survey of legislators and bureaucrats, 70 percent of the respondents (n = 111) agreed that the post-1995 NHI system was more equitable than the previous health care program. Tung-Liang Chiang and Shou-Hsia Cheng found that after the implementation of the NHI, the number of medical care visits by those from the middle-income groups and the lowest quartile increased by 47 and 31 percent, respectively. The rate of utilization among those from the top-quartile income group increased by only 11 percent.[1] In terms of the redistributive impact of the NHI program, Chiang found that in 1998, the value of medical care benefits received by the richest quintile was less than this group's payroll contributions to the NHI, a ratio of 0.96. The ratio of benefits received to insurance premiums paid among those households from the poorest quintile, on the other hand, was 1.75. Overall, the differences between benefits received and premiums paid increased as household income decreased, leading Chiang to conclude that "the poor pay less but get more; the rich pay more but get less."[2]

With respect to its financial status, however, the new universal insurance program faced serious challenges. Soon after the NHI program began operation, on March 1, 1995, many cost-containment mechanisms built into the system were tabled. Proposed payment systems for providers, such as the global budget scheme, were delayed until more detailed data were available. In the meantime, the reversion to the fee-for-service (FFS) payment scheme led doctors to continue "overdoctoring" their patients.[3] Furthermore, the referral system, which was intended to discourage patients from first seeking medical treatment for common ailments at the more expensive hospitals, was scrapped in April just after the NHI was implemented. The copayment scheme, which was based on differential user fee rates calculated as percentages of the total cost of a treatment or physician visit, was scaled back and replaced with a less onerous flat-rate levy.[4] Compared with the Korean copayment scheme (see Chapter 5), Taiwan's was virtually free.[5] Patients thus continued to overuse medical services. The total number of patient visits in 1999 amounted to more than 322 million, or approximately eleven visits per person, a figure much higher than the OECD average.[6] The absence of demand-side and supply-side cost-containment mechanisms contributed to wasteful and costly behavior on the part of both consumers and providers.

In its first three years of operation, the NHI was able to bring in a surplus. The rate of decline in the annual surplus and the reserve fund, however, was dangerously rapid. In 1998, the NHI posted a deficit, and in the following year the program's reserve fund was into the negative (Table 6.1). To make matters worse, NHI's centralized nature made it politically difficult for the government to manipulate other revenue-generating measures, such as raising premium rates. In Korea, for example, the authoritarian government historically eschewed the public integration of health insurance precisely to deflect political blame for unpopular measures onto the individual health insurance societies. In democratic Taiwan, where universal health insurance was managed by the state, the game of blame avoidance was not an option. In short, the KMT felt it had to do something to resolve the looming financial crisis. After all, the NHI was the KMT's creation and now its responsibility.

THE RISE AND DEMISE OF RETRENCHMENT

On February 26, 1997, the cabinet-level Department of Health (DOH) presented its Two-Year Report to the Executive Yuan, as mandated by Article 89 of the National Health Insurance Act. The report highlighted the alarming increase in outpatient visits, escalating health care expenditures, the impending financial crisis in the health insurance fund, and the implications of this fiscal dilemma for the state.[7] The critical question

TABLE 6.1.
Finances of the NHI, 1995–1999 (in millions of NT dollars)

Year	Revenue	Expenditure	Surplus/Deficit	Reserve
1995	199,150	161,671	37,479	—
1996	247,463	229,409	18,054	25,145
1997	256,843	250,810	6,033	5,680
1998	269,481	271,043	−1,562	3,376
1999	300,362	300,651	—	−21,528

Source: Bureau of National Health Insurance, *National Health Insurance Annual Statistical Report* (Taipei: Bureau of National Health Insurance, June 2000). See also Teh-Wei Hu and Chee-Ruey Hsieh, "An Economic Analysis of Health Care Reform in Taiwan," paper presented at the Fourth Annual Social Welfare Policy Conference, National Taiwan University, Taipei, October 1–2, 1999.

for health care policymakers was how to reduce the financial responsibility of the NHI scheme or shift it away from the state. The government feared that increases in premium rates would create a political backlash, and this political consideration limited the state's choices of policy instruments.[8] Media coverage of the NHI's financial problems did not reflect well on the KMT regime's performance. Furthermore, local elections at the end of 1997 and key legislative elections the following year gave the regime little time in which to tinker with the NHI's financing mechanisms. In early 1997, the DOH solicited reform ideas from health policy scholars in Taiwan, ending up with nine proposals.[9] That March, the DOH commissioned the Chung-Hwa Economic Research Institute (Zhong Hua Jing Ji Yan Jiu Yuan) to formulate a new reform plan, and in April, the research institute presented its privatization scheme to the Department of Health.[10]

Minister of Health Chang Po-Ya opposed the competitive insurance idea. Having been the head of the DOH since 1990, Chang was strongly in favor of maintaining the single-carrier system implemented in 1995. She supported a publicly administered, single-pipe, though private-sector-owned, insurance system (*gong ban, min yi*).[11] Under this mixed system, the state would continue to play a significant regulatory role, guaranteeing the provision of basic health care services. The insurance carrier, which was under the public authority of the Bureau of National Health Insurance (BNHI), would be brought over to the private sector. Simply put, financial responsibility in health insurance would no longer be the business of the state. The government sought to reform the system with as few implications for the general public as possible, especially in terms of accessibility and affordability of medical care. Premier Lien Chan, who was also the head of the cabinet and had personally overseen the design and implementation of the original NHI program, supported the public-private reform proposal. It was approved by the Executive Yuan (cabinet) on July 10, 1997, and delivered to the Legislative Yuan for the bill's first reading.

Shortly thereafter, on September 1, the cabinet was reshuffled. Senior KMT official Vincent Siew was named premier and took the reigns of the Executive Yuan.[12] Chang Po-Ya was dismissed as minister of health, and Chan Chi-Shean took her place. Chan, a doctor from the private sector, had served on an ad hoc cabinet-level national health insurance advisory board in 1996 and 1997 and was therefore very much involved in the ongoing reform debates in the DOH. Minister Chan was also a proponent of restructuring the NHI into a new privatized and competitive multiple-carrier system. Consequently, the Executive Yuan's original reform proposal for a mixed system was withdrawn from the legislature. At the end of September 1997, the DOH began preparing a privatized and marketized (*duo yuan*) health insurance system. The state's primary objective, in light of the looming financial crisis in the NHI, was to promote a more efficient and cost-effective health care system. Proponents argued that marketization and privatization would improve systemic efficiency and thus financial stability. They also reasoned that socioeconomic equity could be preserved. Simply put, new problems demanded new solutions.

Under the proposed multiple-carrier system, enrollees would pay premium contributions through a centralized financing stream to the NHI Foundation. The proposed reform maintained a single-pipe financing mechanism. Unlike in other occupationally or regionally based multiple-carrier systems, in which enrollees have no choice in their insurance carriers (such as in Korea's decentralized medical insurance structure before the 1998 reforms), consumers in Taiwan's multiple-carrier scheme would have that choice. Regardless of which insurance carrier they joined, enrollees were to pay the same insurance premium rate to the NHI Foundation. Revenues collected as premium contributions, in addition to government subsidies, would then be paid out to the individual carriers. The Bureau of National Health Insurance could continue to operate in this new scheme, but as one of many carriers.

Payments to carriers were to be based on risk-adjusted capitation. In this system, the various carriers would negotiate their respective annual budgets with the NHI Foundation according to the number of enrollees they covered, essentially on a per capita basis. Risk adjustments to this lump-sum payment to carriers would then be factored into the total payment based on the carrier's membership profile, taking into account enrollees' age, occupation, and health history.[13] Carriers were required to contract care providers (hospitals, clinics) for medical services on their own. In other words, the NHI Foundation's primary role was to collect revenues whereas the role of purchasing medical services was to be the responsibility of carriers from the private sector.[14]

Carriers would be required to cover a government-mandated list of basic services, whose cost would be covered by the risk-adjusted payment from the NHI Foundation. All enrollees were guaranteed the provision of the same basic health care services. Carriers could, however, offer supplemental services, for which they would charge additional insurance premiums directly to their enrollees. The basis of market competition was therefore to lie outside the regulated basic benefits schedule. For example, carrier A could offer coverage for optical treatments (eyeglasses, contact lenses) as part of its insurance package and thus collect a supplemental premium from its enrollees. Carrier B might offer coverage for the payment of private rooms for extended inpatient treatment for an additional premium contribution. Carrier C might offer no supplemental benefits and thus require no extra premium on top of the standard contribution rate for basic benefits set by the public authorities in tandem with the NHI Foundation. Consumers could then choose which plan, or in effect, which carrier, best fit their medical needs. This element of choice would force competing carriers to offer the highest-quality supplementary services at the most competitive prices.[15]

Though many believed the privatization and marketization reform was the beginning of a slippery slope toward an institutionalized two-tiered or multitiered social insurance system, proponents of the reform proposal maintained that equity would be preserved under the new scheme.[16] All insured patients, regardless of which private carrier they enrolled in, were to receive the same basic benefits. Moreover, insurance carriers could not deny membership to any potential enrollee, regardless of health, age, or occupation. This clause, in addition to the risk-adjusted capitation provider payment scheme, would prevent risk-averse selection among carriers. Furthermore, in order to ensure accessibility to medical services, the proposed reform stipulated that insurance carriers would have to contract services to a minimum of 80 percent of all medical providers in Taiwan. DOH reformers envisioned individual insurance carriers forming medical care "networks" or "teams" of primary care clinics and hospitals.[17] Through the use of internally enforced referral and gatekeeper mechanisms, carriers themselves could allocate medical care services more effectively within their contracted networks, expending resources more efficiently. Thus, proponents of the DOH reform effort argued that the regulatory aspects of the new system would preserve redistributive equity while encouraging greater efficiency in medical care delivery. Most important, the reform would promote financial stability.

The looming financial crisis of the NHI opened an auspicious window of opportunity for creative policy problem solving.[18] Raising premium rates—a simple adjustment many scholars and bureaucrats suggested would resolve the imminent financial crunch—was politically out of the question, especially so close to important election years. There was a sense of urgency surrounding the imperatives for reform. To many at the top, few alternative policy options were available that could resolve the

NHI's financial problems in the short term. The leadership role of the minister of health, Chan Chi-Shean, combined with the support of new premier Vincent Siew, solidified the executive's position in favor of the multiple-carrier reform.[19] Finally, legacies of KMT-style legislation—for example, the imposition of party discipline, the rubber-stamp legislature, and the historical closeness of the party and the state-bureaucratic apparatus—seemed to suggest that the ruling party would face few obstacles in actualizing its reform agenda. Recall that the KMT had dominated the health care policymaking process only a few years earlier (Chapter 4).

It was in these seemingly fortuitous political and policy contexts that the cabinet delivered the DOH's multiple-carrier proposal to the Legislative Yuan in February 1998. After the reform bill's first reading, the proposal was referred to the Legislative Yuan's Health and Welfare Committee. It was not, however, presented back to the legislature for its second reading. Noted health policy expert Yaung Chi-Liang, a proponent of the multiple-carrier reform, was made deputy minister in early 1999 specifically to rejuvenate the reform effort. Yet the momentum for policy change had already subsided by the time Yaung took office, and the retrenchment bill essentially died in committee. After the election of opposition leader Chen Shui-Bian to the presidency in March 2000, efforts to promulgate a privatized and competitive health insurance system waned.

In sum, the KMT was unable to craft a consensus around the multiple-carrier proposal despite powerful political and economic pressures favoring the reform and the KMT's nominal control over the Executive and Legislative Yuans. How can we explain this remarkable policy non-event? The answer is simple. The health care policymaking process had changed by the late 1990s. The institutional arena for policy decision making had moved away from the executive, and a greater plurality of actors, interests, and ideas emerged in the policymaking process. Gone were the days of executive dominance. The next sections demonstrate how bureaucratic resistance, legislative deadlock, and grassroots mobilization leveled the KMT's once dominant position in the policy process.

THE GO-SLOW TECHNOCRATS

Despite the appearance of ministerial and bureaucratic consensus regarding the multiple-carrier reform, pockets of bureaucratic officials, both inside and outside the DOH leadership, were hesitant about the idea. In some cases, bureaucratic opponents participated in activities that openly challenged the DOH's official position. In the end, unanticipated bureaucratic resistance to the multiple-carrier reform, combined with the efforts of go-slow technocrats in devising tenable reform alternatives, undermined the singular attention paid to, and thus the urgency surrounding, the privatization and marketization effort. Simply put, alternatives provided a way out for opponents of the multiple-carrier reform.

Many bureaucrats felt that the structural implications of the multiple-carrier reform needed to be thought through more carefully. Although some of the key officials in the central Bureau of National Health Insurance publicly expressed tacit support for the multiple-carrier system, many bureaucrats were concerned in private about the rapid pace and structural scope of the reform. This was, after all, no small change. Tsai Shu-Ling, the director of the planning department in the BNHI, warned that the privatization of health insurance was a "one-chance" reform. Therefore, prudent planning was needed first. She explained that once the provision of health insurance was controlled by private sector actors, the state would have few public policy instruments left with which to regulate the activities of the insurance carriers.[20] Tsai Shu-Ling's arguments were shared by influential policy officials in both the DOH and the BNHI.

What emerged, then, was a corps of bureaucrats who advocated a go-slow approach to health care reform. These policymakers contended that the government should consider alternatives before pursuing the privatization and marketization model. The government, they argued, had a wide array of policy instruments at its disposal that had not been effectively used to address structural inefficiencies in the NHI program. Wu Kai-Hsun, one of the original policy planners on the Council for Economic Planning and Development task force of the late 1980s, explains: "We designed a great system back in the 1980s. But because of political considerations, we had to make many concessions, such as dropping the referral system and delaying the implementation of the global budget program. We need to try these reforms first before considering *duo yuan hua* [multiple-carrier] reforms. We have to give the original program a chance before we abandon it."[21] Go-slow technocrats believed that reform from within could resolve the NHI's financial crisis.

Resistance to the multiple-carrier reform emerged among those DOH policymakers who had devoted the last ten years to perfecting the single-carrier system. Many ranking policy experts in the DOH were recruited into the bureaucracy during the early 1990s when the integrated NHI was first devised. Most notably, key officials in the DOH's "NHI small group" (*xiao zu*), including division leaders Lee Yu-Chune and Lo Chi-Ch'ong, had been involved in the NHI policy process since 1990. Whereas in the case of Korea change in the ruling regime led to the complete reworking of the health policy network core, in Taiwan there remained extraordinary continuity among important policymaking bureaucrats despite the 1997 cabinet shuffle and leadership change in the DOH. Moreover, even though the small group was officially chaired by the deputy minister of health, ostensibly an ally of the minister himself, in reality the various division leaders set the policymaking agenda. The minister could request that the small group undertake certain research projects, but in the end it was the division leaders who wielded the greatest influence in deciding the group's policy objectives.[22]

Go-slow bureaucrats thus enjoyed significant insulation from the KMT leadership. They diligently and openly pursued reform alternatives that rivaled and ultimately delegitimated the executive's privatization and marketization proposal. In early 1999, the BNHI and the financing division of the DOH small group selectively increased flat-rate user fees. To contain costs, the reformers increased copay levies for patients who had exceeded an upper limit of annual outpatient visits and prescription drugs. The BNHI also launched a new expenditure-monitoring system in which bureau staff regularly analyzed claims made by medical care providers. Irregularities in service, such as the overprescription of expensive treatments, overly frequent follow-up visits, and large drug prescriptions, were flagged by the BNHI and brought to the attention of the contracted provider.[23]

The most conspicuous experiment in "reform from within" was the expansion of the global budget provider payment scheme. Lee Yu-Chune, director of the payment division in the DOH small group, accelerated the implementation of the global budget program beginning in 1998. Unlike in 1995, when providers were resistant to a prospective payment system, medical care providers began to warm to the idea after the NHI began operation. Indeed, the financial precariousness of the NHI exposed in 1997 gave medical care providers serious incentives to join the global budget system. As one provider representative stated, "At least with the global budget, we know we will get some piece of the pie."[24] Outpatient dental services were incorporated into a global budget scheme beginning in the summer of 1999. Chinese medicine practitioners were included later in 1999, and general primary care physicians were added in 2001. As of 2003, hospitals, which account for the most significant portion of health care expenditures and are the greatest beneficiaries of the fee-for-service payment system, were negotiating their incorporation into the global budget scheme. The gradual implementation of global budgets met few administrative problems.[25] As of late 1999, both dentists and Chinese medicine practitioners expressed satisfaction with the global budget scheme.[26]

Using a variety of policy instruments—adjusting user fees, shoring up the BNHI's expenditure-monitoring system, raising premiums (in 2002) and implementing a prospective payment system for providers—go-slow bureaucrats made the case for real policy alternatives to the multiple-carrier reform. Whereas the annual growth rate in national health expenditures between 1995 and 1998 averaged over 10 percent, in 1999 health care costs increased by about 5 percent. In 2000, national health expenditures rose by only 3 percent and for the first time did not outpace the GDP growth rate. Though the financial crisis in the NHI continues to loom in Taiwan—as tends to be the case for any comprehensive social program—these alternative reforms significantly contained the pace of rising health care costs.[27] Politically, the emergence of alternative policy solutions for greater financial stability in the NHI gradually undermined support for the DOH's multiple-carrier reform. Go-slow technocrats effectively turned their policy expertise into political leverage in the reform process by taking advantage of their bureaucratic autonomy and policymaking expertise. Their efforts and ideas spilled over into the legislative arena, leading to political deadlock among lawmakers in Taiwan.

LEGISLATIVE DEADLOCK

I argued in Chapter 5 that policy change in Korea was possible during the late 1990s because President Kim Dae-Jung was able to ensure compliance within the Ministry of Health and Welfare and among his own party's rank and file. In Taiwan, in contrast, weakened party leaders in both the ruling and opposition camps undermined efforts at legislative consensus building. Party leaders were unable to formulate internal consensus regarding the direction of health care reform and consequently failed to build any coherent policy coalitions in the Legislative Yuan. Individual legislators presented competing reform proposals in the increasingly fragmented legislature throughout 1997 and 1998. By the fall session of the 1999 legislature, fourteen members' bills had been introduced, in addition to the reform bill proposed by the DOH. Of the members' bills, six were from Democratic Progressive Party legislators, five were from the KMT, one was from the New Party, and two were from independent legislators.[28] Compromise and consensus in health care reform were extremely difficult to achieve under such circumstances.

The number of competing legislative bills, and the substantive range of the reform ideas, reflected the fragmentation of the legislature and the individualization of legislative politics in the area of health care reform. Among DPP legislators, for instance, reform proposals ranged from a partial insurance system (Shen Fu-Hsiung) to an entirely market-based insurance scheme (Lee Ying-Yuan) to a general tax-funded universal program (Chien Chi-Hsieh).[29] There was clearly no opposition platform in health care reform. In fact, the DPP leadership played a marginal role in coordinating the health care reform effort. In late 1997 and early 1998, the DPP legislative caucus formed a health care reform group, but according to former DPP legislator Liu Chin-Shin, the group was unable to forge a party consensus and instead simply "agreed to disagree."[30] Interviews with DPP members revealed that legislators tended to pursue their own social policies, reflective of their personal ideologies, constituencies, or political clients.[31]

What was most surprising was the extent to which party leaders in the ruling KMT were similarly unable to craft any party consensus around the multiple-carrier reform proposal despite the fact that the reform bill was endorsed by the executive branch. In the past, leaders' authority to discipline their legislative rank and file facilitated efficient policymaking in the KMT party-state. However, the dominance of the ruling party leadership in legislative politics had begun to wane by the latter half of the 1990s even though the KMT continued to control a majority of seats in the legislature.

Individual KMT legislators were vocal in their opposition to the multiple-carrier reform proposal. Huang Chao-Shun, a senior KMT legislator and vice-director of the KMT Central Policy Committee (CPC), argued, for instance, that the proposal would open the doors to large, profit-seeking financial conglomerates in the area of health insurance. She expressed concern that the proposed reform worked against the purpose of universal social insurance by failing to protect the health care provision of "economically marginalized" (*ruo shi*) groups such as the elderly, children, and low-income households.[32] KMT legislator Lin Yaw-Hsing was skeptical that private sector firms would even take on the role of insurance carrier. He believed that if they did accept such a role, they would participate only in market conditions that were conducive to profit making. Lin feared that under those circumstances the introduction of private sector insurance carriers would diminish the quality of health services.[33] Shyu Jong-Shyong, a KMT member of the Legislative Yuan's Health and Welfare Committee, was a little more sympathetic to the government's reform proposal but only in principle. Following the lead of the go-slow technocrats, Shyu felt that the government needed to explore all other reform options before implementing any structural reform.[34]

KMT legislators were willing to break with party policy directives on the issue of health care, and the central party apparatus became less effective in controlling and disciplining its legislators.[35] Legislative deliberation among ruling party legislators and officials remained in the party's Central Policy Committee, at least in the initial stages of policy formulation. However, because KMT legislators increasingly found their own policy niches, they were more vocal in CPC discussions, undermining the historically entrenched hierarchy in the KMT party machinery. It was more and more common for KMT legislators to vote against the party and/or executive line during CPC deliberations. The CPC actually rejected the executive's multiple-carrier reform, an open defiance that was unheard-of only a few years before.[36] Recall that five KMT legislators submitted their own health insurance reform bills to the legislature.

The inability of the political parties to fashion a coalition of reform advocates within the Legislative Yuan, particularly among ruling party legislators, prohibited the bill's passage in the legislature. The erosion of party discipline within the ruling party and the absence of intraparty coordination among opposition legislators contributed to the fragmentation of legislative debate surrounding health care reform. Signatories to members' bills were not divided along party lines; legislators frequently crossed the floor and supported opposing members' policy initiatives in the health care debate.[37] The social policy debate was fought not between political parties—or any other institutionalized political organizations, for that matter—but between legislators, both among individuals and between individuals and their respective party leaders. Three factors contributed to this new pattern of legislative politics: the absence of deeply entrenched socioeconomic cleavages in the political party system, the persistence and worsening of intraparty factionalism, and the institutional incentives faced by individual legislators in Taiwan's unique electoral system.

The Absence of Socioeconomic Cleavages

The political party system in Taiwan is not structured around socioeconomic distributional cleavages. Parties were not (and are not) programmatic in social policy matters. Democratization in Taiwan was primarily driven by demands for a fairer distribution of political power along ethnic lines, particularly in struggles around Taiwanese self-determination.[38] Furthermore, the cross-class composition of both the opposition and ruling parties made it difficult for socioeconomic issues to emerge as a central cleavage between parties.[39] According to my survey data, the vast majority of legislators in both the KMT (73 percent) and DPP (75 percent) identified themselves as from either an "upper-class" or an "upper-middle-class" socioeconomic background, far short of a critical mass for a distinctly class-based party system (n = 33). KMT and DPP legislators share increasingly similar views about the relationship between socioeconomic inequality and political instability, trends in the distribution of income, and evaluations of Taiwan's social welfare regime (see Chapter 7).

Both the ruling and opposition parties have failed to transform socioeconomic issues into distinct party programs, undermining leaders' ability to mobilize legislators within the Legislative Yuan around these sorts of cleavages. The consequences are not trivial. Internally, party coherence on social policy issues is nonexistent, making it difficult for party leaders to impose any sort of discipline over their legislative rank and file when it comes to welfare reform. Externally, the absence of socioeconomic cleavages between the political parties means that it is common for legislators to cross party lines in matters related to social welfare. For example, in late 1999, legislators Shen Fu-Hsiung (DPP), Hau Long-Bin (NP), Chiang Chin-Lan (KMT), and Chang Tsai-Mei (KMT) proposed a new reform based on the idea of medical savings accounts, highlighting yet another incidence of breakdown in party cohesion within both the ruling and opposition parties.

Party Factionalism

Internal factionalism in Taiwan's major political parties has eroded party leaders' political authority over their rank and file, diminishing their capacity to facilitate legislative consensus in important policy areas. Elite conflict within the KMT dates back to the party's founding on mainland China, though it was not until the death of Chiang Ching-Kuo in 1988 and his succession by Taiwan-born Lee Teng-Hui that struggles for party leadership erupted in the public arena. Although Lee experienced major challenges to his authority as both party leader and president early in the immediate posttransition period, he was extremely adept at out-maneuvering his opponents in the party (see Chapter 4). His authority within the KMT, however, was always precarious.

Lee appeared soft on the independence issue, drawing continuous criticism from the "nonmainstream" faction of the KMT. In 1993, a group of young mainlanders in the ruling party, increasingly dissatisfied with Lee's vision of the KMT's future, split off to form the New Party (NP). Some KMT members actually campaigned for NP candidates in the 1995 Legislative Yuan elections, defying the KMT leadership.[40] In 1996, Lee hosted the National Development Conference (NDC), which helped broker some major political compromises between elites from both parties. Participants in the NDC agreed, for instance, on key sovereignty issues, most notably regarding the pursuit of Taiwan's admission into the United Nations and other international organizations. Lee's moves drew severe criticisms from the nonmainstream faction of the KMT, however, signaling not only the breakdown of party unity but also Lee's increasing inability to lead the party in legislative matters.[41]

On the opposition side, factional divisions within the opposition DPP formed before the party's founding in 1986. The radical New Tide and more moderate Formosa factions of the *tangwai*-turned-DPP clashed over political strategy, mobilization tactics, and the centrality of the independence issue in the party's platform.[42] During both the 1990 National Affairs Conference and the 1996 National Development Conference, New Tide members criticized moderate leaders of the DPP for being conciliatory and complicitous in interparty negotiations with the KMT.[43] The issue of Taiwan's independence and its position in the DPP platform remained a thorny issue among DPP factional leaders throughout the 1990s.[44]

Internal divisions within the DPP were exacerbated in legislative politics because of its status as the perennial opposition party (before 2000). Perpetual majorities held by the KMT, particularly during the early 1990s, made it impossible for even a united DPP to veto KMT initiatives. For DPP legislators, there were thus few strategic incentives to form a common alliance during legislative battles. As one DPP insider explains it: "The most important job for the opposition party is to oppose and challenge the ruling party. Our role is by nature to respond and to challenge. And as of right now, in the DPP, our best strategy in opposing KMT policies is to challenge from as many different directions as possible as opposed to unifying in what will always be a losing battle."[45] This oppositional blitzkrieg strategy was best reflected in the ideological range of

DPP proposals in the health care policy debate and the overall lack of party consensus regarding social policy reform.

Institutional Peculiarities

Political fragmentation within parties, and within the political arena more generally, was also a consequence of certain institutional factors built into Taiwan's political system. Most notably, the single nontransferable vote and multimember district (SNTV-MM) electoral system promotes personalist, localist, and factional politics, which together undermine party cohesion. Multimember districts mean that parties must often field several candidates within one electoral district.[46] This type of electoral system requires tremendous internal party coordination, especially in the nomination process. One would therefore intuitively expect strong party leadership.[47] Indeed, both the KMT and the DPP historically used an assortment of top-down coordination mechanisms, including strategic nominations, the mobilization of "vote brokers," the creation of campaign zones within an electoral district, and even outright vote buying.[48] However, in recent years, the parties' hold on the strategic nomination process has begun to wane. After the KMT abandoned its three-year experiment with a closed primary nomination system in 1992, those who did not receive the KMT's official nomination ran anyway. Unofficial candidates often enjoyed the support of KMT members and thus challenged official party candidates, taking away traditional KMT votes. Factional conflicts in the nomination process in both the KMT and DPP further contributed to the erosion of the party unity.

In terms of candidate behavior, the SNTV-MM electoral system promotes a peculiar set of circumstances, or strategic context, for politicians. Multiple nominations within a single district require that candidates from the same party compete against one another.[49] Candidates must therefore differentiate themselves from all other candidates, regardless of party affiliation. Party labels and party platforms are therefore less useful and less meaningful than in other electoral systems. Lin Jih-Wen contends that the optimal candidate strategy is for one to run on and promote particularistic policy programs that are, consequently, often at odds with the party's (nominally) official platform. Candidates also have an incentive to distance themselves from the median position and to instead take radical positions, what Lin calls "noisemaking," in order to distinguish themselves from the field of candidates.[50] Candidates do not have to enjoy wide appeal in order to win legislative elections because under the multimember district system, the minimum-winning threshold for candidates is very small. Before the 1998 elections, when the legislature was made up of 164 seats, the minimum-winning threshold was about 50,000 votes. In larger districts with more contested seats, this threshold was even lower.[51] Given the logic of Lin Jih-Wen's noisemaking model and the small number of votes needed to win a district seat, the more narrow and particularistic the candidate's appeal, the more likely she or he can get elected. Clearly, this sort of institutional arrangement, and more important, candidates' strategic adaptation to these conditions, has made it difficult for parties to coordinate their legislators, both before and after elections.[52]

In Korea, legislators must rely heavily on the party's resources and the leadership's political endorsement. In Taiwan, on the other hand, personal networks, local ties, and the promise and exchange of political pork are far more critical for electoral success. Furthermore, because parties in Taiwan have to nominate so many candidates, the competition for party nominations is not as tight as in Korea.[53] In fact, it is often quite difficult for parties to field enough qualified candidates for elections in Taiwan. Moreover, legislative candidates in Korea have to demonstrate, first and foremost, loyalty to the party leader. In Taiwan, legislative candidates have found themselves campaigning independently of their parties and have thus gained a degree of autonomy in policymaking vis-à-vis the party leadership.[54] In contrast to the Korean case, the electoral system in Taiwan promotes more individually minded and politically independent legislators who are less beholden to party patronage and increasingly less dependent on party resources.

The perception of legislators' influence in Taiwan has changed drastically in recent years. According to my elite survey of bureaucrats and legislators, 68 percent of those surveyed (n = 109) believed legislators' influence in the policy process to be increasing; 83 percent of the bureaucrats within that sample (n = 64) also perceived legislative influence to be on the rise. When asked to rank-order policy actors in terms of their influence on the policy process (n = 110), legislators were considered the most influential, outranking the president, the parties, and the bureaucrats. Recall that in Korea, legislative influence was perceived to be declining and National Assembly members were ranked third in influence, far behind the president and the bureaucracy. Indeed, legislative influence in Taiwan may be perceived to be on the rise precisely because of legislators' ability to veto executive initiatives. They are effective because they can cause legislative deadlock.

SOCIETAL MOBILIZATION

Intuitively, greater societal mobilization and effective bottom-up participation in policymaking should go hand in hand with democratic transition. Yet as argued in Chapter 4, civil society actors were not direct
participants in earlier episodes of health care reform in either Taiwan or
South Korea despite the initiation of democratic reform. In more recent
years, however, societal groups and nongovernmental organizations in
both places have played increasingly important roles in policymaking.
The Health Solidarity movement in Korea was directly involved in promulgating and legitimating health care reform. In Taiwan, societal actors
played a similarly critical role in defeating and delegitimating the government's retrenchment reform proposal. To be sure, three-quarters of elite
respondents in Taiwan indicated that they perceived group influence to
be on the rise, and only 6 percent felt it to be on the decline (n = 109).

In March 1998, just weeks after the Executive Yuan delivered its multiple-carrier reform proposal to the legislature, a publication entitled
"Big Business Health Insurance: Citizens without Insurance" was circu-
lated by a group called the NHI Coalition to all legislators and ranking
bureaucratic officials in the Department of Health. Copies were also distributed to cadres within the coalition's unions, social movements, and
other nongovernmental organizations. The manifesto systematically cri-
tiqued the government's multiple-carrier proposal. The NHI Coalition,
an alliance of disparate societal groups united against the multiple-carrier proposal, argued that a private-sector-dominated, competition-based
health insurance system would promote a multitiered system of health
care that unjustly benefited the wealthy. The coalition further argued that
the privatization of health insurance would invariably reduce the government's capacity to regulate health care, despite the government's assurances that state interventions would keep market forces in line with
public interests.

The top priority for the NHI Coalition was to maintain a strong government presence in the regulation and administration of the health insurance system. The manifesto raised issues such as price control, rural access
to high-quality medical care, and equal access to health care. Rather than
shift financial responsibility to the private sector, the coalition argued in
line with go-slow bureaucrats that the government should improve efficiency by reforming the existing single-pipe framework. The document
offered an array of alternative policy solutions, stressing, for example, the
need to implement supply-side or provider-side cost controls such as

global budgets, to streamline administrative costs, and to reformulate the financing system to be less regressive.[55] Above all, the NHI Coalition doubted the government's assurances that the multiple-carrier reform would not compromise redistributive equity.

Institutional Opportunities

Societal actors in Taiwan learned to take advantage of new institutional opportunities for participation in the legislative process.[56] The presence of increasingly autonomous legislators, and a stronger Legislative Yuan more generally, facilitated the emergence of a more assertive civil society. According to elite survey data, 66 percent of respondents (n = 111) agreed with the following statement: "During the policymaking process, the government will often consult with interest groups or interest group leaders"; 76 percent (n = 110) similarly agreed that "with respect to policymaking, societal groups have considerable influence over the policy outcome." Because legislators in Taiwan have become less dependent on central party resources and more reliant on grassroots support for political survival, candidates have an institutional incentive to foster close relations with societal movements and groups. Seventy-two percent of legislators, from both the opposition and ruling camps, meet with interest and/or societal groups at least once a month to discuss policy matters (n = 43); 70 percent (n = 46) reported that it is the interest/societal group that initiates the meetings. A more autonomous legislature has made for a more proactive and politically aggressive civil society.

Coalition Building

Civil society groups in Taiwan forged new broad-based social movement alliances during the late 1990s. This pattern of mobilization was new in Taiwan. As in the Korean experience, civil society in democratizing Taiwan quickly became fragmented.[57] Personality clashes between grassroots leaders, particularistic interests, and the absence of any clear-cut partisan differences related to socioeconomic and redistributive cleavages constrained opportunities for Taiwan's progressive social movements to forge cooperative alliances. Yet despite these challenges, the National Health Insurance Coalition formed in early 1998.

The coalition comprised more than two hundred societal groups, representing workers, children, the aged and disabled, aboriginal groups, women, and an assortment of medical professionals. Not unlike Health

Solidarity in Korea, the NHI Coalition was made up of an array of societal groups that previously had little mutual interest to cooperate. Also like Health Solidarity, the NHI Coalition enjoyed cross-class and cross-cleavage appeal. The coalition joined medical care providers on the one hand with consumer groups such as associations representing labor and the aged on the other. How can we explain the formation of this social movement coalition, given the fragmentation of civil society during the early stages of democratic transition in Taiwan?

First, the legacies of the 1995 NHI program laid the foundation for the NHI Coalition. As already stated, coalition partners, ranging from labor groups to doctors' associations, did not a priori have common or collective interests in the health care debate.[58] According to Paul Pierson, however, preexisting social policies foster new policy advocacy communities within state and society, leading to coalition building to obstruct efforts in welfare retrenchment.[59] Put another way, policy path dependency means that old policies create new interest constellations that resist future policy change. The NHI galvanized otherwise disparate and in some cases competing societal groups around a single policy issue. The 1995 implementation of the national health insurance program also provided a new national arena in which formerly disparate groups were able to engage a common policy debate. The national scope of the NHI program focused the policy debate on the central government.[60] Opposition voices had something to blame and a political target around which to mobilize. Furthermore, the public administration and universal extension of benefits formed a collective expectation that such benefits, in the least, would be maintained. Legislator Shen Fu-Hsiung put it best: "The government's biggest mistake was to make its first attempt at universal health care such a generous program. It is impossible in a democracy to now convince people that what is best for them is to be less generous."[61]

Second, the logic of policy path dependency and the unifying effect of the NHI were significant in bringing together groups within the fractious labor movement. Before the late 1990s, labor organization in Taiwan was fragmented and decentralized. Loose party affiliations and differences in ideology and tactics prevented collective action among workers. The NHI, however, helped bridge the state-sanctioned China Federation of Labor (CFL) and independent movements such as the Taiwan Labor Front (TLF) and the Committee for Action on Labor Legislation (CALL). Tsai Shu-Ling of the BNHI observes that "the NHI has really amalgamated the unions and the labor movement under this single issue. It is the first time that unions actually have something to work on together."[62] Deputy Minister of Health Chang Hong-Jen similarly declares, "The NHI created the labor movement that we see today."[63] All the labor leaders I interviewed reiterated that despite fundamental differences in tactics and enduring personality conflicts, the TLF, the CALL, and even the CFL increasingly work together on issues of shared interest, health care reform being a key policy priority.[64]

Finally, strategic issue framing by NHI Coalition leaders helped disparate actors overcome collective action problems. Issue framing directed political attention to a discrete policy area. Like the Health Solidarity alliance in Korea, the NHI Coalition focused on a single reform issue within the health policy domain rather than a broader set of social welfare policy areas. Coalition leaders did not have larger ambitions to turn the health care coalition into a permanent social movement alliance. It was a short-lived association of political convenience. Furthermore, the NHI Coalition sought to portray its resistance to reform as a position that appealed to all social classes, a tactic used also by Health Solidarity in Korea. The 1997 financial crisis figured into this strategy of issue framing. Although Taiwan survived the crisis relatively unscathed, it alerted social policy activists to the idea that the expansion of social protection at home was necessary in the face of growing economic uncertainty abroad. As in Korea, the financial crisis put inclusive social welfare reform on the policy agenda. Thus, coalition leaders in Taiwan were able to cast a wide, cross-class, cross-cleavage appeal to groups that might not have shared interests in other policy areas. Lastly, the NHI Coalition presented a united front, framed as a negative preference or a common interest in avoiding a certain policy outcome. As Pierson explains, people "will take more chances—seeking conflict and accepting the possibility of greater losses—to prevent any worsening of their current position."[65] In short, popular consensus against a particular system facilitated cooperation among what initially seemed unlikely coalition partners.

Expert Activism

The NHI Coalition was not only a political movement but also a policy-oriented movement. Like Health Solidarity in Korea, the NHI Coalition in Taiwan effectively blended policy expertise with grassroots activism. The coalition attracted a great deal of outside academic support; prominent scholars offered their policy expertise in drafting the coalition's manifesto. In fact, one of the principal contributors to the NHI Coalition's research was (and is) a high-ranking official in the Department of

Health.[66] In addition, many of the participating groups, such as the Taiwan Labor Front, retain permanent staffs of policy researchers. Intergroup cooperation, in this respect, encouraged the sharing of data, ideas, experiences, and proposals and, most important, facilitated contact with other policy specialists. These sorts of exchanges between groups are particularly crucial in health policymaking, not least because the health care policy domain is extraordinarily complex, requiring knowledge of the medical profession, medical technology, finance, and payment systems.

The NHI Coalition's ability to articulate a cogent and sophisticated social policy position, and one with broad-based grassroots support, represented a new style of societal mobilization in Taiwan. Members of the Legislative Yuan, and even bureaucrats in the DOH, had no choice but to contend with these groups. According to many bureaucrats in the DOH and the BNHI, one of the primary reasons for the NHI Coalition's success was the increased level of sophistication in the group's comprehension of health care policy. Elite policymakers further noted that the coalition was able to engage the entire policy debate rather than particular aspects germane only to specific group interests. The NHI Coalition, like Health Solidarity in Korea, thus played an important educative role for otherwise policy-resource-poor and generally uninformed legislators. In the end, the coalition's political influence helped promote deadlock among Taiwan's lawmakers.

CONCLUSION

During the mid to late 1990s, it looked as though the KMT enjoyed a window of opportunity to lead from the top down yet another episode of major health policy change. A looming financial crisis in the medical care system and related challenges in containing escalating health care costs provided justifications for the government's proposed multiple-carrier reform. A sense of urgency surrounding the increasingly cash-strapped NHI strengthened the KMT's contention that change was needed quickly. Furthermore, the emerging global consensus favoring welfare retrenchment, particularly in costly social policy areas such as health care, created an ideational context in which the KMT could divert blame for its efforts in privatizing and marketizing medical insurance in Taiwan. Retrenchment was understood to be inevitable. Finally, given what seemed to be an elite consensus in favor of the multiple-carrier proposal, it appeared as though executive dominance in health care reform was imminent once again. The KMT's continued control of a majority of seats in the Legislative Yuan suggested that the reform would be adopted with few obstacles.

This window of opportunity for health policy change was not as fortuitous as expected, however, particularly for those influential KMT officials who anticipated a smooth reform process. Newly emergent political forces successfully resisted retrenchment, challenging it on three fronts: experts from within the bureaucratic apparatus, an increasingly autonomous legislature, and a maturing civil society. First, go-slow bureaucrats in the DOH and the BNHI pursued alternative reform strategies and, in so doing, undermined support for the much more radical multiple-carrier reform. Second, the inability of party leaders to craft any sort of legislative coalition, especially within the KMT rank and file, resulted in legislative deadlock over the proposed policy change. And finally, the 1998 NHI Coalition mobilized hundreds of different social movements and interest-based groups in opposition to the reform. The combination of these three interrelated dynamics challenged the KMT's dominance in social policymaking.

The significance of this policy non-event cannot be overstated. It clearly demonstrates how the social policymaking process in Taiwan, and policymaking more generally, has become more pluralistic, contested, and indeed democratic. As in Korea, previously excluded actors in the health policy decision-making process emerged as key partners in the resistance to retrenchment during the late 1990s. They skillfully leveraged their policy expertise in opposition to the executive's multiple-carrier reform. Actors adapted to the democratic game and tailored their mobilization strategies to its evolving rules. They took advantage of institutional opportunities to gain a substantive voice in health care policymaking. In short, they learned democracy. In this respect, the KMT's waning authority in policymaking was not so much a reflection of the ruling party's demise as it was the consequence of new challengers taking on and successfully out-maneuvering the KMT at its own game.

CHAPTER 7

DEMOCRACY AND THE
IDEA OF SOCIAL WELFARE

Policymaking, at its core, is the contestation of ideas. Ideas as interpretive frameworks shape different understandings and expectations of how the world works, and also how the world *should* work. Ideas inform the ways problems are defined and what solutions are deemed most appropriate. In Chapter 3, for instance, I argued that the authoritarian states in Korea and Taiwan held to very narrowly defined conceptions of political-economic development, affording little space for redistributive notions of equity. Social welfare was believed to be inimical to rapid and aggregate economic growth, the latter being the top priority for the authoritarian state.

Beginning in the 1990s, however, the idea of development was redefined. The introduction of democratic reform in Taiwan and South Korea reconstituted the idea of development by incorporating more fully considerations about distributive problems and redistributive policy solutions. Furthermore, democratic transformation throughout the late 1980s and 1990s ushered in new understandings about the proper role of government in economic and social development. Democratization brought with it new expectations about one's material quality of life and the role of good governance in achieving these socioeconomic outcomes. In Taiwan and South Korea, the purpose of social policy was redefined, and this ideational change was reflected in the emergence of innovations in health policy. A new consensus regarding the place of social welfare within the broader goals of development helped legitimate welfare deepening in Korea and the resistance to retrenchment in Taiwan.

REDEFINING DEVELOPMENT

Public opinion data in Korea and Taiwan suggest that citizens are increasingly aware of, and consequently opposed to, growing socioeconomic disparity. Similar views are held by the political elites, including bureaucratic officials and politicians. Chung-In Moon observes that in Korea, "the concept of the good society and its underlying template has been radically realigned. The developmentalist ideology couched in terms of growth and security has been devalued. . . . Popular demands for re-distribution, welfare, quality of life and environmental integrity constitute new political and ideological mandates."[1] Moon's observations are also perfectly applicable to present-day Taiwan. Ideational change in both places has led to a consensus among state and society actors about the appropriate place of social welfare in social, economic, and political development. This shift, I contend, represents a significant departure from the previous understandings of development that underpinned policymaking under authoritarianism. In other words, democratization in Taiwan and South Korea not only altered the politics of welfare policymaking (Chapters 4–6) but also changed the very idea of social welfare.

In 1992, 63 percent of public opinion survey respondents in Korea agreed that "the income gap should be narrowed between college and high school graduates." The socioeconomic backgrounds of those respondents ranged from the upper middle class to the urban lower classes. Fifty-six percent of respondents agreed with the following statement: "Failure of government policies is one reason for poverty." Nearly 83 percent of those surveyed felt that large corporations were too powerful, and 64 percent agreed that workers should have more influence in government decision-making processes. Distributive consequences of economic development and political change have become increasingly important problems in the minds of Koreans. Moreover, the perceptions of socioeconomic and political inequity are not delineated along class lines.[2]

In a 1998 survey, 83 percent of Koreans believed that the state, rather than the individual or household, should be responsible for the provision of social welfare and economic security.[3] According to Doh-Chull Shin, Korean citizens expect that democratic governance will lead to a more equitable distribution of wealth.[4] During the late 1990s, four-fifths

(81 percent) of Koreans felt that the reduction of income inequality was even more important than the expansion of political freedom. In other words, on fulfilling the procedural requirements of democracy, Korean citizens have begun to hold to more socioeconomically substantive understandings of democratic citizenship.[5] Growing income inequality and disparities in the distribution of wealth in Korean society are increasingly seen to be undesirable and as negative consequences of rapid economic growth.[6]

A similar attitudinal transformation was also evident in Taiwan during the 1990s. In a 1991 Academia Sinica survey, 44 percent of respondents indicated that they were dissatisfied with the present state of Taiwan's welfare regime; only 28 percent were satisfied. A majority of respondents (51 percent) felt that the level of government welfare expenditure was too low, and less than 1 percent believed it to be too high. Not surprisingly, 69 percent of those surveyed agreed that government welfare expenditures should increase, but only 0.4 percent indicated that such spending should decrease.[7] Three years later, in 1994, the proportion of dissatisfied respondents increased to 50 percent, and those who were satisfied with the state provision of welfare decreased to 20 percent.[8]

According to most people, the government in Taiwan should play a greater role in the provision of social welfare, especially for the elderly, low-income families, and those with disabilities.[9] In 1994, 83 percent of respondents disagreed with the following statement: "So long as churches, temples, and other social organizations play a larger role in providing social welfare, there is less need for the government to play a role."[10] Despite the proliferation of newspaper editorials throughout the 1990s claiming that the expansion of welfare would be too costly for the government, 52 percent of survey respondents in 1994 disagreed with the notion that expanding welfare would cause financial instability for the state while only 31 percent agreed.[11] In 1991, a marginal 2.4 percent of respondents (or 38 out of 1,588 of those surveyed) were "proud" of the existing social welfare policies in Taiwan, and welfare was ranked sixth out of a possible nine policy areas. Policies related to economic growth were ranked first. With respect to which policy areas should be improved, however, social welfare ranked second in priority, behind only environmental protection.[12]

Popular opinion regarding the welfare state and the direction of social policy reform is mirrored in the views of the political elite. According to elite survey data collected in 1999 and 2000, the overwhelming majority of legislators and bureaucrats (n = 242) disagreed with the statement,

"Economic growth in Taiwan/Korea has been accompanied by an equitable distribution of income." A majority of elite respondents in both places (n = 242) disagreed with the notion that continued economic growth inevitably leads to a more even distribution of income. This understanding of the causal relationship between growth and equity runs counter to the trickle-down economic policies of the authoritarian developmental states. It has thus helped legitimate proactive state intervention in the redistribution of economic goods.

New ideas about the desirability of economic redistribution in development have come about in a context of perceived growing disparities within society. In Taiwan, 89 percent of legislators (n = 47) and 73 percent of bureaucrats (n = 64) agreed that in recent years the distribution of income has worsened. The majority of legislator and bureaucrat respondents in Korea (n = 130) likewise agreed with this assertion. Political elites in Taiwan and Korea perceive this condition to be politically undesirable. Around 90 percent of all respondents in both places (n = 242) agreed with the statement, "Societal inequity will lead to political instability."

Consequently, a consensus regarding state involvement in the provision of redistributive social welfare policy has emerged among policymaking elites. Over 90 percent of legislators in Taiwan and Korea (n = 135) agreed with the following statement: "Public welfare is a fundamental characteristic of democracy." Eighty-three percent of bureaucrats in Taiwan (n = 64), and 72 percent of those in Korea (n = 44) agreed also. An overwhelming majority of respondents (n = 241) believed that universal health insurance is a "democratic right." Democracy and the promotion of welfare are increasingly understood to be compatible outcomes, a necessity for legitimate governance. Social citizenship has become a fundamental part of democratic citizenship. Thus, both legislative and bureaucratic elites in Taiwan and Korea believe that there is room for considerable improvement in the area of social policy reform. In fact, over 80 percent of legislators and bureaucrats in Korea (n = 133) disagreed with the assertion that the Korean government could be characterized as a welfare state. In Taiwan, 79 percent of legislators (n = 47) and 61 percent of bureaucrats (n = 64) similarly disagreed.

Over the past ten years or so, an ideational convergence around the idea of social welfare has emerged in democratizing Taiwan and South Korea. The significance of this ideational change cannot be overstated. Policymaking elites and the general public increasingly share views about the proper place of social welfare in democratic governance. This ideational convergence furthermore includes both politicians and bureaucrats. It also cuts across partisan lines and socioeconomic classes. What makes this change so significant, however, is the fact that it has occurred in places where the political left was historically marginalized and where there continues to be an absence of any explicitly left-leaning, pro-labor, or social democratic party. Indeed, the lack of any social welfare statist tradition in Taiwan and South Korea makes this ideational change even more counterintuitive.

The rest of this chapter offers explanations for this new consensus in Taiwan and South Korea, focusing on the relationship between democratic transformation and ideational change. First, democratic change encouraged strategic political actors to make socioeconomic cleavages and redistributive policy issues salient bases of political competition and thus part of mainstream policy debate. Second, the introduction of new social policies during the late 1980s and early 1990s resulted in the formation of new distributional coalitions around a common material interest in welfare state development. It also resulted in new normative expectations, or an ideational legacy, about the role of government in social welfare provision. And third, cross-class mobilization in both Taiwan and South Korea helped mainstream social policy ideas that had earlier been marginalized from policy discourse. Interestingly, legitimating welfare was not a leftist project per se but rather an inextricable part of the democratic project.

STRATEGIC POLITICAL CHOICES

The presence of clearly defined socioeconomic cleavages in the formal political arena—entrenched in the political party system, as the basis of societal mobilization, or as a topic of policy debate among elites—is what typically drives social welfare reform. One might reason, therefore, that the absence of such cleavages provides few incentives for strategic political actors to engage this issue. That may be the case in established democratic polities where salient political cleavages are entrenched and where actors (for example, parties) have assumed stable and programmatic identities. This stability assumption is challenged, however, by the insights of Herbert Kitschelt regarding parties and electoral competition. With respect to the relationship between parties and issue saliency, he writes: "Parties appeal to certain issue stances not just because voters find such issues salient for their choice, but voters' evaluations of salience are at least partially predicated on whether politicians advance alternative positions on an issue dimension."[13] In other words, strategic political entrepreneurs can energize or make salient certain positions or issues that may have otherwise been in equilibrium or not salient at all. Issue structures are malleable, dynamic, and subject to actors' strategic manipulations.

The construction of cleavages and issues is a central, though understudied, aspect of democratic transformation.[14] I contend that the processes of democratization, particularly the institutionalization of political competition, encourage political actors to realign issue structures. In so doing, they reconstitute the bases of competition in politics. In Taiwan and South Korea, democratic transformation and the imperatives of political contestation facilitated the construction of new and salient political cleavages around socioeconomic and redistributive issues.

Generally speaking, before democratic transition, opposition movements mobilize support around the common goal of ending authoritarian rule and installing democratic institutions. Movement leaders situate the democratic ideal as part of their larger political, economic, and social transformative demands. In the case of Taiwan, opposition *tangwai* leaders framed the idea of democracy around Taiwanese ethnic solidarity. In Korea, the prodemocracy alliance of workers, students, and the middle class articulated an integrated vision of social, economic, and political justice. Once democracy was introduced in both places (i.e., after the institutionalization of competitive elections), however, the democracy/authoritarian cleavage became less salient. Civil society quickly fragmented in the absence of a unifying "enemy" after the moment of democratic breakthrough. Political elites were left scrambling as they tried to restructure the lines of competition in the new democratic order.

The Basis of Democratic Competition

The independence versus reunification cleavage emerged as the single most important division in Taiwan's new democracy. However, the sovereignty debate in Taiwan soon resulted in stalemate as voters sought to maintain the status quo.[15] The looming presence of an increasingly aggressive Beijing regime on mainland China also constrained the political choices available to leaders on both sides of the independence issue. In Korea, the socioeconomic cleavages expounded by the prodemocracy activists and *minjung* movement fell by the wayside as middle-class supporters of the alliance abandoned the democracy movement shortly after

1987. Workers were viewed as narrowly self-interested, and students were perceived to be inflexible ideologues. Instead, regional cleavages that centered on the four major party leaders—Roh Tae-Woo, Kim Young-Sam, Kim Dae-Jung, and Kim Jong-Pil—quickly came to dominate the political arena. Personalism reinforced by regionalism became the single most important predictor of electoral politics in Korea after the initiation of democratic reform.

In democratizing Taiwan and South Korea, political competition, at least at the outset, therefore centered on single-dimensional cleavages: ethnicity in the former and regionalism in the latter. Single-dimensional divisions promoted static political competition. It soon became apparent to political entrepreneurs in both places that single-cleavage bases of competition locked in voters and politicians, inhibiting potential challengers from gaining significant electoral advantage in future contests. In Korea, rigid regional voting blocs made it difficult for certain candidates to succeed in electoral competition. In Taiwan, the inability of both the Kuomintang and the opposition Democratic Progressive Party to resolve the sovereignty question rendered the ethnic cleavage increasingly less useful as a strategic basis of political competition. The introduction of new cross-cutting cleavages—or put another way, the diversification of the bases of political competition—restructures the terms of political contestation. In this respect, democratic transition in Taiwan and South Korea provided fertile ground for the emergence of new political cleavages and related policy innovations.

Constructing New Cleavages

In democratizing societies, the absence of socioeconomic cleavages at the outset of democratic transition compels strategic actors to exploit or construct new lines of competition along socioeconomic dimensions and distributive issues to gain a competitive edge over their opponents. Emerson Niou and Peter Ordeshook conclude that in Taiwan, "the issue of nativism, which is largely a conflict over the distribution of political power between mainlanders and native Taiwanese, is one-dimensional, so by limiting its central appeal to that the issue, the [opposition] DPP cannot form a winning electoral coalition as long as the KMT has the internal flexibility [on other issues] to co-opt the majority." Drawing from spatial theories of electoral behavior, Niou and Ordeshook suggest that for the DPP to gain any advantage in political competition, it must "increase the issue space's dimensionality." In other words, the party "must find new issues to divide the electorate."[16] Tse-Min Lin and his colleagues concur, reasoning that a candidate's "chance of winning [elections] is increased when there are cross-cutting issues that can be exploited."[17] Both studies suggest that the introduction or construction of socioeconomic cleavages and redistributive issues that cut across otherwise static bases of competition, such as ethnic division in Taiwan, is an effective way for political entrepreneurs to gain votes. The same strategic political logic can be applied to Korea.

The absence of well-entrenched socioeconomic cleavages at the outset of democratic transition in Taiwan and South Korea meant that there was a lack of a priori party identification with socioeconomic and redistributive issues. Therefore, socioeconomic dimensions were ideal bases of political competition for all political actors, regardless of party affiliation. Political entrepreneurs from both the opposition and ruling camps strategically adopted social welfare causes in order to win new distributional coalitions. For example, the absence of strict party lines on these sorts of issues and the inherent ideological flexibility of the posttransition political order in both Taiwan and Korea allowed otherwise conservative leaders to initiate the universalization of health insurance during the late 1980s. Social policy, simply put, was a winning strategy. Since then, political actors in Taiwan and South Korea have continued to adopt socioeconomic issues as central platforms in their political campaigns. They have focused on various social policy areas, including pensions, health care reform, the eradication of corruption, and policies relating to social justice more generally.[18]

The nonprogrammatic nature of the emerging party systems in Taiwan and South Korea facilitated the mainstreaming of social welfare issues in electoral politics. However, individual political entrepreneurs, not political parties, were the principal agents to construct socioeconomic cleavages in the posttransition period in democratizing Taiwan and Korea. The absence of left-right programmatic parties provided the political space for individual politicians to elevate social policy issues onto the national political stage. Socioeconomic issues have become more prevalent in politics over the past decade or so, yet they have not become programmatic party cleavages. Ironically, this may be a good thing for proponents of welfare reform, as the programmatic entrenchment of such cleavages may polarize and potentially radicalize the politics of social welfare development.

It was the *process* by which socioeconomic dimensions of competition emerged in Taiwan and Korea that helped foster an ideational convergence around social welfare. The introduction and subsequent strategic articulation of socioeconomic issues and social policy reform ideas by political entrepreneurs in the interest of political gain had an important ideational effect on the development of the welfare state. First, the process of constructing socioeconomic and redistributive cleavages helped set the course of social policy reform in both places. It facilitated new policy innovations (such as global budgets in Taiwan) and the effective rearticulation of old policy ideas (such as the integration reform in Korea) in social policymaking processes. Second, the introduction of socioeconomic cleavages provided actors with a new policy language and the analytical tools and concepts with which to engage social policy debates. By bringing social policy ideas into the political mainstream, actors in both state and society began a process of policy learning, a process that was critical to the dynamics of policy innovation and change during the late 1990s. Third, and most important, the fact that political elites increasingly discussed social welfare policy in elite and popular forums beginning in the 1990s helped bring previously marginalized social policy ideas and redistributive principles into the political and policy mainstreams. Interestingly, the 1997 Asian financial crisis was understood by policy activists as an imperative for, rather than an impediment to, greater social protection in the face of continued economic globalization. The crisis, and in particular how it was understood by political actors, helped further mainstream the idea of social welfare deepening. In these changing political and economic contexts, social policy was a winning political strategy and the related principles of the welfare state were winning ideas.

POLICY PATH DEPENDENCY

The ideational shift about the place of social welfare in Taiwan and South Korea also involved changing expectations among citizens about good democratic governance. I argue in this section that the legacy effects of social policy path dependency helped entrench new ideas about social welfare in Taiwan and South Korea. Path dependency has two types: institutional and ideational.

Institutional Path Dependency

According to Edwin Amenta and Theda Skocpol, the creation of the welfare state restructures distributional coalitions and political alliances.

Social policy feedback reconstitutes the game of politics, affecting subsequent efforts at social welfare reform or retrenchment.[19] Drawing from this idea of policy feedback, Paul Pierson contends that social welfare policies form new advocacy coalitions with a common interest in preserving, if not deepening, welfare reform. He writes that "the policy induced emergence of elaborate social and economic networks" has the effect of "increas[ing] the cost of adopting once possible alternatives," thus "inhibit[ing] exit from the current policy path."[20] Preexisting social policies form new constellations of interests, which in turn shape subsequent social policymaking processes.

As argued in Chapter 4, the introduction of democracy in Taiwan and South Korea during the late 1980s prompted the consolidating regimes to offer significant social policy concessions, particularly in health care. The Roh Tae-Woo regime in Korea immediately universalized health insurance, and the KMT government in Taiwan began planning for what eventually became a significantly revamped universal health care system. As predicted by Pierson and others, these welfare reforms restructured distributional interest coalitions. In Korea, the introduction of universal, though decentralized, health insurance prompted broad-based societal coalitions to push for the integration reform in the late 1990s. Similarly, in Taiwan, the 1995 implementation of national health insurance solidified cross-class support for maintaining the program's integrated structure. In both cases, the institutionalization of universal health care was instrumental in bringing together disparate societal actors to push for welfare deepening in Korea and to resist retrenchment in Taiwan.

Ideational Path Dependency

Earlier reform efforts in Taiwan and South Korea also legitimated new ideas about the role of government in social welfare, particularly governance at the central level. They left a legacy of ideational path dependency. In the past, government intervention in social policy matters was understood by policymakers to be inimical to rapid economic growth, but by the 1990s, this policy narrative, or causal story, no longer resonated with the general public. People learned that equity and growth need not be antithetical. Furthermore, the universalization of medical insurance during the early period of democratic transition transformed the perception that social protection was reserved for the privileged into the expectation that social security was a right of democratic citizenship. Put another way, the logic of policy path dependency shaped new ideas and normative expectations about certain socioeconomic and redistributive outcomes, what I call ideational or normative path dependency.

Not only is the prior implementation of certain policies critical in reconstituting ideas and expectations about social welfare, but policy proposals themselves represent important ideational cues. Social policy proposals and public debate about these proposals deepen normative expectations for social welfare reform. These cues and their significance are even more meaningful in increasingly transparent and accountable democracies. Simply put, people can mobilize.

In 1988, the Korean government introduced the National Pension Program (NPP), which covered only a small portion of the population. Though the redistributive effect of this new policy was relatively insignificant at the time, the momentum gained by workers and farmers in the health care policy arena spilled over into the area of pension reform. The expectation for universal pensions emerged in Korea shortly thereafter, prompting President Kim Dae-Jung to promise a new universal pension program during his election campaign in late 1997.[21] Kim's commitment to pension reform, in turn, only strengthened expectations about the health insurance integration reform. In Taiwan, local elections in late 1993 similarly sparked a new debate about old-age benefits and pension reform. After DPP candidates floated an idea for a universal pension program in early October 1993, the KMT leadership was forced to respond with its own plans to expand the provision of pension benefits. Debate between candidates escalated, and promises became more extravagant. As Ku Yeun-Wen observes, "In a short period—less than one month—pensions became a big issue all over the island and the size of the allowance grew and grew."[22] The point is that ideational path dependencies are not limited to the legacies of policies that are already in existence but are also constituted by policy utterances or cues made in increasingly competitive political contexts. It should come as no surprise that in 2003 pension reform was among the highest policy priorities in Taiwan and Korea.

In sum, policy path dependency is critical in shaping future social policy debates and policymaking processes. Prior social policies restructure distributional coalitions around material interests and shape the ideas that underpin future debates. These ideas reflect changing normative expectations about good governance and the state's role in providing social welfare. From this process of ideational change emerges a new and legitimate vocabulary—giving political meaning to ideas such as universalism, equitable, accessible, inclusion—which in turn establishes the terms of future social policy debates. In the specific contexts of Taiwan and South Korea, efforts to resist retrenchment or to deepen the welfare state were facilitated by the institutional and ideational legacies of earlier episodes of health care reform.

CROSS-CLASS COALITION BUILDING

Cross-class coalitions in Taiwan and South Korea not only provided the political foundations for group mobilization but also legitimated the idea of social welfare reform. This legitimation occurred despite historical antipathies in both Taiwan and South Korea toward what were perceived to be leftist policy ideas.

Political Learning and Coalition Building

In Chapters 5 and 6, I argued that new patterns of societal mobilization in Taiwan and Korea during the late 1990s were critical to resisting retrenchment in the former and welfare deepening in the latter. I describe them as new because in the immediate posttransition period, civil society in both places was fragmented, a pattern common to many democratizing societies. In Korea, the defection of middle-class activists in the late 1980s led to the collapse of the cross-class coalition that had successfully pushed for democratic reform in the summer of 1987. The radicalization of labor further marginalized workers from the formal political arena. In Taiwan, the proliferation of new societal groups in the late 1980s resulted in their inability to forge what Yun-Han Chu calls "horizontal linkages" within civil society.[23] Labor in Taiwan was similarly fragmented, continually failing in its efforts to mount collective action campaigns. Particularistic interests, personality clashes, ideational conflicts, and segmented organization inhibited effective cooperation between groups.

Despite these fragmentary trends among societal actors early in the democratization process in Taiwan and Korea, new patterns in coalition building soon emerged. Groups quickly learned that intergroup cooperation was instrumental to effective societal mobilization. In the case of Korea, activists learned that the success of the farmers' movement in winning health insurance during the late 1980s was due to its alliance with other rural groups, church organizations, and progressive medical professional movements. In Taiwan, during the run-up to the 1995 Legislative Yuan elections, about fifty social movement groups formed the

Social Movement and Legislative Coalition (*she hui yun dong li fa lian meng*). Though the coalition disbanded shortly after the elections, civil society activists learned that when they pooled resources and articulated a unified voice on key issues, the government was more responsive to societal initiatives.

The emergence of Health Solidarity and the National Health Insurance Coalition were the results of lessons learned from earlier attempts at coalition building within civil society. What was most striking, however, was the cross-class composition of these broad alliances. Health Solidarity in Korea comprised "moderate" middle-class organizations such as the Citizens' Coalition for Economic Justice and People's Solidarity for Participatory Democracy, as well as "radical" groups such as the independent Korean Confederation of Trade Unions. Similarly, the NHI Coalition in Taiwan was made up of more than two hundred nongovernmental organizations, including "new" social movement groups such as the women's movement, independent labor organizations such as the Taiwan Labor Front, and professional medical associations, most notably the National Primary Care Physicians Association.

There are several reasons why these coalitions were able to join middle-class and professional activists with working-class movements. First and foremost, the legalization of associational life provided the political space to form such alliances. Both Health Solidarity and the NHI Coalition drew on the dense network of activists that had held together the democracy movements during the 1970s and early to mid-1980s. The narrow focus of each coalition, health care reform, allowed coalition leaders to bring together like-minded reformers on a specific issue, putting aside other differences. This was most apparent in the inclusion of labor in both Health Solidarity and the NHI Coalition.

Reinventing Labor

In the early stages of democratic reform in Taiwan and South Korea, workers were marginalized from the political mainstream, in part by their own doing. In terms of political tactics, labor movements were exclusionary and, in the case of Korea, perceived as too radical. Workers in Korea were extremely militant, particularly during the period before and just after the initiation of democratic reform. In 1987 alone, more than 3,700 labor disputes were reported in Korea.[24] Though workers in Taiwan were less militant in their tactics—the number of labor demonstrations peaked at 296 in 1988—the labor movement tended to mobilize on its own.[25]

Cooperation with other civil society organizations was eschewed, viewed by labor leaders as a political compromise. Tactically, labor pushed itself to the political margins early in the democratization process.

The labor movements in both places were concerned with issues that pertained only to the condition of workers rather than socioeconomic justice more broadly defined. Jongryn Mo recounts how labor demands in Korea were narrowly focused on certain policy issues that although important to the rights and well-being of workers, did not resonate with the general public.[26] For instance, Korean workers did not join the farmers' health care reform alliance during the late 1980s when mobilization in the countryside reached a peak. Labor leaders reasoned that since workers already received health insurance benefits, farmers' demands for universal health care were not directly germane to workers' interests. Labor organizations instead focused their demands on wages and improved working conditions.[27] The independent labor movement in Taiwan was similarly particularistic in its policy demands. Lin Liang-Rong, a senior officer at the Taiwan Labor Front, recounts that during the 1980s, "workers were very narrow-minded. They were only concerned with their own shop floor experiences."[28] Between 1988 and 1989, over 60 percent of labor demands concerned salary bonuses and wage increases.[29]

For these reasons, the labor movements in both Taiwan and Korea were perceived to be self-serving. They were viewed by some as betrayers of the democratic ideals that had underpinned the opposition movements during the time of political transition. Simply put, labor did not play the game of democratic politics or policymaking particularly well in the immediate posttransition era. As I suggested in Chapter 2, the learning curve in democratization is very steep.

Labor leaders soon learned, however, that in order to gain in democracy, they needed to develop new mobilization strategies and, more important, new ways of thinking about labor issues and social policies. In Korea and Taiwan, the independent labor movements learned that by cooperating with other civil society groups and increasing the scope of the movement's policy goals, labor could be more successful in gaining concessions from the state. Lin Liang-Rong, of the Taiwan Labor Front (TLF), explains:

When the TLF was founded in the early 1980s, our primary goal was to mobilize workers to stand up and fight for important labor and political rights. After the passage of the Labor Standards Law, however, we wanted to broaden the scope of the labor movement. Labor activism should no longer have been about negotiating at the level of the enterprise or on the shop floor, but rather, the labor movement needed new leadership in order to cooperate with other groups and together negotiate with the government in important labor and social policy matters.[30]

Groups such as the TLF in Taiwan learned to compromise, both with other social movement organizations and with the government. In Korea, the independent labor movement, particularly its more radical vanguard, the Korean Confederation of Trade Unions (KCTU), similarly reaped the benefits of cooperating with other groups in certain situations and on select issues beginning in the 1990s. This is not to say, however, that the KCTU has not continued to be an independent, and sometimes militant, labor movement. It still often works in isolation rather than cooperate with other groups.[31] Woo-Hyun Yoon, director of the KCTU's policy division, explains: "The KCTU continues to represent the more basic rights and interests of workers and farmers. That has not changed since the early 1990s. However, we also welcome cooperation with the civic groups ['moderate' organizations] on these larger, more national issues, like corruption, chaebol policy, and social welfare, including the integration of health insurance."[32]

In both Taiwan and Korea, coalition building between the labor movement and other more moderate social movement organizations broadened the base of issues around which workers mobilized. Labor was no longer solely concerned about matters that directly and exclusively pertained to workers. Tactically, the formation of broad-based coalitions moderated the image of the independent labor movement. Cross-class coalition building also helped legitimate the material interests of workers, and labor's coalition partners gained from the grassroots mobilization of the labor movement. The reinvention of the labor movement ultimately proved to be a win-win solution for both workers and nonlabor groups in their push for inclusive social policy reform.

Through the process of continued policy learning, the labor movements in Taiwan and Korea also became much more policy-oriented organizations, or what I refer to as expert-activists. As Dietrich Rueschemeyer and his colleagues point out, equalizing the distribution of skill and expert knowledge contributes to a more democratic process of policy decision making.[33] The KCTU, for example, is staffed by dozens of policy researchers. Both the KCTU and the TLF have forged connections with other international organizations. The TLF retains a permanent staff of researchers and has its disposal a corps of outside academic experts. In the fall of 2000, the TLF formed the Labor and Social Policy Research Association (*lao dong she hui zheng ce yan jiu xie hui*), which uses TLF researchers in addition to outside scholars to conduct studies on social and labor policy.

Coalition building also strengthened the policymaking capabilities of labor organizations and their alliance partners. For instance, in explaining why doctors pursued an alliance with workers in the 1998 NHI Coalition, Shi Hsian-Yan, resident of the National Primary Care Physicians Association, notes that physicians increasingly felt that labor's demands were no longer particularistic to workers' interests alone. Doctors were also impressed by the labor movement's expertise in health policy. Shi comments that "in the past, my impression of the labor movement was that it was an uneducated group of blue-collar workers who did nothing but incite violence, create chaos in the economy, and launch meaningless protests. Now it seems that you need at least a Ph.D. or master's degree to even be a part of the new labor movement."[34] Lee Yoong-Jung, of the Citizens' Coalition for Economic Justice (CCEJ) in Korea, similarly observes that "while the labor movement [in Korea] is primarily concerned with the effects of social welfare policy on workers and farmers, they have a great knowledge of the policies in general. They take their policy research very seriously."[35] Policy learning and policy expertise helped moderate the image of labor, making it a viable partner for coalition building.

Mainstreaming the Idea of Welfare

The formation of cross-class alliances can be attributed in part to the leadership role played by middle-class and professional activist organizations. However, the reinvention of labor, through leaders' strategic attempts to moderate tactics, broaden issue areas, and gain policy expertise, also factored significantly in successful cross-class coalition building. The political upshot was greater societal involvement in the process of health care reform. In the realm of ideas, the inclusion of workers in Health Solidarity and the NHI Coalition, and indeed, the remarkable transformation of labor as a political force, helped mainstream and legitimate the idea of social welfare. These cross-class alliances fostered a universal conception of social citizenship that was *class-blind*. The fact that the 1997 financial crisis had a cross-class effect—that is, both blue- and white-collar workers were afflicted—only deepened the sense that social welfare reform was universally beneficial. Simply put, the socioeconomic implications of globalization were understood to be class-blind.

Welfare state scholars have long pointed out the importance of cross-class coalition building in the development of the welfare state. Alliances forged between the working and middle classes were required to amass enough political capital to force positive social policy change.[36] However, the process of making cross-class alliances is important to legitimating ideas about social welfare. This is particularly the case in societies where the left is underrepresented in the formal political arena and where ideas associated with the left have been historically marginalized from mainstream politics and policy discourse.

Mainstreaming the idea of welfare was critical in shaping health care reform in Korea and Taiwan during the late 1990s. As I have pointed out, actors who were opposed to the content of the medical insurance integration reform in Korea were nonetheless in favor in principle of equity-enhancing reform. Even in Taiwan, the proponents of the privatization and marketization proposal of the late 1990s couched the reform effort as a way of promoting, or at least maintaining, socioeconomic equity. In both places, the idea of equity in social policy was firmly entrenched in policymaking debates. Considerations about distributive equity had become an inescapable part of social policy dialogue.

The cross-class composition of Health Solidarity and the NHI Coalition was instrumental in mainstreaming welfare and crafting a societal and political consensus in favor of social policy reform. Health Solidarity in Korea and the NHI Coalition in Taiwan recast the idea of social welfare as one that enjoyed both working-class and middle-class support. Civic groups in Korea such as the Citizens' Coalition for Economic Justice and People's Solidarity for Participatory Democracy (PSPD), both of which were key members of Health Solidarity, are themselves broad-based coalitions that comprise middle-class activists, professionals, scholars, and socioeconomically marginalized groups. The PSPD, for example, acts as a political watchdog over the government, paying particular attention to social policies, corruption, the abrogation of civil liberties, and constitutional reform.[37] The CCEJ similarly monitors governmental activities, though the group's central concerns are policy issues relating to the environment, gender equality, industrial policy, and social welfare.[38] Coalition-building processes in which labor and the middle class were integral partners in pushing social policy reform demonstrate the degree to which the idea of social welfare reform transcended class in both Taiwan and South Korea.

Cross-class coalition building in Korea helped sell the idea of health insurance integration as a reform that would benefit all, not just the working class. In Taiwan, the NHI Coalition, led by the Taiwan Labor Front, stressed that the privatization and marketization of health care would hurt not only lower-income wage earners but also children, women, and the aged. In both cases, societal coalitions rearticulated—or reinvented—the idea of welfare as a social good for society as a whole. Welfare reform, and health care reform in particular, was no longer perceived to be strictly a "farmers' grievance" or a "labor" issue or a "leftist" policy. Rather, equitable social policy was increasingly seen as a social right, couched in the language and expectations of democratic citizenship. The idea of welfare was not presented in class-based rhetoric. Indeed, the civil society articulators of welfare reform in Taiwan and Korea cut across class lines.

Broad-based, cross-class movements such as Health Solidarity and the NHI Coalition deradicalized the idea of social welfare, an important strategy given the historical antipathies to the left in Korea and Taiwan. Lee Yoong-Jung of the CCEJ emphasizes that progressive civic groups such as the CCEJ and PSPD "try very hard not to be labeled leftist organizations. It is important that organizations such as ours avoid this leftist label if we are to maintain our influence in mainstream politics." Lee goes on to explain that "one of the strengths of the CCEJ is that we look at issues from a very broad perspective, giving consideration to the government's position, the needs of the Korean people, and the role of civil society.... We work for all citizens and not only for the single interests of, for example, labor."[39] Liu Chin-Hsin of the Taiwan Labor Front echoes Lee's reasoning: "Social welfare should not be treated as a class issue. It is a principled issue."[40] By eschewing ideological labels, and thus defusing any sort of ideological battle in social policy reform, societal groups in Taiwan and South Korea, and the cross-class coalitions they built, successfully mainstreamed perceptions about the idea of the social welfare state.

CONCLUSION: IDEAS AND SOCIAL POLICY

Ideas have an important constitutive effect on how social problems are defined, policy solutions justified, expectations shaped, and reform trajectories legitimated. Health care reform in Taiwan and South Korea was reinforced by an important transformation in the idea of social welfare. Survey data highlight converging attitudes and ideas about welfare among both state and societal actors. This attitudinal shift is all the more extraordinary considering the historical marginalization of the left in East Asian politics. Three key points help explain this shift and tie together the processes of ideational change with the politics of democratic change.

First, democratization and the imperatives of political competition compelled strategic political entrepreneurs to make salient new cleavages with which to gain competitive advantage over other political contestants. Ironically, the prior absence of socioeconomic cleavages in the formal political arena helped promote the construction of distribution-based cleavages. Parties and individual actors were not a priori identified with any particular stance. Distributional issues were fair game for all competitors in this ideologically flexible context. They also proved to be winning issues, ratcheting up promises for more social policy reform and mainstreaming what were once marginal ideas.

Second, policy path dependencies, or the normative and ideational legacies of earlier health care reforms, locked governments into a certain reform trajectory. Most notably, the initial introduction of universal health care in the immediate posttransition period reoriented normative expectations within both state and society about maintaining, if not deepening, social welfare reform. People in Taiwan and South Korea not only sought to protect their benefits in health care but also expected that their interests would be protected by the state.

Finally, the formation of cross-class coalitions in Taiwan and South Korea was integral to the legitimation or mainstreaming of social welfare ideas. Crafting these cross-class alliances required that labor reinvent itself as both a willing and contributing partner. This process helped blunt any perceptions of single-class claims for greater redistribution. The idea of welfare was deradicalized, articulated as an idea that transcended class lines. Ironically, the burgeoning welfare states in Taiwan and Korea developed in spite of a weak political left. In fact, welfare state deepening and resistance to retrenchment during the late 1990s were possible precisely because ideas about welfare were portrayed distinctly without reference to the left.

CHAPTER 8

DEFENDING DEMOCRACY

People expect democracy to bring greater socioeconomic justice. According to Adam Przeworski, the "first connotation of 'democracy' among most survey respondents in Latin America and Eastern Europe is 'social and economic equality.'"[1] For democracy to survive and to thrive, conflicts over economic distribution need to be speedily resolved.[2] Inequality destabilizes democracy. Yet resolving these distributional conflicts is easier said than done. To be sure, empirical data from real-world experiences suggest that democracy has not lived up to its billing in most places around the world. Inequality is on the rise in many parts of the developing and democratizing worlds.[3] Defending democracy as a vehicle for greater equity is not an easy task.

There are several reasons why our intuitive expectations about the relationship between democracy and socioeconomic justice would seem to fail us. First, the conventional wisdom on globalization and the imperatives of global economic competition is that they are supposed to have undermined states' capacity to intervene in the workings of the market for the purposes of redistributing wealth. Economic theory tells us that to remain competitive, states have to be lean and markets relatively unfettered. Productive efficiency and market fitness have won out over equity. Welfare state retrenchment and the race to the bottom in redistributive social policy legislation have increasingly become the norm.

The construction of redistributive welfare states in the current global context seems more and more unlikely.[1]

Second, there is little consensus among empirical researchers that a positive relationship even exists between democratic forms of governance and equity.[5] Other factors, such as the level of economic development, a country's place in the world economy, or the current dominance of the neoliberal ethos, mediate the causal impact of democracy on socioeconomic outcomes. In the cases of Taiwan and South Korea, for example, sustained economic growth in the postwar period has provided the fiscal bases and the macroeconomic foundations more generally for effective welfare state expansion, an economic structural condition that many other late developers, such as those in Latin America, have simply not enjoyed. Democracy alone, it appears then, is no panacea for flattening socioeconomic disparities.

Finally, the relationship between democratization and equity, and the introduction of political equality to economic justice, remain undertheorized. Because comparative research on democratization has largely focused on how democracy is installed, scholars of democratic change have only just begun to evaluate the performance of new democracies and to examine the impact of democratic reform on other aspects of political, social, and economic life.[6] With respect to the politics of welfare reform, this dearth of research may be due to the lack of suitable cases.

Despite these reasons for skepticism, this book attempts to shed a more positive light on the effects of democratic transition on socioeconomic equity. Universal health care, implemented during the early stages of democratic transition in Taiwan and South Korea, has had a significant redistributive effect in both places. The Korean government's effort to integrate medical insurance during the late 1990s was an attempt to strengthen the redistributive impact of social insurance even further. Resisting retrenchment in Taiwan maintained social solidarity in health care provision. The fact that major health care reform occurred during the last decade and a half, when neoliberal economic theory has become so dominant, casts serious doubt on the determinism of the globalization thesis.

Democratic transition in Taiwan and South Korea has opened up new social and economic possibilities. In this respect, this book defends democracy. That major health care reform, and social policy change more generally, was initiated after the moment of democratic breakthrough in Taiwan and South Korea suggests that the politics of democratic transition had something to do with welfare state development in the region. The fact that continued social welfare reform thereafter mirrored the course of democratic change in both places seems to reaffirm some sort of relationship between democratization and equity. Yet to defend democracy and its role in social policy reform requires that we go beyond coincidences in timing. A political explanation is needed. We need to show how the politics of democratic change reconstituted the politics of social policymaking in Taiwan and Korea. After all, the politics of welfare reform is all about making hard choices, choices that are even more difficult given the current era of globalization and a conventional wisdom that favors welfare state retrenchment.

The empirical chapters in this book have provided a dense and detailed examination of health care reform in Taiwan and South Korea, spanning the authoritarian developmental state through the current democratic era. When we step back from the details of the cases, however, the argument is actually quite simple. Health care reform in Taiwan and South Korea is best explained as a causal chain, a sequence of political and policy events. After all, democratic transformation, as I have argued throughout this book, involves a dynamic process of change.

During the first phase of health care reform, under authoritarianism, the state pursued a political-economic strategy of selective social policy compensation for economically productive sectors of the population (Table 8.1). The authoritarian developmental states were, on the whole, welfare laggards, as the idea of redistributive social welfare was subsumed under high-growth objectives. After the moment of democratic breakthrough, however, the imperatives of political competition, or more accurately, anticipated competition, compelled the incumbent regimes to initiate a trajectory of universal health care reform. I have argued that the

TABLE 8.1.
Three Phases of Reform

	Phase 1 (1950s–1980s	Phase 2 (late 1980s)	Phase 3 (late 1990s)
Political development	Authoritarian rule	Procedural democracy	Substantive democracy
Reform outcome	Selective compensation	Universal trajectory	Welfare deepening & resisting retrenchment
Policymaking pattern	Directed by the authoritarian state	Preempted by the democratizing state	Inclusive decision making

early stages of democratic transition had a profound impact on health policy agenda setting even though the legacies of authoritarian state dominance continued to keep policy networks relatively exclusive. The third phase of reform, during the late 1990s and roughly a decade after democratic transition had begun in Taiwan and South Korea, involved new patterns of health care policymaking. Previously marginalized actors such as civil society groups, professional bureaucrats, and legislators gained unprecedented access to the health policy network, resulting in further welfare state deepening in Korea and resistance to retrenchment in Taiwan.

I have also argued that changing conceptions of social welfare and its proper place in democratic governance reinforced these health care reform trajectories in Taiwan and South Korea. In this way, democratic transformation also had a major impact on normative expectations of the democratic welfare state. The introduction of democracy revalued the state at a time when the pressures of economic globalization were supposed to have weakened it. In fact, the connection made by policymakers in Taiwan and Korea between globalization on the one hand and the 1997 financial crisis on the other actually strengthened popular sentiments in favor of welfare state deepening. Simply put, globalization necessitated social policy reform, a causal story that was embraced by political entrepreneurs throughout the process of setting the social policy agenda. In the context of democratic Taiwan and South Korea, this story made the most political sense. The politics of economic insecurity has resulted in more, not fewer, welfare reform initiatives.

As an empirical contribution, this book provides an important account of social policy change in East Asia, a story that has not been explored elsewhere. As a theoretical project, this book charts new territory in the study of democratization by examining the transformative impact of democratic change on other substantive aspects of the quality of life, such as social welfare, participatory politics, and political economy more generally. Democratization is not the outcome to be explained. Rather, it is treated as a causal variable that entails its own chain of political logics, which in turn have a constitutive impact on social, economic, and political transformation.

The arguments developed in this book also add to the existing welfare state literature. Other factors mattered in the development of the welfare state in Taiwan and South Korea, to be sure. The course of economic development, the state of health care infrastructure, the availability of tenable social policy ideas, and the level of state capacity all had an influence on welfare state formation in Taiwan and South Korea. However, this book situates these conditions in their proper political context, illuminating why certain choices were preferred to others. It could have been very easy for policymakers to eschew welfare reform and to have justified these choices with neoliberal economic rhetoric. Yet they did not. Therefore, this book has contended from the start that explanations for welfare development in East Asia need to be couched in the politics of democratic change. Furthermore, variable pathways of democratic change facilitated specific patterns of health care policy reform in Taiwan and South Korea. This perspective is a novel one in the conventional welfare state canon.

This chapter develops a theory of democratic change and welfare reform. I offer seven theoretical assertions about the relationship between democratization and social welfare. These causal arguments are inductively generated from the specific cases of Taiwan and South Korea. In terms of larger comparative research agendas, the arguments provide what I think are important hypotheses to evaluate in other national contexts. Thus, the ensuing discussion is framed in conceptual language so as to be relevant to regions and experiences in other parts of the world.

THE LOGIC OF POLITICAL COMPETITION

According to its most minimalist definition, democracy is about institutionalized political contestation.[7] The consequences of political contestation—for example, through regular electoral competition—are not trivial. Democratic competition fundamentally alters the political game. This, in turn, has a significant impact on the politics of social policy agenda setting. The universal extension and enforcement of the right to vote, for instance, provide opportunities for previously excluded citizens to engage the political process. They also institutionalize the use of a new political currency. Alternative resources such as prestige, coercive capabilities, affluence, and patronage ties will continue to play a role in political decision making; it would be naive to think otherwise. Indeed, political corruption, vote buying, and rent-seeking clientelism continue to be a part of democratic practice in Taiwan and South Korea. Nonetheless, the right to vote, and the right to political participation more generally, gives all citizens, by virtue of their citizenship and nothing else, a share in the stock of political capital. The basis of political legitimacy is thus reconstituted.

Critics of such minimalist conceptions of democracy are right to point out that the de jure institutionalization of political competition does not automatically result in the de facto practice of meaningful contestation. This is absolutely true. For one, the rules of the game are never neutral; institutional crafting is not an impartial process. Jack Knight, in his study of institution building, argues that "the main goal of those who develop institutional rules is to gain strategic advantage vis-à-vis other actors, and therefore, the substantive content of those rules should generally reflect distributional concerns."[8] In the specific context of democratization, outgoing regimes tend to craft the rules of the new political game to ensure their survival into the democratic era. In both Taiwan and South Korea, electoral rules favored the incumbent parties, allowing them to remain central players despite authoritarian breakdown. Second, the institutions of political competition do not necessarily guarantee that there will be viable competitors, especially in the period just after democratic breakthrough. As we have seen, the opposition parties in Taiwan and South Korea were hardly challengers to the incumbent ruling parties. Finally, learning democracy takes time. Previously excluded actors are forced to learn and adapt to the new political game over time, thus giving the incumbent regime an unfair advantage, at least in the short term.

Since the terms of political competition may be skewed at the outset, the democratic virtue of any political competition at all must therefore lie in the possibility of alternatives or alternation, no matter how remote the possibility may be. Regardless of the specific rules of the game or the resulting degree of competition, the mere presence of alternative ideas, parties, programs, or individual candidates promotes some meaningful contestation, certainly more than during the authoritarian era. Indeed, as Geraint Parry and George Moyser put it, "it is the mere fact of the election—the opportunity to throw the rascals out, the chance of exercising a veto—which matters."[9] The existence of choice, regardless of how far-fetched or untenable some of the choices may be, gives the right to political participation its value. It may take time for real alternatives to emerge in young democracies, as evidenced by the fact that in both Taiwan and South Korea the incumbent regimes were at first able to hold on to power. Nonetheless, as long as there is choice, or the possibility of future choice, voters can impose "electoral sanction," either prospectively or retrospectively. In other words, the institutionalization of political competition creates conditions of political uncertainty.[10]

Political uncertainty entails a set of political responses unique to democracies. For one, institutionalized uncertainty, ideally, promotes accountability. Political survival is not guaranteed, which in turn makes political performance a premium. In both Taiwan and South Korea, for example, the incumbent parties were voted out of power within the first decade of democratic consolidation despite the overwhelming advantages they enjoyed at the start. Second, political uncertainty alters the logic of the political game. Under authoritarian rule, for instance, political power holders eliminate or co-opt their dissenters, often through repressive measures. Democratic governments and aspirants to government, on the other hand, need to win support. Retrospective electoral sanctions vote out governments that perform poorly, and prospective voting brings in new governments with the hopes of better performance. Lastly, democratic accountability ensures that the prospects of political survival reflect a society-wide consensus. Performance standards are defined by citizens, and most important, by a universally enfranchised citizenry.

Political actors are forced to adapt to this new strategic context. Democratic accountability makes actors responsive to societal demands, and agenda setting is therefore the function of consensus building.[11] This is simply good strategy. Democracy also encourages forward thinking. We can therefore expect that actors will anticipate future challenges and that democratic states may preemptively initiate policy reform in anticipation of citizens' demands. Reform agendas are reconstituted, and policy innovation is politically rewarded. *Among late democratizers, therefore, the institutionalization of political competition, and thus conditions of political uncertainty, compel newly democratic regimes to initiate some social policy reform, no matter how secure (or insecure) the regime may be at the time* (assertion 1). Even in cases in which there are no tenable alternatives to the governing regime at the outset of democratic transition, the mere prospect of future challenges induces this same logic of policy reform and agenda setting. The empirical evidence confirms this assertion.

Democratization in Latin America, for instance, forced new initiatives in social policy reform. In Chile, the center-left Concertación Alliance won the first post-Pinochet elections in 1990 on a policy platform of "growth with equity."[12] The electoral success of Brazilian Workers' Party presidential candidate Luis Inacio da Silva (Lula) in 1989 pushed centrist candidate Fernando Collor de Mello to adopt social policy reforms as part of the government's democratic mandate.[13] In Mexico, Institutional Revolutionary Party (PRI) president Carlos Salinas launched the National Solidarity Program (PRONASOL), a social spending campaign, after nearly losing the 1988 presidential elections to leftist candidate Cuauhtémoc Cardenas.[14]

The impact of elections on social policy agenda setting was evident outside Latin America as well. During the late 1970s, the center-right government of Spain incorporated a social democratic policy agenda in
order to bring the labor unions into an electoral pact with the governing
party, the Union de Centro Democrático (UCD).[15] Immediately after the
lifting of apartheid and the initiation of democratic crafting in South
Africa, the government attempted to implement new social policies as
part of its reconstruction and development program.[16] The promise of
greater equity has been a key feature in democratic projects in other parts
of Africa as well, particularly in ethnically divided states.[17] Among post-
communist states in eastern Europe and the former Soviet Union, the
preservation or strengthening of social safety nets in the "dual transition"
to democracy and the market economy has been a major issue in electoral competition.[18]

The experiences of democratizing Taiwan and South Korea also support the assertion that political competition creates political incentives
for social welfare expansion. Social policy reform in Taiwan and Korea
was pursued as both an anticipatory and a responsive strategy by policy
decision makers. In the immediate postdemocratic breakthrough period,
the Kuomintang and Democratic Justice Party regimes initiated universal health care. Though the emerging opposition parties did not immediately vie for power, incumbent regimes in Taiwan and South Korea
nonetheless anticipated future challenges and thus preemptively
launched social welfare reform to win new bases of support. Later on,
during the 1990s, the governments were forced to play a more responsive role, taking their cues from below. New social movement groups
demanded medical insurance integration in Korea. In Taiwan, civil society actors, legislators, and recalcitrant bureaucrats successfully mobilized
against retrenchment, forcing the KMT government to backpedal on its
privatization reform efforts.

During both the late 1980s and the late 1990s, the institutionalization
of political competition reconstituted social policy agendas. One could
argue that it was the state's initiatives that drove welfare reform, as statist
perspectives on the welfare state would suggest. Where the statist
approach falls short, however, is in explaining why states, particularly
previously conservatives regimes such as the KMT in Taiwan and the DJP
in Korea, would be motivated to launch this new social policy trajectory
in the first place. Here procedural democracy—even the most minimalist
conceptions of democracy—matters most. Governments and/or their
challengers turned to social policy as a way of gaining short-term political

support. In addition, the universal extension of the right to political participation demanded social policy solutions that were more inclusive and, in the cases of Taiwan and South Korea, universal in scope. The authoritarian logic of crisis and selective compensation, discussed in Chapter 3, was therefore less viable in the context of democratization.

CONSTRUCTING CLEAVAGES

This book has highlighted how socioeconomic issues became a part of, even entrenched in, mainstream politics in Taiwan and South Korea. They became enduring bases of political competition and policy contestation. Political competition over certain cleavages—or in effect, the political attention paid to particular issues—kept certain ideas on the larger political agenda and thus increased the likelihood of further reform.

How do certain issues become salient competitive dimensions in the first place? Political cleavage formation is an agent-driven process, in that the choices that actors make determine which cleavages become salient in political competition. Constructing cleavages is therefore strategic. *Under conditions of political uncertainty and institutionalized political competition, strategic political actors will turn socioeconomic issues into salient bases of political contestation* (assertion 2). Several factors account for this strategic turn to socioeconomic cleavages. First, former lines of conflict may not resonate as well in new democratic settings; they simply may no longer be winning issues. The main political cleavage during the authoritarian period, for instance, is one that divides those who support democratic reform and their opposing conservative hard-liners. After the moment of democratic breakthrough, however, the cleavage between democratic activists and supporters of the old regime becomes less salient. Political actors, from both the incumbent and opposition camps, are thus forced to find new conflict dimensions and new issues over which to battle.

Second, socioeconomic lines of conflict fit better into the dominant ideological categories that differentiate social class interests in most societies. Political entrepreneurs may find that left-right ideological cues (and parties, if they exist) are effective means for mobilizing political support. Third, socioeconomic cleavages can reinforce or magnify other existing bases of political conflict and, as a result, strengthen preexisting lines of political contestation and conflict. For instance, regionalism in Korea and Brazil, ethnic conflict in Malaysia and Indonesia, and racial tensions in

South Africa are experienced in terms of socioeconomic disparity and have been articulated in those terms in times of political conflict.

Most important, political competition creates incentives for strategic entrepreneurs to diversify the bases of competition in order to gain competitive or electoral advantage over others. This strategy is especially useful where unidimensional lines of conflict have become static. In Taiwan, for instance, the main cleavage during the early stages of democratic transition was over Taiwanese claims for independence versus reunification with China. This cleavage quickly became static as voters tended to support the status quo—neither independence nor reunification. Strategic political actors thus turned to socioeconomic cleavages and redistributive social policy as a way of carving out new political constituencies. Exploiting these cross-cutting cleavages not only helped deepen democratic consolidation in Taiwan and South Korea but also turned socioeconomic issues into salient political cleavages. In sum, by diversifying the bases of competition, strategic political actors inadvertently constructed new cleavages, which in turn restructured the basis of policy contestation and social policymaking.

What was particularly interesting about the experiences of Taiwan and South Korea was that socioeconomic cleavages became important bases of competition despite the fact that these lines of conflict were previously nonexistent in East Asian politics. Because of geostrategic considerations, the left was marginalized from mainstream politics in authoritarian Taiwan and South Korea. Its position vis-à-vis communist China and North Korea promoted a political and popular atmosphere in which the left was demonized and even considered unpatriotic. A history of growth with relative equity, especially in Taiwan, also dampened the development of class-based conflict before democratic transition. Furthermore, the absence of any explicitly left-leaning political party meant that leftist conceptions of socioeconomic order were never a part of the formal political agenda. Weak unions, and a fragmented civil society more generally, inhibited any bottom-up mobilization around social welfare ideas. To be sure, democratic transition in Taiwan was driven by the dynamics of ethnic conflict. And though the *minjung* movement in Korea initially expounded a social democratic vision, the collapse of the movement alliance in 1987 signaled the abandonment of that reform agenda. Under these conditions, the fact that socioeconomic cleavages emerged in democratizing Taiwan and South Korea at all was quite remarkable.

Political entrepreneurs in Taiwan and South Korea constructed socioeconomic cleavages and drew attention to social policy ideas in order to gain competitive advantage over political opponents. I want to add another point here: *The likelihood that political actors will mobilize around socioeconomic cleavages is much greater when these competitive dimensions are introduced into political societies where no such cleavages existed before* (assertion 2, addendum). In Taiwan and South Korea, the prior absence of socioeconomic dimensions in the formal political arena provided the issue space in which strategic actors could effectively promote new socioeconomic policy ideas. Because left-right conflict did not exist before or around the time of democratic transition, any political actor of any political affiliation was able to exploit social policy reform ideas. Ideology, party identities, or political programs did not constrain social policy innovation on the part of any political actors in Taiwan and South Korea. As we have seen, the socially conservative DJP and KMT swiftly co-opted policy ideas from the opposition in order to win over key constituencies. They universalized health care even though these same regimes were the very ones that had earlier eschewed the idea of universal social welfare. They made this policy turnaround because the democratic political system encouraged them to do so.

Civil society movements also took advantage of this ideological and issue space and pushed social policy reform agendas from the bottom up. In Korea, Health Solidarity helped initiate new health care reform during the 1990s. The NHI Coalition in Taiwan was instrumental in leading social movement groups and politicians to resist the executive's retrenchment proposal. Social movement groups in both places appealed to parties, politicians, and bureaucrats of all political affiliations. In the end, the scramble among political entrepreneurs to use these new social policy ideas for competitive gain resulted in the continual "ratcheting up" of social policy reform. Because there were no political constraints (ideology, party programs), strategic policymakers essentially tried to outdo one another in social policy reform (and continue to do so). In a counterintuitive way, the absence of entrenched socioeconomic cleavages in Taiwan and South Korea reversed the race to the bottom and in fact encouraged a race upward. Social welfare's appeal was broadened in mainstream politics.

BROADENING WELFARE'S APPEAL

The power-resources perspective on the class-mobilization thesis in welfare state development puts a great deal of causal weight on the size of the working class. It also assumes that the working class is homogenous, at least in its political economic interests. Yet as we know, the size of the manufacturing working class in East Asian newly industrialized countries, as elsewhere, no longer constitutes a majority. Industrial diversification and labor market segmentation through continued industrial upgrading beginning in the 1970s have problematized any notion of a working-class identity. In the case of Taiwan, easy upward mobility, the proliferation of small and medium-sized enterprises (SMEs), and the geographical dispersion of these SMEs have further weakened the conventional class-mobilization thesis. The political demobilization of both unions and the independent labor movement in Taiwan and Korea during the authoritarian period, and even up through the early stages of democratic transition, undermined labor's political participation. Simply put, if labor was to be the driving force in welfare reform in East Asia, it desperately needed political allies.

Here power-resources theory and the modified class-mobilization thesis offer important insights. Gosta Esping-Andersen argues that a "class coalition" approach to understanding welfare state development is critical. He suggests that "we have to think in terms of social relations, not just social categories." According to Esping-Andersen, the mere existence of a working class does not guarantee effective societal mobilization.[19] Rather, coalitional politics drives political mobilization for the welfare state. This was certainly the case in South Korea and Taiwan. The Health Solidarity Coalition in South Korea was forged among middle-class civic groups (such as the Citizens' Coalition for Economic Justice and the People's Solidarity for Participatory Democracy), other new social movements, and the independent labor movement. In Taiwan, the National Health Insurance Coalition comprised more than two hundred social activist groups, ranging from the independent labor movement to women's organizations to child protection groups to professional medical associations. *Cross-class coalition building is necessary for social welfare reform* (assertion 3).

Coalition building was critical to new social policy innovations for several reasons. At one level, cross-class cooperation strengthened the movements' political leverage. In both Taiwan and South Korea, the sheer size of the NHI Coalition and Health Solidarity meant that policymakers could no longer block civil society's participation in policy decision making. Moreover, intergroup cooperation facilitated policy learning among coalition members. The sharing of ideas, experiences, and data, and most important, the inclusion of policy experts, allowed Health Solidarity and the NHI Coalition to play important educative roles, especially during legislative deliberations. The combination of policy expertise and grass-roots credentials—what I have called expert activism—made both coalitions formidable political forces. Finally, cross-class and cross-cleavage coalition building cut across, and thus dampened, other salient and potentially divisive political and economic cleavages among societal actors. Intergroup cooperation in Taiwan made ethnic divisions less salient, at least in the area of social policy, as was the case in Korea with respect to regional tensions.

Cross-class coalition building also shaped how state and society understood the place of social welfare reform in terms of the larger goals of political economic development. The process of coalition building helped mainstream the idea of redistributive welfare. For one, proponents of welfare reform in Taiwan and South Korea did not express health policy change as an ideological project. They did not need to. As argued earlier, the East Asian political system afforded the ideological flexibility for the emergence of new socioeconomic cleavages and the ideational space for new social policy initiatives. Advocates of socioeconomic transformation thus deliberately eschewed the rhetoric of the conventional left, both as a point for political mobilization and as an ideological justification for welfare reform. Advocates of welfare reform did not attempt to undermine capitalist development. Equitable health care was not incommensurate with economic growth. Health policy change was, in this sense, deradicalized.

This mainstreaming was not trivial. The consequences of health care reform (and resisting retrenchment) were understood to be inclusive socioeconomic arrangements. They were not perceived to benefit a single social class at the expense of others. Cross-class coalition building framed the idea of social welfare reform in the language of democratic citizenship, expressed as an expectation of democratic governance. *A strong political left is therefore not necessary for social welfare development. In fact, the presence of a strong or radicalized left may be detrimental to the prospects for welfare state development in the context of democratic change* (assertion 4). Indeed, in democratizing Latin America, the new left, better known as the "renovated left," has moderated its tactics, abandoned its ideological orthodoxy, and come to accept neoliberal economic realities. More and more, leftist parties are winning elections in the region because of such strategic reorientation. In this way, the new left in Latin America, as in East Asia, has staked the future of social democracy on its ability to play the new democratic game, replacing revolutionary radicalism with strategies that build on the normative appeal of cross-class inclusion.[20]

POLICY PATH DEPENDENCY

Policy change in Taiwan and South Korea reflected the legacies of earlier policy decisions. For instance, I argued in Chapter 4 that the decentralized health insurance system in Korea prohibited the Roh Tae-Woo regime from instituting any major structural reform at that time. Hence, universal health insurance in Korea was achieved through the addition of new insurance funds. In Taiwan, on the other hand, the relatively centralized administration of social insurance predating the universalization reform allowed the KMT government to implement a much more structurally ambitious reform plan that resulted in not only the universalization of health care but also the financial and administrative integration of medical insurance. Past choices mattered. As Edwin Amenta and Theda Skocpol argue: "Not only does politics create social policies; social policies also create politics. That is, once policies are enacted and implemented, they change the public agendas and the patterns of group conflict through which subsequent policy changes occur."[21] Policies "feed back" into politics and thus create patterns of policy path dependency. Reform efforts in Taiwan and South Korea during the late 1990s reflected these sorts of policy path dependencies. *Once a democratizing government initiates some social welfare reform, it is difficult for these states either to reverse this reform trajectory or to inhibit even more reform in the future because of policy path dependency* (assertion 5).

Paul Pierson argues that "welfare states create their own constituencies."[22] He reasons that once social policies are put into place, new interest coalitions will form around those policies to ensure against any future changes.[23] Pierson's insights capture the health care reform experiences of Taiwan and South Korea, particularly during the late 1990s. After universal health care was achieved in both places—a reform effort that was initiated by the state itself, though under political pressure from within society—new interests converged around the redistributive effects of social insurance. This led to demands in Korea during the late 1990s for even greater redistribution through medical insurance integration. In Taiwan, the legacy of the 1995 NHI drew together varied social movement groups, a corps of progressive-minded bureaucrats, and increasingly autonomous legislators to form a formidable political alliance against health care retrenchment in 1998.

The logic of policy path dependency in Taiwan and South Korea not only created new interest-based support for maintaining or deepening health care reform but also nurtured powerful normative expectations

about appropriate health care policy. Prior policy decisions thus constituted ideational path dependencies as well. After having enjoyed the benefits of universal health insurance, people changed their expectations
about health care and their understandings about the purpose of health
care policy throughout the 1990s. Redistribution in health policy was
expected, considered appropriate, and most of all desired. In South Korea,
the benefits of universal health care created demands for greater socioeconomic redistribution. In Taiwan, the redistributive effects of the NHI program fueled expectations that such benefits should be maintained.

LEARNING DEMOCRACY

Democratization reconstitutes how the political game is played. The institutionalization of political competition changes not only the objective of
the political game but also the political currency with which the game is
played. The legalization of associational life and the opening up of political space facilitate the creation of new actors and strengthen the standing of previously marginal actors. Democratic reform also brings about
institutional change. The rules of the game, both formal and informal,
are redefined. By extension, then, democratic transition reconstitutes
policymaking processes. It restructures policy networks, the institutional
framework in which these networks are embedded, and the rules that govern decision-making processes. Democratic change additionally facilitates the construction of new cleavage structures through which
redistributive policy ideas can become salient and mainstream. In short,
political change opens up opportunities for policy change.[24]

Policy change occurs when actors take advantage of these windows of
opportunity to float and advocate new policy ideas. In this book, we have
looked at two types of opportunities, political and policy. Political opportunities are, as Sidney Tarrow puts it, "dimensions of the political environment that provide incentives for people to undertake collective action
by affecting their expectations for success or failure."[25] Democratic transition is potentially full of these sorts of opportunities. Changes to the
rules of the political game, for instance, open up new channels for the
indirect or direct participation of previously marginal actors in the policy process. Policy windows of opportunity open up when actors articulate innovative policy ideas that draw attention to either new social
problems or new solutions that resolve existing policy challenges. In this
respect, new policy ideas are also the bases of policy change.

Opportunities for policy change are rare, however. They are not automatic; rather, they are made. Politically speaking, we have seen how democratic transition alone does not guarantee more inclusive patterns of representation and participation (i.e., Taiwan during the late 1980s). Instead, the introduction of democracy provides only new strategic contexts in which actors can devise new strategies for political representation and effective policymaking participation. It is not surprising, therefore, that some actors continue to be shut out of the policy process despite democratic reform. Actors need to learn and adapt. Similarly, the emergence of innovative policy ideas, or what Deborah Stone refers to as new policy narratives, is also not automatic. Policy knowledge, expertise, and the ability to articulate new policy alternatives must be learned over time. *Only through continual learning can political actors (i) adapt to new political contexts, (ii) innovate new policy ideas, and (iii) consequently take advantage of or open up opportunities for policy change* (assertion 6).

Learning is central to politics. Political learning and strategic adaptation are very much a part of the democratization process. As argued earlier, the terms of democratic transition are often engineered by political elites, usually from the outgoing ancien régime. Many actors are thus excluded from the democratic crafting process from the start.[26] Learning to play by someone else's rules is not easy. In Taiwan, for instance, the KMT "managed" democratic transition. Therefore, the ruling party was able to adapt to the democratic game more quickly and more effectively than the nascent opposition party and other civil society actors. The experience in Taiwan was not unique in this way. The opposition parties in Korea, for instance, were similarly slow to adapt when incumbent president Roh Tae-Woo unexpectedly initiated democratic transition in the summer of 1987.

Yet actors can learn and do adapt. Herbert Kitschelt and his colleagues point out that "the uncertainties of political action in the new democracies are high, but political actors explore the new setting not simply in a randomized trial-and-error mode but in a directed fashion that makes rational use of information. With each additional round of competition, the actors gain a better understanding of their strategic options."[27] Douglass North, using the game metaphor, elaborates:

> Given a set of formal and informal rules and enforcement characteristics that broadly define the way the game is played, what can we say about the play that we observe? Obviously a critical factor is the skill of the players and the knowledge they possess of the game. Even with a constant set of rules,

the games played will differ if they are played between rank amateurs and professionals. . . . The contrasts come from the differences between communicable knowledge and tacit knowledge . . . and from learning by doing in the case of repeated team play.[28]

Actors can learn new strategies with which to play the political and policy-making game and, more important, can transmit these strategies among different groups of actors. Some actors learn more quickly than others; some never learn at all and are therefore pushed out of the policy process.

Policy learning involves actors' cognitive capacities to identify problems, connect problems with tenable policy solutions, and articulate these new policy narratives or ideas in a convincing way. Policy learning is about gaining expertise in policy matters. In this respect, knowledge, expertise, and information are potential sources of policy influence and of political power more generally. Learning promotes a greater pluralism and contestation of ideas, facilitating opportunities for innovative policy change. In the context of democratization, policy learning undermines the knowledge and information monopoly enjoyed by the authoritarian developmental state. Through learning, previously marginalized actors can challenge the state by articulating real policy alternatives. Again, the proliferation of information—through, for instance, free media and greater transparency in policy deliberations—does not automatically guarantee new expertise among all actors in the policy process. Policy innovation is, in part, the product of policy learning.

In Taiwan, Department of Health bureaucrats learned to leverage their policy expertise. Go-slow bureaucrats offered alternative policy solutions to the KMT's privatization scheme. Their efforts not only helped soften the fiscal crisis in the National Health Insurance system but also undermined the political urgency surrounding the retrenchment reform proposal. In the formal political arena, legislators in Taiwan learned how to play the electoral game. They gained a tremendous amount of policy-making authority by strategically adapting to the multimember district electoral system. By relying less on party resources and leadership patronage and more on local networks, politicians turned party politics in Taiwan on its head, creating a political space in which legislators could play a more autonomous role in policy decision making. Legislators in Taiwan also gained policy expertise, to the extent that they are now considered the most influential policymakers, outranking the president and the bureaucracy. Using this influence, legislators were critical in logjamming the government's multiple-carrier proposal during the late 1990s.

Political actors in Korea similarly learned how to take advantage of the democratic rules of the game in order to influence policy outcomes. President Kim Dae-Jung was especially quick to learn and adapt to new political circumstances. Kim, recognizing that many officials in the bureaucracy were opposed to the medical insurance integration reform idea, reorganized the state apparatus in early 1998. Using his powers of political appointment, he restaffed the Ministry of Health and Welfare with his political allies. Kim was also forced to forge new legislative alliances within the National Assembly. He ensured strict party discipline through his institutionally derived authority as party leader and president. Most important, Kim assembled a coalition for reform, bringing together important legislators, bureaucrats, and civil society actors. For the first time, nongovernmental actors were invited to be a part of the health policy network, earning Kim's integration reform efforts a fair degree of grassroots support and wide political legitimacy. Learning from past failed attempts to legislate the integration reform, Kim recognized that civil society participation was crucial for effective policy change.

Societal actors were perhaps the most effective students of the democratic game. Because of conflicting interests, enmity among social movement leaders, and the breakdown of the authoritarian regime, civil society in Taiwan and South Korea effectively collapsed soon after the moment of democratic breakthrough. Such fragmentation is not uncommon in cases of democratic transition, and the experiences of Taiwan and Korea were not unique in this regard. However, social activist groups in Taiwan and South Korea soon learned new mobilization strategies.

First, they learned that broad-based coalition building was crucial if nongovernmental organizations were to gain any sort of influence in the policy process. Both Taiwan's NHI Coalition and the Health Solidarity Coalition in Korea increased the political clout of societal actors. The independent labor movements, once marginalized for being too radical, modified their interests, tactics, and images in order to cooperate with other reform-minded groups, at least in the area of health policy. Second, the NHI Coalition and Health Solidarity raised their policymaking profile by gaining policy expertise. Through political and policy learning, they transformed themselves into effective expert activists. Finally, these coalitions strategically "connected" with health care policymaking networks, adopting tactics that best fit their political institutional contexts. The NHI Coalition in Taiwan targeted both KMT and opposition party leaders in its effort to block the multiple-carrier reform. Health

Solidarity forged a tacit alliance with the Kim Dae-Jung regime. In the end, both strategic adaptations—as different as they were—were successful in achieving each group's objectives in health care reform.

In sum, actors learned how to play the policymaking game, adapting to specific, and thus variable, contexts of democratic change in each place and at different points in time. Political and policy learning among actors in Taiwan and South Korea were instrumental in altering preexisting patterns of policymaking, in shifting network boundaries, and in affecting policy outcomes. Yet the full effects of learning and adaptation emerged only recently, in the late 1990s, or about a decade after the initiation of democratic transition. Part of this delay can be explained by the fact that democratic crafting is an ongoing process, lasting much longer than the moment of democratic breakthrough. Authoritarian legacies linger, just as democratic bargains are continually renegotiated.[29] Indeed, democratic transition is a process, not an end in itself. More important is the fact that learning and strategic adaptation, quite simply, take time. They are not automatic processes. *Therefore, we should expect a lag time between the introduction of democracy and the realization of fairer representation and effective participation in the democratic policy process* (assertion 7). Because democratization is not accomplished overnight, the effects of learning by doing and strategic adaptation may necessarily lag behind otherwise momentous institutional and political change.

It is important to stress that the learning process is far from finished in Taiwan and South Korea. The challenges of improving democratic governance are ongoing. The near failure in implementing the medical insurance integration reform in Korea alerted policymakers there to the need for even more compromise among contending interests. Policy authority needs to be further diffused, reducing its concentration in the presidency. Parties need to be further democratized so that legislators can, in fact, make policy. Interestingly, the challenges of democratic governance in Taiwan could not be more different. There the failure of the government even to legislate the multiple-carrier reform indicates, on the one hand, the inclusion of a wider range of actors in the policy process yet, on the other hand, the significant institutional obstacles to making policy. Long-standing party factionalism, an electoral system that undermines party unity, and a generally fragmented political system continue to threaten the minimal coherence required for policy consensus. Taiwan's current politics is made for vetoing policy but inadequately equipped to make policy. Indeed, during the 2003 legislative session, only 17 of 106 "priority" bills were passed.[30]

CONCLUSION: REVITALIZING THE STATE

For those concerned about the future of the welfare state and issues of socioeconomic redistribution, the recent social policy developments in democratizing Taiwan and South Korea give reason for optimism. In the first place, the universalization of health care during the 1980s and 1990s was a major achievement. Continued welfare state deepening in Korea and resistance to retrenchment in Taiwan were even more impressive, particularly given the increasingly hostile environment for social welfare. Though still far from the welfare state benchmark of the northern European states, social policy reform in Taiwan and South Korea has taken an encouraging direction. It is one that is also very counterintuitive. These two cases cast doubt on socially and culturally deterministic arguments about the incompatibility of the welfare state and Asian societies. Even more important, especially in the broader comparative sense, the dynamics of welfare state development in Taiwan and South Korea provide a powerful rejoinder to the economic determinism of the globalization thesis, which suggests the inevitability of welfare state retrenchment. The 1997 financial crisis, for example, was interpreted in Taiwan and South Korea as an imperative for welfare state deepening rather than a reason for scaling back state intervention.

These two cases should not simply be dismissed as inexplicable anomalies. They need to be explained, and any lessons they may offer need to be distilled for other democratizing countries. They need to be theorized. To that end, the arguments assembled throughout this book teach us that there are *political* reasons why a burgeoning welfare state has emerged in these two unlikely places. More specifically, this book points to the politics of democratic transition as the key variable for welfare state development in Taiwan and Korea.

Democratic transition in Taiwan and South Korea had an impact on social policymaking. The institutionalization of political competition—a process some lament as being *only* procedural democracy—reconstituted the health care policy agenda. Policymakers in Taiwan and South Korea initiated major health policy reform, both in anticipation of and in response to the pressures of political competition. The imperatives of democratic competition and, more important, ongoing competition compelled strategic actors to introduce and then mainstream political cleavages around social welfare issues. Cross-class coalition building broadened welfare's appeal in both Taiwan and South Korea. Furthermore, the logic of policy path dependency ensured that the welfare state trajectory established during the late 1980s was sustained through the late 1990s. Though the effects of path dependency in health care policy were not a direct consequence of democratic reform, the articulation of such normative expectations for and political mobilization around universal health care were possible only under democratic conditions.

I believe democratic transition in Taiwan and South Korea has saved the developmental state. Contrary to expectations that democratic reform strips the state of its institutional capacity and political autonomy, democratic change has revitalized or even strengthened the state in Taiwan and South Korea. After the moment of democratic breakthrough, the imperatives of building democratic legitimacy reenergized the state's capacities to lead reform, capacities that even the pressures of economic globalization could not diminish. Furthermore, the institutionalization of political participation in Taiwan and South Korea drew newly enfranchised citizens into politics and the policymaking process. Citizens invested time and effort in remaking the democratizing state, requiring in turn that the state earn their consent to govern legitimately. Greater accountability, furthermore, meant that the performance of the state was necessary for its political survival. In the context of Taiwan and South Korea, then, the democratic developmental state has taken on the shape of a limited though deepening welfare state. Democracy sparked this new developmental trajectory, and I believe the logic of democratic deepening in Taiwan and Korea will ensure its continuation. And this is, ultimately, democracy's greatest defense.

NOTES

1. DEMOCRATIZATION AND THE WELFARE STATE

1. James Midgeley, "Industrialization and Welfare: The Case of the Four Little Tigers," *Social Policy and Administration* 20 (1985); *Social Welfare in Asia*, ed. J. Dixon and H. S. Kim (London: Croom Helm, 1985).

2. Catherine Jones, "The Pacific Challenge: Confucian Welfare States," in *New Perspectives on the Welfare State in Europe*, ed. Jones (London: Routledge, 1993).

3. Paul Pierson, *The New Politics of the Welfare State* (Oxford: Oxford University Press, 2001); Gosta Esping-Andersen, *Welfare States in Transition: National Adaptations to Changing Global Economies* (London: Sage, 1996); Geoffrey Garrett and Peter Lange, "Political Responses to Interdependence: What's 'Left' for the Left?" *International Organization* 45 (1991).

4. Thomas Biersteker, "The 'Triumph' of Liberal Economic Ideas in the Developing World," in *Global Change, Regional Response: The New International Context of Development*, ed. Barbara Stallings (Cambridge: Cambridge University Press, 1995).

5. Ian Holliday, "Productivist Welfare Capitalism: Social Policy in East Asia," *Political Studies* 48 (2000); World Bank, *The East Asian Miracle* (Oxford: Oxford University Press, 1993).

6. Between 1999 and 2000, I conducted an original comparative elite survey of bureaucrats and legislators in Taiwan (in 1999) and South Korea (2000). The self-administered paper survey was distributed to all legislators in the Legislative Yuan in Taiwan and the National Assembly in Korea. For the bureaucratic sample, two groups of bureaucrats were targeted in each administration. In Taiwan, the survey was randomly distributed to the Department of Health (DOH) Small Group on Health Policy, comprising about twenty officials. The survey was also distributed randomly throughout three divisions of the Bureau of National Health Insurance (BNHI): finance, medical affairs, and planning/evaluation. In Korea, the bureaucratic sample consisted of officials from the National Health Insurance Corporation's (NHIC) Inte-

gration Committee and the Ministry of Health and Welfare (MOHW) Health Insurance Division. The survey, which comprised more than sixty attitudinal and network/contact measures, was administered in Chinese and Korean. The total sample size from both countries was 249 respondents, 133 from Korea and 116 from Taiwan.

7. National Statistical Office, *Korea Statistical Yearbook* (Seoul: National Statistical Office, 1997); Bank of Korea, *Economic Statistics Yearbook* (Seoul: Bank of Korea, 2000); Council for Economic Planning and Development, Executive Yuan, *Taiwan Statistical Data Book* (Taipei: CEPD, 1999).

8. Figures calculated from the sources in note 7.

9. Lee Chang, "Setting National Priorities: Welfare vs. Defense," *Korean Social Science Journal* 16 (1990); Council for Economic Planning and Development, *Taiwan Statistical Data Book.*

10. On recent social policy reforms in Taiwan and South Korea, see Huck-Ju Kwon, "Democracy and the Politics of Social Welfare: A Comparative Analysis of Welfare Systems in East Asia," in *The East Asian Welfare Model: Welfare Orientalism and the State,* ed. Roger Goodman, Gordon White, and Huck-Ju Kwon. (London: Routledge, 1998).

11. Guillermo O'Donnell and Philippe Schmitter, *Transitions from Authoritarian Rule: Tentative Conclusions* (Baltimore: Johns Hopkins University Press, 1986), 45; Juan Linz and Alfred Stepan, *Problems of Democratic Transition and Consolidation* (Baltimore: Johns Hopkins University Press, 1996), 12–13; Adam Przeworski, Michael Alvarez, Jose Antonio Cheibub, Fernando Limongi, "What Makes Democracies Endure?" *Journal of Democracy* 7 (1996): 43.

12. Walter Korpi, *The Democratic Class Struggle* (London: Routledge, 1983); Seymour Martin Lipset, *Political Man: The Social Bases of Politics* (New York: Doubleday, 1960).

13. Robert Jackman, "Elections and the Democratic Class Struggle," *World Politics* 39 (1986).

14. Evelyne Huber, Dietrich Rueschemeyer, and John D. Stephens, "The Paradoxes of Contemporary Democracy: Formal, Participatory, and Social Dimensions," in *Transitions to Democracy,* ed. Lisa Anderson (New York: Columbia University Press, 1999).

15. Charles Andrain, *Public Health Policies and Social Inequality* (New York: New York University Press, 1998), 6–8.

16. The proportion of the world's population over the age of 65 increased from 5.3% in 1965 to 6.6% in 1995 and is projected to reach over 10% by 2025. In East Asia, a notably graying region, the proportion of population over 65 increased from 4.1% in 1965 to 5.8% in 1995 and is expected to be 11% in 2025. In Korea, the percentage of over-65 citizens was 6.8 in 2000, up from 3.1 in 1965. Similarly, the percentage of people over 65 in Taiwan was 8.2 in 1998, having increased from 2.5 in 1965. See Jacques van der Gaag and Alexander Preker, "Health Care for Aging Populations: Issues and Options," in *Choices in Financing Health Care and Old Age Security,* ed. Nicholas Prescott, World Bank Discussion Paper No. 392 (Washington D.C.: World Bank, 1998), 8; Hye-Hoon Lee and Kye-Sik Lee, "A Korean Model of Social Welfare Policy: Issues and Strategies," in *An Agenda for Economic Reform in Korea: International Perspectives,* ed. Kenneth Judd and Yoong-Ki Lee (Stanford: Hoover Institution Press, 2000), 207; Council for Economic Planning and Development, *Taiwan Statistical Data Book.*

17. Deborah Stone, *Policy Paradox: The Art of Political Decision Making* (New York: W. W. Norton, 1997), chap. 2; H. Peyton Young, *Equity: In Theory and Practice* (Princeton: Princeton University Press, 1994); John Rawls, *A Theory of Justice* (Cambridge: Harvard University Press, 1971).

18. William Hsiao, "Comparing Health Care Systems: What Nations Can Learn from One Another," *Journal of Health Politics, Policy, and Law* 17 (1992).

19. World Health Organization, *The World Health Report, 1999* (Geneva: World Health Organization, 1999), 39.

20. Adam Wagstaff and Eddy van Doorslaer, "Equity in the Finance of Health Care: Methods and Findings," in *Equity in the Finance and Delivery of Health Care: An International Perspective*, ed. Adam Wagstaff, Eddy van Doorslaer, and Frans Rutten (Oxford: Oxford University Press, 1993).

21. William Hsiao and Jui-Fen Lu, "Taiwan's National Health Insurance: The Trade-Offs between Equity and Efficiency," paper presented at National Taiwan University, Taipei, October 1–2, 1999, 20.

22. Ian Gough, *The Political Economy of the Welfare State* (London: Macmillan, 1979); James O'Connor, *The Fiscal Crisis of the State* (New York: St. Martin's Press, 1973); Clause Offe, *Contradictions of the Welfare State* (Cambridge: MIT Press, 1990).

23. Philips Cutright, "Political Structure, Economic Development, and National Social Security Programs," *American Journal of Sociology* 70 (1965); Harold Wilensky, *The Welfare State and Equality* (Berkeley: University of California Press, 1967).

24. Michael Howlett and M. Ramesh, *Studying Public Policy: Policy Cycles and Policy Subsystems* (Oxford: Oxford University Press, 1995), 106–7.

25. Gosta Esping Andersen, *Three Worlds of Welfare Capitalism* (Princeton: Princeton University Press, 1990); John D. Stephens, *Transition from Capitalism to Socialism* (New York: Macmillan, 1979).

26. Ruth Berins Collier, *Paths toward Democracy: The Working Class and Elites in Western Europe and South America* (Cambridge: Cambridge University Press, 1999), 2.

27. Sidney Tarrow, *Power in Movement: Social Movements, Collective Action, and Politics* (Cambridge: Cambridge University Press, 1994).

28. Ellen Immergut, *Health Politics: Interests and Institutions in Western Europe* (Cambridge: Cambridge University Press, 1992); Margaret Weir, Ann Shola Orloff, and Theda Skocpol, eds. *The Politics of Social Policy in the United States* (Princeton: Princeton University Press, 1988).

29. Huck-Ju Kwon, *The Welfare State in Korea: The Politics of Legitimation* (New York: St. Martin's Press, 1999), 31–35; Yeun-Wen Ku, *Welfare Capitalism in Taiwan: State, Economy, and Social Policy* (New York: St. Martin's Press, 1997), 21–30.

30. Peter Evans, *Embedded Autonomy: States and Industrial Transformation* (Princeton: Princeton University Press, 1995); Robert Wade, *Governing the Market: Economic Theory and the Role of Government in East Asian Industrialization* (Princeton: Princeton University Press, 1990).

31. Holliday, "Productivist Welfare Capitalism."

32. Steve Chan, "Democracy and Inequality: Tracking Welfare Spending in Singapore, Taiwan, and South Korea," in *Inequality, Democracy, and Economic Development*, ed. Manus Midlarsky (Cambridge: Cambridge University Press, 1997), 243 (emphasis added).

33. See Gerardo Munck, "Review Article: Democratic Transitions in Comparative Perspective," *Comparative Politics* 26 (1994).

34. Edward Friedman, "Democratization: Generalizing the East Asian Experience," in *The Politics of Democratization: Generalizing East Asian Experiences*, ed. Friedman (Boulder: Westview Press, 1994); Giuseppe Di Palma, *To Craft Democracies: An Essay on Democratic Transition* (Berkeley: University of California Press, 1990).

2. A DYNAMIC POLICYMAKING FRAMEWORK

1. Steve Chan, "Income Inequality among LDCs: A Comparative Analysis of Alternative Perspectives," *International Studies Quarterly* 33 (1989).

2. John Kingdon, *Agendas, Alternatives, and Public Policies*, 2d ed. (New York: Addison Wesley Longman, 1995), 109.

3. Deborah Stone, *Policy Paradox: The Art of Political Decision Making*, 2d ed. (New York: W. W. Norton, 1997), 188. See also Stone, "Causal Stories and the Formation of Policy Agendas," *Political Science Quarterly* 104 (1989).

4. Stone, "Causal Stories," 295.

5. Giandomenico Majone, *Evidence, Argument, and Persuasion in the Policy Process* (New Haven: Yale University Press, 1989), 10.

6. Frank Baumgartner and Bryan D. Jones, *Agendas and Instability in American Politics* (Chicago: University of Chicago Press, 1993).

7. Douglass North, *Institutions, Institutional Change, and Economic Performance* (Cambridge: Cambridge University Press, 1990).

8. Majone, *Evidence*, 10; Charles Lindblom, "The Science of Muddling Through," *Public Administration Review* 19 (1959).

9. Sven Steinmo and Jon Watts, "It's the Institutions Stupid! Why Comprehensive National Health Insurance Always Fails in America," *Journal of Health Politics, Policy, and Law* 20 (1995).

10. Gosta Esping-Andersen, *Three Worlds of Welfare Capitalism* (Princeton: Princeton University Press, 1990).

11. David Wilsford, "States Facing Interests: Struggles over Health Care Policy in Advanced Industrial Democracies," *Journal of Health Politics, Policy, and Law* 20 (1995).

12. Paul Pierson, "The New Politics of the Welfare State," *World Politics* 48 (1996).

13. Albert S. Yee, "The Causal Effects of Ideas on Policies," *International Organization* 50 (1996): 69.

14. Judith Goldstein and Robert Keohane, "Ideas and Foreign Policy: An Analytical Framework," in *Ideas and Foreign Policy: Beliefs, Institutions, and Political Change*, ed. Goldstein and Keohane (Ithaca: Cornell University Press, 1993), 9.

15. Robert Henry Cox, "The Social Construction of an Imperative: Why Welfare Reform Happened in Denmark and the Netherlands, but Not Germany," *World Politics* 53 (2001): 474.

16. Peter Hall, "Policy Paradigms, Social Learning, and the State: The Case of Economic Policy-Making in Britain," *Comparative Politics* 25 (1993).

17. Michael Howlett and M. Ramesh, *Studying Public Policy: Policy Cycles and Policy Subsystems* (Oxford: Oxford University Press, 1995), 122.

18. Gertrude Himmelfarb, *The Idea of Poverty: England in the Early Industrial Age* (New York: Knopf, 1984), 8.

19. H. Peyton Young, *Equity: In Theory and Practice* (Princeton: Princeton University Press, 1994), 3; T. H. Marshall, *Class, Citizenship, and Social Development* (Chicago: University of Chicago Press, 1977), 78.

20. John Rawls, "Justice as Fairness: Political not Metaphysical," *Philosophy and Public Affairs* 14 (1985).

21. See, for example, Soonwon Kwon, "Economic Justice and Social Welfare: New Principles of Economic Policy," in *Democratization and Globalization in Korea: Assessments and Prospects*, ed. Chung-In Moon and Jongryn Mo (Seoul: Yonsei University Press, 1999).

22. Joseph Wong, "Deepening Democracy in Taiwan," *Pacific Affairs* 76 (2003).

23. Stephen Brooks and Alain Gagnon, *Social Scientists, Policy, and the State* (New York: Praeger, 1990).

24. Alan Cigler and Burdett Loomis, *Interest Group Politics*, 5th ed. (Washington, D.C.: Congressional Quarterly Press, 1998).

25. Carol Weissert and William Weissert, *Governing Health: The Politics of Health Policy* (Baltimore: Johns Hopkins University Press, 1996).

26. Peter Katzenstein, "Domestic Structures and Strategies of Foreign Economic Policy," *International Organization* 31 (1977).

27. Randall Ripley and Grace Franklin, *Congress, the Bureaucracy, and Public Policy* (Homewood, Ill.: Dorsey Press, 1978).

28. Hugh Heclo, "Issue Networks and the Executive Establishment," in *The New American Political System*, ed. Anthony King (Washington, D.C.: American Enterprise Institute for Public Policy Research, 1978).

29. Paul Sabatier, "An Advocacy Coalition Framework of Policy Change and the Role of Policy-Oriented Learning Therein," *Policy Sciences* 21 (1988).

30. Howlett and Ramesh, *Studying Public Policy.*

31. Barbara Wake Carroll and Terrance Carroll, "Civic Networks, Legitimacy, and the Policy Process," *Governance: An International Journal of Policy and Administration* 12 (1999).

32. Douglas Chalmers, Scott Martin, and Kerianne Piester, "Associative Networks: New Structures of Representation for the Popular Sectors," in *The New Politics of Inequality in Latin America: Rethinking Participation and Representation,* ed. Douglas Chalmers et al. (Oxford: Oxford University Press, 1997).

33. John Heinz, Edward Laumann, Robert Salisbury, and Robert Nelson, "Inner Circles or Hollow Cores? Elite Networks Policy Systems," *Journal of Politics* 52 (1990).

34. Sabatier, "Advocacy Coalition Framework."

35. Michael Atkinson and William Coleman, "Policy Networks, Communities, and Problems of Governance," *Governance* 5 (1992): 172.

36. Ibid., 172–73.

37. Dietrich Rueschemeyer, John Stephens, and Evelyn-Huber Stephens, *Capitalist Development and Democracy* (Chicago: University of Chicago Press, 1992), 42.

38. Kingdon, *Agendas.*

39. John C. Campbell, *How Policies Change: The Japanese Government and the Aging Society* (Princeton: Princeton University Press, 1992), 30–31.

40. Sidney Tarrow, *Power in Movement: Social Movements, Collective Action, and Politics* (Cambridge: Cambridge University Press, 1994), 18. See also Herbert Kitschelt, "Political Opportunity Structure and Political Protest: Anti-nuclear Movements in Four Democracies," *British Journal of Political Science* 16 (1986).

41. Kingdon, *Agendas,* 169.

42. Bryan Jones, *Reconceiving Decision-Making in Democratic Politics: Attention, Choice, and Public Policy* (Chicago: University of Chicago Press, 1994), 3.

43. Carolyn Hughes Tuohy, *Accidental Logics: The Dynamics of Change in the Health Care Arena in the United States, Britain, and Canada* (Oxford: Oxford University Press, 1999), 123.

44. Sabatier, "Advocacy Coalition Framework," 20–29.

45. Peter Hall, "Conclusion: The Politics of Keynesian Ideas," in *The Political Power of Economic Ideas: Keynesianism across Nations,* ed. Hall (Princeton: Princeton University Press, 1989).

46. Baumgartner and Jones, *Agendas,* 4.

47. North, *Institutions,* 4.

48. Sven Steinmo, Kathleen Thelen, and Frank Longstreth, *Structuring Politics: Historical Institutionalism in Comparative Analysis* (Cambridge: Cambridge University Press, 1992); Peter Hall and Rosemary Taylor, "Political Science and the Three New Institutionalisms," *Political Studies* 10 (1996).

49. Jack Knight, *Institutions and Social Conflict* (Cambridge: Cambridge University Press, 1992), 40.

50. Herbert Simon, *Administrative Behavior: A Study of Decision-Making Processes in Administrative Organizations,* 2d ed. (New York: Macmillan, 1957).

51. Ellen Immergut, *Health Politics: Interests and Institutions in Western Europe* (Cambridge: Cambridge University Press, 1992), 7; Robert Keohane and Helen Milner, "Internationalization and Domestic Politics: An Introduction," in *Internationalization and Domestic Politics*, ed. Keohane and Milner (Cambridge: Cambridge University Press, 1996), 4.

52. Marian Dohler, "Policy Networks, Opportunity Structures, and Neo-conservative Reform Strategies in Health Policy," in *Policy Networks: Empirical Evidence and Theoretical Considerations*, ed. Bernd Marin and Renate Mayntz (Boulder: Westview Press, 1991).

53. Kurt Weyland, *Democracy without Equity: Failures of Reform in Brazil* (Pittsburgh: University of Pittsburgh Press, 1996).

54. Baumgartner and Jones, *Agendas*, 32.

55. Carlos Vilas, "Participation, Inequality, and the Whereabouts of Democracy," in *The New Politics of Inequality in Latin America*, ed. Douglas Chalmers et al. (Oxford: Oxford University Press, 1997).

56. Tse-Min Lin, John Higley, and Tong-Yi Huang, "Elite Settlements in Taiwan," *Journal of Democracy* 9 (1998).

57. Hee-Min Kim, "Rational Choice Theory and Third World Politics: The 1990 Party Merger in Korea," *Comparative Politics* 30 (1997); David Brady and Jongryn Mo, "Electoral Systems and Institutional Choice: A Case Study of the 1988 Korean Elections," *Comparative Political Studies* 24 (1992).

58. Adam Przeworski, *Democracy and the Market: Political and Economic Reform in Eastern Europe and Latin America* (Cambridge: Cambridge University Press, 1991).

59. Herbert Kitschelt, "Partisan Competition and Welfare State Retrenchment: When Do Politicians Choose Unpopular Policies?" in *The New Politics of the Welfare State*, ed. Paul Pierson (Oxford: Oxford University Press, 2001).

60. Giuseppe Di Palma, *To Craft Democracies* (Berkeley: University of California Press, 1990), 45.

61. Samuel Huntington, *The Third Wave: Democratization in the Late Twentieth Century* (Norman: University of Oklahoma Press, 1991), chap. 3.

62. Huang Te-Fu, "Elections and the Evolution of the Kuomintang," in *Taiwan's Electoral Politics and Democratic Transition: Riding the Third Wave*, ed. Hung-Mao Tien (Armonk, N.Y.: M. E. Sharpe, 1996); Gary Cox, *Making Votes Count: Strategic Coordination in the World's Electoral Systems* (Cambridge: Cambridge University Press, 1997).

63. Brady and Mo, "Electoral Systems."

64. Seymour Martin Lipset and Stein Rokkan, "Cleavage Structures, Party Systems, and Voter Alignments," in *Party Systems and Voting Alignments: Cross-National Perspectives*, ed. Lipset and Rokkan (New York: Free Press, 1967). See also Herbert Kitschelt et al., *Post-Communist Party Systems: Competition, Representation, and Inter-party Collaboration* (Cambridge: Cambridge University Press, 1999); Tse-Min Lin, Yun-Han Chu, and Melvin Hinich, "Conflict Displacement and Regime Transition in Taiwan: A Spatial Analysis," *World Politics* 48 (1996).

65. Anthony Downs, *An Economic Theory of Politics* (New York: Harper Collins, 1957).

66. Robert Jackman, "Review Essay: Elections and the Democratic Class Struggle," *World Politics* 39 (1986): 135–42.

67. David Collier and Steven Levitsky, "Democracy with Adjectives: Conceptual Innovation in Comparative Research," *World Politics* 49 (1997).

68. Rueschemeyer, Stephens, and Stephens, *Capitalist Development*, 76.

3. AUTHORITARIANISM AND THE ORIGINS OF SOCIAL INSURANCE

1. David Kang, *Crony Capitalism* (Oxford: Oxford University Press, 2001).

2. The Committee on Social Security (CSS) originated before the 1961 coup as an informal group of scholars and civil servants that met weekly to discuss issues of social development, including social welfare. In March 1962, the group was formally named the Committee on Social Security by order of President Park and subsequently was officially made an advisory body to the minister of health and social affairs. See Huck-Ju Kwon, *The Welfare State in Korea: The Politics of Legitimation* (New York: St. Martin's Press, 1999), 161 n. 63.

3. The SCNR demanded that the CSS complete its policy proposals in time for President Park's New Year's address in 1963.

4. Chan-Ung Park, "Institutional Legacies and State Power: The First State Health Insurance Movements in Great Britain, the United States, and Korea," Ph.D. diss., University of Chicago, 1997, 343.

5. Cited in Huck-Ju Kwon, *Welfare State*, 54.

6. It should be pointed out, however, that the Industrial Accidents Insurance program provided medical care benefits only in the case of workplace accidents and only after the claimant could prove that the injury was caused by an accident at work and that the cause of the accident was from the workplace itself. The IAI program extended coverage only to those workers employed by large-scale enterprises (five hundred-plus employees). See Hye-Hoon Lee and Kye-Sik Lee, "A Korean Model of Social Welfare Policy: Issues and Strategies," in *An Agenda for Economic Reform in Korean and International Perspectives*, ed. Kenneth Judd and Young-Ki Lee (Stanford: Hoover Institution Press, 2000), 217.

7. Soonwon Kwon, *Social Policy in Korea: Challenges and Responses* (Seoul: Korea Development Institute, 1993), 184–85.

8. Park Chong-Kee, *Social Security in Korea: An Approach to Socio-Economic Development* (Seoul: Korea Development Institute, 1975), 79.

9. Cited in Chan-Ung Park, "Institutional Legacies," 357.

10. A U.S. aid loan, granted in 1975, was designated by American authorities for the improvement of public health care in Korea. See Huck-Ju Kwon, *Welfare State*, 57.

11. On the domestic factors leading to the passage of the 1976 medical insurance program, see Chan-Ung Park, "Institutional Legacies," 358–61.

12. Myongsei Sohn, Seung-Hum Yu, and Yong-Hak Kim, "Network Analysis of Korean Health Insurance Policymaking Process," *Yonsei Medical Journal* 33 (1992): 125–27.

13. Ibid.

14. Chan-Ung Park, "Institutional Legacies," 369.

15. Copay rates for dependents of the insured (those who were not independently insured at their own workplace or were not eligible for insurance, such as children, unemployed spouses, or the aged) were 10% higher (50% for outpatient treatment and 40% for inpatient care). See Soonwon Kwon, *Social Policy*, 267.

16 Later in that year, the multiple HIS were placed under one umbrella organization, the National Federation of Medical Insurance (NFMI), though the individual insurance societies continued to operate independently.

17. Cited in Chan-Ung Park, "Institutional Legacies," 406.

18. Lin Wan-I, *The Welfare State: A Historical and Comparative Analysis* (Taipei: Great Current Press, 1994), 183 [in Chinese].

19. Chiang Tung-liang, *Health Care Policy: Taiwan's Experience* (Taipei: Great Current Press, 1999), 95 [in Chinese].

20. Gordon Hou-sheng Chan, "Taiwan," in *Social Welfare in Asia*, ed. J. Dixon and H. S. Kim (London: Croom Helm, 1985), 334–35.

21. See Wu Kai-hsun, "A Review of Health Insurance Programs in Taiwan," in *Health Insurance*, ed. Yaung Chi-liang (Taipei: Great Current Press, 1998), 179–81 [in Chinese].

22. Beginning in the early 1960s, health insurance coverage was extended to retired government employees.

23. For instance, in 1994 the number of inpatient stays for those under the age of 15 and those over 65 (347 per 1,000 people) was higher than the number of stays for those between the ages of 15 and 64 (312 per 1,000 people). The number of outpatient visits per year was likewise higher for those under 15 and those over 65 (46 per 1,000 people) in 1994 than for those aged 15 to 64 (37 per 1,000 people). Tung-Liang Chiang, *Health Care Policy*, 43.

24. Calculated from figures cited in Sungkyun Lee, "A Comparative Study of Welfare Programs for Old-Age Income Security in Korea and Taiwan," Ph.D. diss., University of Wisconsin-Madison, 1997, 143.

25. Measures included increasing the minimum wage, ensuring a safe workplace (the Law for Labor Security and Health was passed in 1974), the improvement of welfare services for workers, and the reform of the labor insurance scheme. Cited in Sungkyun Lee, "Comparative Study," 145.

26. Shelley Rigger, *Politics in Taiwan: Voting for Democracy* (London: Routledge, 1999), 114–15.

27. Ching-Yuan Tsai, "Accent on the People," *Free China Review* (1979): 15.

28. Council for Economic Planning and Development, Executive Yuan, *Taiwan Statistical Data Book* (Taipei: CEPD, 1999), 299.

29. Sungkyun Lee, "Comparative Study," 152.

30. Lin Kuo-Min, "From Authoritarianism to Statism: The Politics of National Health Insurance in Taiwan," Ph.D. diss., Yale University, 1997, 138–39.

31. In 1983, voluntary health insurance was extended to those working in firms with 5 to 15 employees.

32. In the pilot program for farmers' insurance, the "farmer associations" acted as the insurer unit. Premiums were set very low, at 5.5% of the lowest insured wage bracket under the LI scheme, because of the difficulty of getting accurate income reporting from farm wages. The farmer paid 30% of the premium, the state 60%, and the farmer associations 10%. See Lin Kuo-Min, "Authoritarianism," 103–4.

33. In 1980, there were close to 40,000 insurance units under the LI scheme and 5,250 in the GEI program.

34. Chan-Ung Park, "Institutional Legacies," 344; Tung-Liang Chiang, *Health Care Policy*, 77.

35. Kuo-Min Lin shows that between 1976 and 1992, the growth rate of private sector health care expenditures was twice as rapid as national economic growth and three times as fast as the consumer price index. Lin, "Authoritarianism," 94.

36. Hagen Koo, "Strong State and Contentious Society," *State and Society in Contemporary Korea*, ed. Koo (Ithaca: Cornell University Press, 1993), 239.

37. Jung-En Woo, *Race to the Swift: State and Finance in Korean Industrialization* (New York: Columbia University Press, 1991), 98.

38. Chung Kil-Chung notes, for example, that the chairman of the Economic Planning Board during the late 1960s declared that "whoever speaks up for the issue of pollution is a traitor." Cited in Chung, "The Ideology of Economic Development and Its Impact on the Policy Process," *Korean Journal of Policy Studies* 1 (1986): 34 n. 14.

39. Park Chung-Hee, *Our Nation's Path: Ideology of Social Reconstruction* (Seoul: Dong-A Publishing, 1962), 20–21.

40. Yong-Duck Jung, "Distributive Justice and Redistributive Policy in Korea," *Korean Social Science Journal* 11 (1984).

41. Chen-Kuo Hsu, "Ideological Reflections and the Inception of Economic Development in Taiwan," in *The Role of the State in Taiwan's Development*, ed. Joel Aberbach et al. (Armonk, N.Y.: M. E. Sharpe, 1994).

42. According to former minister of labor (and member of the Economic Planning Board) Hyung-Koo Lee, before the 1970s state and society shared in the belief that aggregate economic growth would promote a "trickle-down" effect in terms of distributive outcomes. See Hyung-Koo Lee, *The Korean Economy: Perspectives for the Twenty-First Century* (Albany: State University of New York Press, 1996), 71.

43. Yeun-Wen Ku, *Welfare Capitalism in Taiwan: State, Economy, and Social Policy* (New York: St. Martin's Press, 1997), 146.

44. Hou-Sheng Chan, "The Relationship between Social Security Systems and Economic Development: Hong Kong, Singapore, and Taiwan," *Journal of Sociology, National Taiwan University* 13 (1979); Roger Goodman and Ito Peng, "The East Asian Welfare States: Peripatetic Learning, Adaptive Change, and Nation-Building," in *Welfare States in Transition: National Adaptations in Global Economies*, ed. Gosta Esping-Andersen (London: Sage, 1996).

45. Kent Calder, *Crisis and Compensation: Public Policy and Stability in Japan* (Princeton: Princeton University Press, 1988), 20.

46. Peter Flora and Jens Alber, "Modernization, Democratization, and the Development of Welfare States in Western Europe," in *The Development of Welfare States in Europe and America*, ed. P. Flora and A. J. Heidenheimer (New Brunswick: Transaction Publishers, 1981); Theda Skocpol and Edwin Amenta, "States and Social Policies," *Annual Review of Sociology* 12 (1986).

47. James Malloy, *The Politics of Social Security in Brazil* (Pittsburgh: University of Pittsburgh Press, 1979), 160–61. See also Kurt Weyland, *Democracy without Equity: Failures of Reform in Brazil* (Pittsburgh: University of Pittsburgh Press, 1996), 104–5; Dietrich Rueschemeyer, John Stephens, and Evelyne Huber-Stephens, *Capitalist Development and Democracy* (Chicago: University of Chicago Press, 1992), 290.

48. Yeun-wen Ku, *Welfare Capitalism in Taiwan: State, Economy, and Social Policy* (New York: St. Martin's Press, 1997), chaps. 5 and 6; Kuo-Min Lin, "Authoritarianism," 78–79; Lin Wan-I, *The Welfare State: A Historical-Comparative Analysis* (Taipei: Great Current Press, 1994), 181–82 [in Chinese].

49. Huck-Ju Kwon, *Welfare State*, 19–20.

50. Hagen Koo, "The State, Minjung, and the Working Class in South Korea," in *State and Society in Contemporary Korea*, ed. Koo (Ithaca: Cornell University Press, 1993).

51. In his argument of crisis and compensation, Calder emphasizes that the implementation of new social welfare programs in democratic Japan was the result of a long process of deliberation and policy experimentation that preceded the crisis. Calder, *Crisis*, 361–64.

4. DEMOCRATIC BREAKTHROUGH AND UNIVERSAL HEALTH CARE

1. See Robert Bedeski, *The Transformation of South Korea: Reform and Reconstruction in the Sixth Republic under Roh Tae-Woo, 1987–1992* (London: Routledge, 1994).

2. See Tien-Hung Mao, "Taiwan's Transformation," in *Consolidating the Third Wave Democracies: Regional Challenges*, eds. Larry Diamond, Marc Plattner, Yun-Han Chu, and Hung-Mao Tien (Baltimore: Johns Hopkins University Press, 1997).

3. Health insurance coverage for workers in firms with one hundred or more employees was extended between 1981 and 1982. In 1988, firms with five or more employees were brought into the employee-based health insurance system.

4. In 1992, there were 154 employee insurance societies, 136 urban self-employed insurance schemes, and 130 rural self-employed insurance societies in addition to the single government employees' insurance program.

5. The proportion of Koreans living under the poverty line decreased from 41% in 1965 (55% in urban areas) to 14.6% in 1976. Soonwon Kwon, *Social Policy in Korea: Challenges and Responses* (Seoul: Korea Development Institute, 1993), 96.

6. See Eun-Mee Kim, *Big Business, Strong State: Collusion and Conflict in South Korean Development, 1960–1990* (Albany: SUNY Press, 1997), and Jung-En Woo, *Race to the Swift: State and Finance in Korean Industrialization* (New York: Columbia University Press, 1990).

7. For instance, the gini coefficient (a statistical measure of income inequality) in 1965 was 0.370, though by 1985 it had increased to 0.410. Soonwon Kwon and Kwang Choi, "Social Welfare and Distribution Policies," in *The Korean Economy, 1945–1995: Performance and Vision for the Twentieth Century,* eds. Dong-Se Cha, Kwang-Suk Kim, and Dwight Perkins (Seoul: Korea Development Institute, 1997), 563. See also Joung-Woo Lee and David Lindauer, "Relative Deprivation and the Distribution of Wages," in *The Strains of Economic Growth: Labor Unrest and Social Dissatisfaction in Korea,* ed. David Lindauer et al. (Cambridge: Harvard University Press, 1997), 58.

8. According to a census study conducted in 1989–90 by the Korea Development Institute, the gini coefficient calculated from household income in 1988 was 0.40. However, if real property assets (real estate) are included in the calculation, the coefficient increases to 0.60. If financial assets (bank deposits, bonds, stocks) are included, the gini coefficient increases to 0.77. According to Soonwon Kwon, the top income quintile (20%) held 78% of all financial assets and 61% of all real property assets in Korea. See Kwon, "Korea: Income and Wealth Distribution and Government Initiatives to Reduce Disparities," Korea Development Institute Working Paper No. 9008, June 1990.

9. Jang-Jip Choi, "Political Cleavages in South Korea," in *State and Society in Contemporary Korea,* ed. Hagen Koo (Ithaca: Cornell University Press, 1993), 29.

10. Yin-Wah Chu, "Labor and Democratization in South Korea and Taiwan," *Journal of Contemporary Asia* 28 (1998); Hagen Koo, "The State, Minjung, and the Working Class in South Korea," in *State and Society in Contemporary Korea,* ed. Koo (Ithaca: Cornell University Press, 1993), 143.

11. Sung-Joo Han and Ok-Nim Chung, "Economic Management and Democratization," in *Driven by Growth: Political Change in the Asia-Pacific Region,* rev. ed., ed. James Morley (Armonk, N.Y.: M. E. Sharpe, 1999), 207.

12. Korea's GNP growth rate increased from 5.6% in 1982 to 9.5% one year later. The inflation rate was drastically reduced from 21.3% in 1981 to just 3.4% by 1983. Cited in Alice Amsden, *Asia's Next Giant: South Korea and Late Industrialization* (Oxford: Oxford University Press, 1989), 56.

13. On the rebirth of social movements during the 1980s, see Martin Hart-Landsberg, *The Rush to Development: Economic Change and Political Struggle in South Korea* (New York: Monthly Review Press, 1993), chap. 11.

14. The NKDP won 50 of the 184 contested district seats with 29% of the popular vote; the ruling DJP won 87 district seats with 35% of the vote. Because of the skewed seat bonus that favored the ruling party, the opposition NKDP won only 17 of 92 proportional representation (PR) seats compared with the 61 (of 92) that the DJP took in those elections. According to the electoral rules prior to the 1987 reforms, two-thirds of the PR seats (or 61 of 92) automatically went to the winningest party, which

historically ensured that the ruling party could gain a legislative majority even without a majority showing in the popular vote. See B. C. Koh, "The 1985 Parliamentary Election in South Korea," *Asian Survey* 25 (1985).

15. Bedeski, *Transformation;* Hart-Landsberg, *Rush.*

16. Tun-Jen Cheng and Eun-Mee Kim, "Making Democracy: Generalizing the South Korea Case," in *The Politics of Democratization: Generalizing East Asian Experiences,* ed. Edward Friedman (Boulder: Westview Press, 1994), 134; Bronwen Dalton and James Cotton, "New Social Movements and the Changing Nature of Political Opposition in South Korea," in *Political Oppositions in Industrializing Asia,* ed. Garry Rodan (London: Routledge Press, 1996), 279.

17. See Jongryn Mo, "Democratization, Labor Policy, and Economic Performance," in *Democracy and the Korean Economy,* ed. Chung-In Moon and Jongryn Mo (Stanford: Hoover Institution Press, 1999).

18. James Cotton, "East Asian Democracy: Progress and Limits," in *Consolidating the Third Wave Democracies: Regional Challenges,* eds. Larry Diamond, Marc Plattner, Yun-Han Chu, and Hung-Mao Tien (Baltimore: Johns Hopkins University Press, 1997), 101.

19. Byung-Kook Kim, "Korea's Crisis of Success," in *Democracy in East Asia,* eds. Larry Diamond and Marc Plattner, (Baltimore: Johns Hopkins University Press, 1998); Soo-Hyun Chon, "Political Economy of Regional Development in Korea," in *State and Development in the Asian-Pacific Rim,* ed. Richard Appelbaum and Jeffrey Henderson (London: Sage, 1992).

20. Sunhyuk Kim, "State and Civil Society in South Korea's Democratic Consolidation: Is the Battle Really Over?" *Asian Survey* 37 (1997).

21. Jongryn Mo, "Political Learning and Democratic Consolidation: Korean Industrial Relations, 1987–1992," *Comparative Political Studies* 29 (1996).

22. Jungung Choi, John Higley, Tong-Yi Huang, and Tse-Min Lin, "Elite Settlement and Democratic Consolidation in Korea and Taiwan," in *Democratization and Globalization in Korea: Assessments and Prospects,* ed. Chung-In Moon and Jongryn Mo (Seoul: Yonsei University Press, 1999), 97.

23. Roh Tae-Woo's DJP gained only 125 seats out of a possible 299. Kim Young-Sam's RDP and Kim Dae-Jung's PPD won 59 and 70 seats, respectively.

24. Between 1980 and 1982, the number of employee insurance societies decreased from 602 to 146. The average membership size of each society increased from just over eight thousand members in 1980 to over sixty thousand in 1982, demonstrating the effects of the consolidation reform.

25. After the ruling party fared poorly in the 1985 National Assembly elections, President Chun announced a welfare reform package in 1986, including the implementation of a pension program and the universalization of health insurance. See Sungkyun Lee, "A Comparative Study of Welfare Programs for Old-Age Income Security in Korea and Taiwan," Ph.D. diss., University of Wisconsin-Madison, 1997, 177–78.

26. Huck-Ju Kwon, *The Welfare State in Korea: The Politics of Legitimation* (New York: St. Martin's Press, 1999), 61–63.

27. Author interview with Cho Hung-Jun, Health Solidarity (July 19, 2000).

28. The seven main medical organizations that were linked to the health insurance reform movement were the Association of Physicians for Humanism, the Association of Dentists for a Healthy Society, the Pharmacists' Council for Attaining a Healthy Society, the Association of Young Christian Physicians, the Church Council of Medical Care for the Poor, the Korean Academy for Health and Society, and the Korean Academy for Labor and Health.

29. In early 1988, the three parties compromised on a new single-member district system with a reformed proportional representation component. The new electoral system comprises 299 winnable seats, one-quarter of which are at-large seats. Unlike in the past when two-thirds of the at-large seats were automatically given to the winning party, the new system allocates one-half (38 of 75) of at-large seats for the winning party, and the rest are distributed proportionally to the other parties. There are two contending explanations for the ruling party's decision to accept the opposition's reform proposal. David Brady and Jongryn Mo argue that Roh's acquiescence was driven by a rational-strategic calculation that the opposition parties would likely split the electoral vote–as they had done in the 1987 presidential elections. Cheng and Tallian contend that Roh's decision was swayed by public opinion and that his decision to concede the electoral reform was to distance himself from the legacies of the Chun regime by portraying himself as a reformer. See Tun-Jen Cheng and Mihae Lim Tallian, "Bargaining over Electoral Reform during the Democratic Transition," in *Rationality and Politics in the Korean Peninsula,* ed. Hee-Min Kim and Woo-Sang Kim (East Lansing: Michigan State University International Studies, 1994); David Brady and Jongryn Mo, "Electoral Systems and Institutional Choice: A Case Study of the 1988 Korean Elections," *Comparative Political Studies* 24 (1992).

30. See Hart-Landsberg, *Rush.*

31. For urban dwellers, most of whom moved into the cities from elsewhere, the regional background of a district candidate (who might also originate from elsewhere) was a significant factor in voting decisions. The regional background of an assembly candidate in rural areas was more likely to be common to the voter, thus making regionalism a less relevant determinant of rural electoral behavior.

32. See Hart-Landsberg, *Rush,* 260–64.

33. Jongryn Mo, "Democratization."

34. Jong-Chan Lee, "The Politics of National Health Insurance, 1961–1989," Ph.D. diss., Johns Hopkins University, 1993, 212.

35. Author interview with Kim Yong-Ik, Health Solidarity (July 26, 2000).

36. Alan Wachman, *Taiwan: National Identity and Democratization* (Armonk, N.Y.: M. E. Sharpe, 1994), 92–122.

37. Shelley Rigger, "Mobilizational Authoritarianism and Political Opposition in Taiwan," in *Political Oppositions in Industrializing Asia,* ed. Garry Rodan (London: Routledge Press, 1996).

38. *Tangwai* literally means "outside the party."

39. Ramon Myers and Linda Chao, *The First Chinese Democracy: Political Life in the Republic of China on Taiwan* (Baltimore: Johns Hopkins University Press, 1998).

40. Bruce Dickson, *Democratization in China and Taiwan: The Adaptability of Leninist Parties* (Oxford: Oxford University Press, 1997).

41. Hung-Mao Tien and Tun-Jen Cheng, "Crafting Democratic Institutions in Taiwan," *China Journal* 37 (1997): 18.

42. By 1975, the ethnic composition of the party had begun to reverse, and by the mid-1980s, two-thirds of the ruling party had been born in Taiwan. In 1984, 12 of the 31 members of the Central Standing Committee and 7 members of the executive cabinet (including the vice-premier and the ministers of justice, the interior, and communication) were ethnic Taiwanese. In 1985, the majority of KMT cadres in the party's local field offices had been born in Taiwan. See Huang Te-Fu, "Elections and the Evolution of the Kuomintang," and Bruce J. Dickson, "The Kuomintang before Democratization: Organizational Change and the Role of Elections," both in *Taiwan's Electoral Politics and Democratic Transition: Riding the Third Wave,* ed. Hung-Mao Tien (Armonk, N.Y.: M. E. Sharpe, 1996); Edwin Winckler, "Institutionalization and Participation on Taiwan: From Hard to Soft Authoritarianism?" *China Quarterly* 99 (1984).

43. Shelley Rigger, *Politics in Taiwan: Voting for Democracy* (London: Routledge, 1999).

44. Chiang Ching-Kuo himself stated, "No political party can maintain its advantage forever if it does not reflect the public opinion and meet the people's demand." Cited in Andrew Nathan with Helena V. S. Ho, "The Decision for Reform in Taiwan," in *China's Transition,* ed. Nathan, Ho, and Tian-jian Shi (New York: Columbia University Press, 1998), 94.

45. Dickson, *Democratization,* 213.

46. In 1986, KMT candidates won 58 of 72 contested Legislative Yuan seats, and in 1989, the ruling party won 72 of 101. In both elections, the DPP did not win more than 20% of the contested seats or more than 30% of the popular vote.

47. Myers and Chao, *First Chinese Democracy,* 159.

48. Tse-Min Lin, John Higley, and Tong-Yi Huang, "Elite Settlements in Taiwan," *Journal of Democracy* 9 (1998): 151–53.

49. Lu Ya-Li, "Political Opposition in Taiwan: The Development of the Democratic Progressive Party," in *Political Change in Taiwan,* ed. Tun-Jen Cheng and Stephen Haggard (Boulder: Lynne Reinner, 1992), 129.

50. See Tien and Cheng, "Crafting," 16.

51. Yun-Han Chu, *Crafting Democracy in Taiwan* (Taipei: Institute for National Policy Research, 1992), 84.

52. Hsin-Huang Michael Hsiao, "Political Liberalization and the Farmers' Movement in Taiwan," in *The Politics of Democratization: Generalizing East Asian Experiences,* ed. Edward Friedman (Boulder: Westview Press, 1994).

53. See Lin Kuo-Min, "From Authoritarianism to Statism: The Politics of National Health Insurance in Taiwan," Ph.D. diss., Yale University, 1997, 113–19.

54. In the Taiwan tax system, wage reporting for the purpose of income tax is separate from wage reporting for the purpose of labor insurance. Thus, it is not uncommon for employers to report two different wages when calculating an employee's income tax contributions and his or her labor insurance contribution.

55. Author interviews with Yaung Chi-Liang, deputy minister, Department of Health and Council for Economic Planning and Development Task Force, Executive Yuan (November 24, 1999); Chiang Tung-Liang, Council for Economic Planning and Development Task Force, Executive Yuan (November 15, 1999); and Wu Kai-Hsun, chair, Medical Care Cost and Arbitration Committee, Department of Health, and Council for Economic Planning and Development Task Force, Executive Yuan (November 3, 1999).

56. Council for Economic Planning and Development, *Task Force Report: National Health Insurance Research and Planning* (Taipei: CEPD, June 1990), 12 [in Chinese]; see also Lin Kuo-Min, "Authoritarianism," 312.

57. Under the government employees' insurance system, nine separate health insurance schemes were available to dependents, retirees, and retired dependents of both government employees and private schoolteachers. Under the farmers' insurance (FI) system, there were nominally two separate health insurance programs, one for farmers and another for rural village and municipal councilors. The labor insurance program provided only one health insurance scheme for both employed and self-employed workers.

58. CEPD, *Task Force Report,* 50, 104–5.

59. Ibid., 78–82.

60. A fiscal-based financing mechanism was not adopted because both high-income and low-income earners consistently evaded paying income taxes. Thus, financing health insurance through the general tax pool would perpetuate inequities between different wage groups. Also, Taiwan's total tax revenue is comparatively lower

than that of most other industrialized countries. Among the Organization for Economic Co-operation and Development (OECD) countries in 1990, Taiwan's tax revenue as a proportion of GDP was second lowest at 20.1%, second only to Korea's 18.1% (Denmark had the highest ratio of tax to GDP at 45.7%). What is even more problematic is that Taiwan's tax-to-GDP ratio has declined since 1990, reaching a low of 15.8% in 1997, the lowest among all OECD countries (Korea's ratio had increased to 19.5%). Figures are from Chu Tzer-Ming, "Analysis of Financing Social Insurance in Taiwan," paper presented at the International Symposium on Reform and Perspectives of Social Insurance, Taipei, September 29, 2000.

61. For example, if the average number of household dependents was two persons, then enrollees and employers would have to pay a contribution amount equivalent to three persons' premium: 1 (enrollee) plus 2 (average number of dependents).

62. CEPD, *Task Force Report*, 39–40.

63. Author interview with Wu Kai-Hsun.

64. Lin Kuo-Min, "Authoritarianism," 346–47.

65. Ibid., 362–65.

66. Chan Jin-Yueh, "The Legitimation Process of National Health Insurance Policy in Taiwan," M.A. thesis, Institute of Health and Welfare Policy, National Yang-Ming University, 1995, 34 [in Chinese]. For more detail on each legislator's reform bill, see *Legislative Yuan Bulletin: No. 169, The National Health Insurance Law* (Taipei: Legislative Yuan, 1994), 27–118 (in Chinese).

67. Author interview with Ku Yu-Ling, Committee for Action on Labor Legislation (October 27, 1999).

68. In the government's proposal, Article 20 stated that the premium rate range was to be 4.5–6% of the wage earner's payroll. Some legislators, however, felt that the bottom range should be lowered, to 4% or even 2.8%.

69. Chan Jin-Yueh, "Legitimation," 77–81.

70. Ibid., 84.

71. The Legislative Yuan worked for thirty hours straight between July 18 and 19, finally passing the bill in the early afternoon of the 19th. See *Legislative Yuan Bulletin*, 890–909.

72. Dickson, *Democratization*, 167–68.

73. Lin Kuo-Min, "Authoritarianism," 386.

74. See Tun-Jen Cheng and Yung-Ming Hsu, "Issue Structure, the DPP's Factionalism, and Party Realignment," in *Taiwan's Electoral Politics and Democratic Transition: Riding the Third Wave*, ed. Hung-Mao Tien (Armonk, N.Y.: M. E. Sharpe, 1996). See also Linda Gail Arrigo, "From Democratic Movement to Bourgeois Democracy: The Internal Politics of the Taiwan Democratic Progressive Party in 1991," in *The Other Taiwan: 1945 to the Present*, ed. Murray A. Rubinstein (Armonk, N.Y.: M. E. Sharpe, 1994).

75. Author interview with Hsieh Wen-Sheng, director, Democratic Progressive Party (DPP), Social Development Committee (October 13, 1999).

76. Author interview with Shi Xian-Yan, president, Primary Care Physicians Association of Taiwan (November 29, 1999).

77. Author interviews with Lin Liang-Rong, education outreach officer, Taiwan Labor Front (October 18, 1999); Kuo Kuo-Wen, secretary-general, Taiwan Labor Front (October 19, 1999), and Wu Young-Yie, Committee for Action on Labor Legislation (December 1, 1999).

78. Author interview with Son Yu-Liam, researcher, Taiwan Labor Front (October 12, 1999).

79. Author interview with Ku Yu-Ling, Committee for Action on Labor Legislation (October 27, 1999).

5. COALITION BUILDING IN KOREA

1. *1998 Medical Insurance Statistical Yearbook* (Seoul: National Federation of Medical Insurance, 1999).

2. All inpatient treatments, which tended to be expensive in the first place, carried a 20% copay levy. Outpatient levies ranged from 26 to 55% of the total medical cost per visit, depending on the type of medical facility. Cited in *Medical Insurance in Korea, 1997* (Seoul: National Federation of Medical Insurance, 1997), 11–12.

3. Ik-Hee Han, "Equity and the Korean Health Care Policy," *Korean Health Economic Review* 6 (2000): table 7.

4. Ok-Ryun Moon and Soonman Kwon, "Health Care Policy and Reform in Korea," unpublished monograph, School of Public Health, Seoul National University, March 1999, 31.

5. Ik-Hee Han, "Equity," table 9.

6. *1998 Medical Insurance Statistical Yearbook.*

7. Soonwon Kwon and Wataru Suzuki, "Approach toward a Unified Health Insurance System: What Can Japan Learn from the Korean Experience?" Discussion Paper no. 502 (Institute of Social and Economic Research, Osaka University, 2000), 5 n. 5.

8. See Ik-Hee Han, "Equity," table 5.

9. One reason for low utilization rates among self-employed workers is the relatively small number of medical facilities in rural areas (8% of all hospital beds and 4.2% of all physicians in 1996), where a large portion of self-employed workers live (24.4% of the Korean population in 1996). See Tchoe Byong-Ho, "Overview of National Health Insurance in Korea," paper presented at the International Workshop on Health Policy and Program Management, Seoul, November 2–15, 1999, 4.

10. *1998 Medical Insurance Statistical Yearbook*, 380–85.

11. In 1980, 229 of the 602 EIS had fewer than 1,000 enrollees; 75 % had fewer than 3,000 members; and only 35 of the 602 EIS (or 6% of the total) had more than 10,000 insured members. Cited in Jong-Chan Lee, "The Politics of National Health Insurance in South Korea, 1961–1989," Ph.D. diss., Johns Hopkins University, 1993, 164.

12. The proposal required that all insurance societies with fewer than 3,000 members merge with other small funds. As a result, the number of EIS decreased from 602 in 1980 to 146 two years later. The average size of each EIS increased from just over 8,000 members in 1979 to over 61,000 members in 1982.

13. The NAMIS launched its campaign against the integration idea as early as October of that year with the publication of "Background and Theory of Administrative Separatism in National Health Insurance" in the association's monthly journal, *Medical Insurance.* The following month, a second article, "Arguments against the Unification of the Administrative System of Health Insurance," appeared in the same journal. The NAMIS contended that the separated system of health insurance organization promoted greater efficiency by preventing the sluggish bureaucratization of publicly managed welfare. The NAMIS also pointed to the "welfare disease" of the European welfare states as evidence of global trends toward welfare state retrenchment and the diminishing capacity of statist policy instruments in the provision of effective and efficient social policy. See Lee, "Politics," 166–68 and nn. 17, 18.

14. Author interview with Young-Lee Goh, director, Environment and Welfare Department, Federation of Korean Industries (July 3, 2000).

15. See Eun-Mee Kim, *Big Business, Strong State: Collusion and Conflict in South Korean Development* (Albany: SUNY Press, 1997), chap. 6.

16. In 1988, a group of academics formed the Society for Social Security Studies and prepared a policy pamphlet endorsing the integrated health insurance reform.

The pamphlet was subsequently published in the *Korean Journal of Social Policy* 11 (1989).

17. DJP legislators who supported the integration reform came primarily from rural areas.

18. Kim Jong-Pil's party originally opposed the integration reform legislation. However, after twenty days of demonstrations staged by the NCMII coalition and its social movement allies outside the party's headquarters, Kim acceded to the reformers' demands.

19. Author interview with Cho Yong-Jik, chairman, National Health Insurance Corporation (June 7, 2000).

20. Author interview with Kim Gamlip, deputy director, Pensions Policy Division, Ministry of Health and Welfare (June 7, 2000).

21. Author interview with Kim Jong-Dae, former director-general, Policy and Planning Division, Ministry of Health and Welfare (June 7, 2000).

22. The Federation of Korean Medical Insurance Societies, which succeeded the National Association of Medical Insurance Societies, was reorganized into the National Federation of Medical Insurance (NFMI) on January 1, 1988.

23. See Hee Min Kim, "Rational Choice Theory and Third World Politics: The 1990 Party Merger in Korea," *Comparative Politics* 29 (1997).

24. Sung-Joo Han, "The Korean Experiment," *Journal of Democracy* 2 (1991): 98.

25. Cited in Man-Woo Lee, *The Odyssey of Korean Democracy, 1987–1990* (New York: Praeger, 1990), 132. See also Heng Lee, "Uncertain Promise: Democratic Consolidation in South Korea," in *The Politics of Democratization: Generalizing East Asian Experiences,* ed. Edward Friedman (Boulder: Westview Press, 1994), 154–55.

26. Jongryn Mo, "Democratization, Labor Policy, and Economic Performance," in *Democracy and the Korean Economy,* eds. Chung-In Moon and Jongryn Mo (Stanford: Hoover Institution Press, 1999).

27. Jongryn Mo, "Political Learning and Democratic Consolidation: Korean Industrial Relations, 1987–1992," *Comparative Political Studies* 29 (1996).

28. Tun-Jen Cheng and Eun-Mee Kim, "Making Democracy: Generalizing the South Korea Case," in *The Politics of Democratization: Generalizing East Asian Experiences,* ed. Edward Friedman (Boulder: Westview Press, 1994), 140.

29. Sung-Deuk Hahm and Kwang-Woon Kim, "Institutional Reforms and Democratization in Korea: The Case of the Kim Young-Sam Administration, 1993–1998," *Governance* 12 (1999): 481–82.

30. Soonwon Kwon, "Economic Justice and Social Welfare: New Principles of Economic Policy," in *Democratization and Globalization in Korea: Assessments and Prospects,* ed. Chung-In Moon and Jongryn Mo (Seoul: Yonsei University Press, 1999).

31. Jongryn Mo, "Democratization."

32. The bill was passed during a midnight session of the National Assembly when no opposition members were present. The bill took six minutes to pass in its entirety. Kim Jong-Pil, who left the DLP earlier in 1996, stated that the "early morning blitz is the kind that Japan's Tojo, Germany's Hitler and North Korea's Kim Il-Sung once used." Cited in *Far Eastern Economic Review,* January 23, 1997, p. 14.

33. In 1994, the Ministry of Health and Social Affairs was renamed the Ministry of Health and Welfare.

34. The Korean Association for Public Administration offered a blueprint for administrative reform in the late 1980s, stressing that "administrative decentralization is a necessity of political democracy." Bun-Woong Kim, "The Democratization of Public Administration in Korea," *Korean Social Science Journal* 16 (1990): 102. See also Kwang-Woong Kim, "Government Restructuring Has Only Begun," *Korea Focus* 3 (1995).

35. Yong-Duck Jung, "Reforming the Administrative Apparatus in Korea: The Case of the 'Civilian' Government," *Korean Review of Public Administration* 1 (1996): 272–77.

36. Hahm and Kim, "Institutional Reforms," 489.

37. Jaehyun Joo, "Dynamics of Social Policy Change: A Korean Case Study from a Comparative Perspective," *Governance* 12 (1999): 74.

38. After the mergers, the number of regional SEIS decreased from 266 to 227.

39. In an effort to curtail rising health care expenditures, the government implemented a medical care referral system that divided the country into primary and tertiary "medical care service regions." Patients could visit large hospitals in their tertiary care region only after getting a referral from a small hospital or clinic. Differential copay rates—depending on the size of the clinic—helped enforce the referral system. This administratively cumbersome system was dropped in October 1998, after which time patients could visit any provider without a referral, with the exception of forty-one designated "large or university" hospitals. See *Medical Insurance in Korea, 1997,* 14–16; Byongho Tchoe, "Overview," 5–7.

40. Soonwon Kwon and Wataru Suzuki, "Approach," 5 n. 5.

41. The sixteen consolidated units comprised six major cities and ten provincial bodies. Author interview with Moon Ok-Ryun, Seoul National University (July 7, 2000). Professor Moon was one of the subcommittee chairmen on the 1996–97 Health Care Reform Committee. See also Moon Ok-Ryun and Soonman Kwon, "Recent Changes in Health Insurance: Health Sector Reform in Korea," paper presented at the Bangkok Symposium on Health Sector Reform in East Asia, Bangkok, November 16, 1998, 9.

42. Author interview with Choi Min-Sik, Committee for Policy, Social Welfare Division, Millennium Democratic Party (MDP, formerly NCNP) (July 20, 2000).

43. The commission, which Bruce Cumings describes as a "peak bargaining arrangement," was mandated to negotiate the necessary reform measures to steer the Korean economy out of the crisis. See Cumings, "Korea's Other Miracle," *The Nation* 266 (1998): 20.

44. Author interview with Kim Jeung-Soo, Grand National Party legislator (July 27, 2000).

45. Officially, the Health Solidarity Coalition was not established until the summer of 1999. However, since the membership ranks of the National Solidarity Alliance and Health Solidarity were the same, and the official founding of Health Solidarity was essentially only a change in name, I refer to the 1994 alliance as Health Solidarity.

46. Author interview with Cho Hong-Jun, Health Solidarity (July 19, 2000).

47. The KCTU was established in 1995, though it was not legally recognized until the Kim Dae-Jung era in 1999. At the time of its formation, the KCTU consisted of 861 unions and 400,000 workers. As of 1999, membership had increased to 1,300 trade unions and 530,000 members.

48. Author interview with Kim Yong-Ik, Health Solidarity (July 26, 2000).

49. Author interview with Yoon Woo-Hyun, director-general, Policy Division, Korean Confederation of Trade Unions (June 8, 2000).

50. Sunhyuk Kim, "State and Civil Society in South Korea's Democratic Consolidation: Is the Battle Really Over?" *Asian Survey* 37 (1997): 1142.

51. Kyoung-Ryung Seong, "Civil Society and Democratic Consolidation in South Korea: Great Achievement and Remaining Problems," in *Consolidating Democracy in South Korea,* ed. Larry Diamond and Byung-Kook Kim (Boulder: Lynne Reinner, 2000), 92.

52. Author interview with Cho Hung-Jun, Health Solidarity (July 19, 2000).

53. Author interviews with Lee Yoon-Jung, director, Social Welfare Policy Division, Citizens' Coalition for Economic Justice (May 31, 2000), and Yoon Woo-Hyun,

director-general, Policy Division, Korean Confederation of Trade Unions (June 8, 2000).

54. Chung-In Moon and Song-Min Kim, "Democracy and Economic Performance," in *Consolidating Democracy in South Korea,* ed. Larry Diamond and Byung-Kook Kim (Boulder: Lynne Reinner, 2000), 164.

55. Choi Min-Sik recounts how other influential anti-integration officials Moon Kyung-Tae and Yun Sung-Tae were shuffled out of the MOHW after the election of Kim Dae-Jung in early 1998. Author interview with Choi Min-Sik, Policy Committee, MDP (July 20, 2000).

56. According to my survey data, all but two of the health insurance division bureaucrats agreed that the reformed health insurance system was more equitable than the preexisting program.

57. Author interview with Chun Chang-Bae, Integration Task Force, National Health Insurance Corporation (June 6, 2000).

58. Author interview with Lee Hye-Hoon, health policy fellow, Korea Development Institute (May 29, 2000).

59. Author interview with Choi Min-Sik.

60. See Kim Byung-Kook, "Electoral Politics and Economic Crisis," in *Consolidating Democracy in South Korea,* eds. Larry Diamond and Kim Byung-Kook (Boulder: Lynne Reinner, 2000).

61. Park Chan-Wook, "The Organization and Workings of Committees in the Korean National Assembly," *Journal of Legislative Studies* 4 (1998): 221–22.

62. Ibid.

63. Multiple-term members among the key players in the health care debate, such as Hwang Seong-Gun, Hwang Kyu-Sun, Kim Hong-Shin, and Lee Seung-Jae, ensured a high degree of continuity within the committee during the late 1990s.

64. Park, "Organization," 221–22.

65. According to my survey data, there was a significant consensus among ruling party legislators in favor of the integration reform. Around 75% (n = 27) agreed that a reformed and integrated medical insurance scheme would be more equitable than the previous system.

66. Among GNP legislators surveyed (n = 47), 47% agreed that integration would promote greater equity and 43% disagreed.

67. David Steinberg, "Korea: Triumph and Turmoil," *Journal of Democracy* 9 (1998): 80. See also Chan-Wook Park, "The National Assembly of the Republic of Korea," *Journal of Legislative Studies* 4 (1998).

68. The interviewee asked to remain anonymous.

69. The 1988 reform changed the dual-member district system into a single-member electoral district scheme (see Chapter 4).

70. In the pre-1988 electoral system, there were 92 at-large seats won through proportional representation (PR). After the reform, however, the number of PR seats decreased to 74.

71. This new generation of legislators has been called the "386" generation because they are all in their thirties, went to university during the 1980s, and were born in the 1960s.

72. See Chan-Wook Park, "Elections in Democratizing Korea," in *How Asia Votes,* ed. John Fuh-Sheng Hsieh and David Newman (New York: Chatham House, 2002).

73. Ok-Ryun Moon and Soonman Kwon, "Recent Changes," 10.

74. According to SNU professor of health economics Yang Bong-Min, only about 5% of the self-employed sector can be classified as high-income earners. He cites others who suggest that only about 2% can be considered high-income earners. For proponents of the integration reform, the assumption is that most self-employed workers,

including farmers, tend to be poorer than other workers. Author interview with Yang Bong-Min, Citizens' Coalition for Economic Justice (and Seoul National University) (July 12, 2000).

75. Author interview with Chung-Kil Oh, director, Policy Division, Federation of Korean Trade Unions (May 30, 2000).

76. Author interviews with Yong-Lee Goh, director of Environment and Welfare Department, Federation of Korean Industries (July 3, 2000), and Kim Pan-Joong, Social Welfare Division, Korean Employers Federation (June 7, 2000).

77. The Supreme Court decided in favor of the integration reform in late June 2000. It found that the integration of the reserve funds of different insurance societies was not in violation of private property laws. Author interviews with Cho Yong-Jik, chairman, National Health Insurance Corporation (June 7, 2000), and Lee Sang-Yong, director, Health Insurance Division, Ministry of Health and Welfare (June 8, 2000).

78. See Eun-Young Choi, Jin-Soo Kim, and Woo-Baek Lee, "Health Care System in Korea," KIHASA Consultant Papers no. 98–05 (Korean Institute for Health and Social Affairs, December 1998), 72; Byoung-Yik Kim, "Korean Experiment for the Unification of Multiple Medical Insurers: A Road to Success or Failure," paper presented at the International Symposium on National Health Insurance, Seoul, June 9, 2000, 12–13.

79. Author interview with Lee Hye-Hoon.

80. Park Yoon-Bae, "Integration of Health Insurance Postponed," *Korea Times* (July 13, 1999).

81. In private, GNP legislators told me that they opposed the delay in administrative integration because the postponement would put the integration start date after the April 2000 National Assembly elections. The GNP hoped that popular discontent with the integration reform, particularly on the heels of the scaled-back pension reform in 1998, would cut electoral support for the ruling party. Author interviews with Oh Yang-Soon, GNP legislator (July 20, 2000), and her chief of staff, Lee Min-Kyung (July 27, 2000).

82. Among bureaucrats and legislators surveyed in 2000 (n = 132), 57% of respondents perceived the president's influence in policymaking to be increasing and only 30% felt the reverse was true. Respondents rank-ordered the president as the single most influential actor in the policy process.

83. Paul Pierson, "The New Politics of the Welfare State," *World Politics* 48 (1996): 154.

6. RESISTING RETRENCHMENT IN TAIWAN

1. Tung-Liang Chiang and Shou-Hsia Cheng, "The Effect of Universal Health Insurance on Health Care Utilization in Taiwan," *Journal of the American Medical Association* 278 (1997): 92.

2. Tung-Liang Chiang, "Taiwan's Universal Health Insurance: What Has Been Achieved? What Hasn't? and Where to Go?" Paper presented at the International Symposium on National Health Insurance, Seoul, June 9, 2000, 143.

3. Between 1995 and 1997, 34% of primary care physicians claimed to see more than fifty patients per day, spending on average five to seven minutes with each patient. Department of Health, Executive Yuan, *National Health Insurance Two Year Report* (Taipei: Department of Health, Executive Yuan, February 1997), 130 [in Chinese].

4. For outpatient services, flat-rate copay levies ranged from NT$50 (US$2) for visits to a primary care clinic to NT$150 (US$6) for visits to large medical centers. User

fee levies for dental and Chinese medicinal treatments were NT$50, irrespective of the level of medical care provider. Emergency care levies ranged from NY$150 at the clinic level to NT$420 (US$17) at large medical centers.

5. Recall that in Korea, approximately 60% of all health care financing came from consumers' out-of-pocket payments. In Taiwan, on the other hand, only about 30% of the total health care bill is paid out-of-pocket. Tung-Liang Chiang and Chih-Liang Yaung, "Recent Health Care Reforms in Taiwan: The Global Budget Policy," paper presented at the HHIP Conference, Bangkok, December 5, 2001.

6. Bureau of National Health Insurance, *National Health Insurance Annual Statistical Report* (Taipei: Bureau of National Health Insurance, June 2000).

7. Department of Health, Executive Yuan, *The National Health Insurance Two-Year Progress Report* (Taipei: Department of Health, Executive Yuan, 1997) [in Chinese].

8. By law, the DOH could unilaterally increase premium rates from the existing 4.25% to 6%.

9. The proposals ranged from those seeking to maintain but adjust the current single-carrier system to those mandating serious structural reform, such as the privatization of the single insurance carrier, the introduction of insurance market competition, and/or the implementation of an American-style HMO system. On the various privatization proposals, see Hwang Min-Ling, "A Study of Basic Health Care Services and Supplemental Health Insurance under the Proposed NHI Multiple-Carrier System," M.A. thesis, National Taiwan University, 1998, 12–17 [in Chinese].

10. Department of Health, Executive Yuan, *A Review of Taiwan's National Health Insurance Reform Design* (Taipei: Department of Health, internal document, April 15, 1997) [in Chinese].

11. On the *gong ban min yi* proposal, see ibid., 21–22.

12. At the 1996 National Development Conference, the three political parties agreed on a new reform that prohibited Lien Chan from holding the positions of vice-president and premier simultaneously. Thus, he was forced to relinquish control over the Executive Yuan.

13. On the different types of prospective payment systems, see Lu Ann Aday et al., *Evaluating the Health Care System: Effectiveness, Efficiency, and Equity*, 2d ed. (Chicago: Health Administration Press, 1998), 56–59, 136–37.

14. On the DOH's second reform proposal, see the Executive Yuan's bill in *Bulletin of the Legislative Yuan* (Taipei: March 18, 1998), 6–60 (in Chinese); see also "NHI 'Structure' Small Group Report," in *National Health Research Institute Forum* (Taipei: National Health Research Institute, 1998), 21–24 [in Chinese].

15. Author interview with Yaung Chi-Liang, deputy minister, Department of Health, Executive Yuan (November 24, 1999).

16. See "NHI 'Structure' Small Group Report." See also Department of Health, Executive Yuan, *Review of Taiwan's National Health Insurance Reform Design.*

17. Yaung Chi-Liang, "National Health Insurance Structural Reform Note," in *National Health Research Institute Forum* (Taipei: National Health Research Institute, 1998), 168–70 [in Chinese].

18. According to Paul Pierson, opportunities for welfare state retrenchment rarely occur, particularly for those policies that are popular with the general public. However, he writes, "moments of budgetary crisis may open opportunities for reform. Advocates of retrenchment will try to exploit such moments to present reforms as an effort to save the welfare state." Pierson, "The New Politics of the Welfare State," *World Politics* 48 (1996): 177.

19. During the fall of 1999, I interviewed all four members of the original planning task force sponsored by the Council for Economic Planning and Development

(1988–90). With the exception of Wu Kai-Hsun, all the original members expressed some support for a privatized or semiprivatized reform package.

20. Author interview with Tsai Shu-Ling, director, Department of Planning and Evaluation, Bureau of National Health Insurance (October 5, 1999).

21. Author interview with Wu Kai-Hsun, chairman, Medical Care Cost Arbitration Committee, Department of Health (November 3, 1999).

22. Author interview with Julie Ma, research associate, DOH Small Group, Department of Health (November 11, 1999).

23. Laurie Underwood, "Stronger Prescription Needed," *Topics* (2000): 38.

24. Author interview with Lin Jaung-Geng, president, Chinese Medical Professionals Union (November 4, 1999).

25. Author interview with Lee Yu-Chune, DOH Small Group, Department of Health, Executive Yuan (October 2, 2000).

26. Author interviews with Huang Shun-Te, president, National Dentists Association (December 13, 1999); and Lin Jaung-Geng, president, Chinese Medical Professionals Union (November 4, 1999).

27. Chiang and Yaung, "Recent Health Care Reforms."

28. See *Bulletin of the Legislative Yuan* (Taipei, October 16, 1997) [in Chinese]. See also *Bulletin of the Legislative Yuan, Health and Welfare Committee Report*, (Taipei, September 1999) [in Chinese].

29. *Bulletin of the Legislative Yuan* (October 16, 1997), 553–648.

30. Key participants included Shen Fu-Hsiung, Lee Ying-Yuan, Chien Shi-Chieh, Liu Chin-Shin, and Hong Chi-Chang. Author interview with Liu Chin-Shin, former DPP legislator (October 18, 1999).

31. Author interviews with DPP legislators Lee Ying-Yuan (November 16, 1999), Hong Chi-Chang (December 15, 1999), Shen Fu-Hsiung (November 16, 1999), Chien Shi-Chieh (October 26, 1999), and Liu Chin-Shin (October 18, 1999).

32. Author interview with Huang Chao-Shun, KMT legislator (November 11, 1999).

33. Author interview with Lin Yaw-Hsing, KMT legislator (December 1, 1999).

34. Author interview with Shyu Jong-Shyong, KMT legislator (December 2, 1999).

35. Author interview with Lin Yu-Hsiang, deputy director, KMT Central Department for Policy Research (and former KMT legislator) (June 10, 1999).

36. Author interview with Huang Chao-Shun, KMT legislator (November 11, 1999). See also Gerald McBeath, *Wealth and Freedom: Taiwan's New Political Economy* (Brookfield, Vt.: Ashgate, 1998), 105; Ching-Ping Tang and Shui-Yan Tang, "Democratizing Bureaucracy: The Political Economy of Environmental Impact Assessment and Air Pollution Prevention Fees in Taiwan," *Comparative Politics* 32 (2000): 89.

37. With the exception of Chien Shi-Chieh's reform bill, which was endorsed only by DPP members, the signatories for the other thirteen members' bills were a mix of ruling and opposition party legislators.

38. Hong Chi-Chang, a member of the DPP and the New Tide faction, explains: "The parties in Taiwan are not as rigid as they are in, say, Europe. In Europe, the lines are clearly drawn between the left and the right. However, in Taiwan, the founding ideologies of the three parties, the DPP, the KMT, and recently the New Party, were based on ethnic politics. Because of this, legislators from all three parties care about social welfare issues." Author interview (December 15, 1999).

39. Though the DPP considers the working class one of its principal allies, the membership composition of the party suggests that lower-income strata are only one portion of the DPP's constituencies. Shelley Rigger, "Mobilizational Authoritarianism and Political Opposition in Taiwan," in *Political Opposition in Industrializing Asia*, ed. Garry Rodan (London: Routledge, 1996), 316; Tun-Jen Cheng, "Is the Dog Barking?

The Middle Class and Democratic Movements in the East Asian NICs," *International Study Notes* 15 (1990).

40. Thomas Gold, "The Waning of the Kuomintang State on Taiwan," paper presented at the State and Society in East Asia Network Conference, Copenhagen, September 27–29, 1996.

41. Tse-Min Lin, John Higley, and Tong-Yi Huang, "Elite Settlements in Taiwan," *Journal of Democracy* 9 (1998): 156–57.

42. Linda Chao and Raman Myers, *The First Chinese Democracy: Political Life in the Republic of China on Taiwan* (Baltimore: Johns Hopkins University Press, 1998), 164–66.

43. Ibid., 200–201. See also Yu-Shan Wu, "Taiwan's Constitutional Framework and Cross-Straits Relations," paper presented at the American Political Science Association Meeting, Boston, September 2–5, 1999, 14.

44. Shelley Rigger, *From Opposition to Power: Taiwan's Democratic Progressive Party* (Boulder: Lynne Reinner, 2001).

45. Author interview with Hsueh Rui-Yuan, chief of staff to DPP legislator Hong Chi-Chang (November 3, 1999).

46. The average number of seats per district during the 1998 Legislative Yuan elections was 5.68.

47. Hu Fu and Chu Yun-Han, "Electoral Competition and Political Democratization in Taiwan," paper presented at the Conference on Democratization in the ROC, Taipei, January 1989.

48. See Rigger, *From Opposition to Power,* 84–97. See also John Fuh-Sheng Hsieh, "Continuity and Change in Taiwan's Electoral Politics," in *How Asia Votes,* ed. Hsieh and David Newman (New York: Chatham House, 2001), 57–58.

49. For more details, see Rigger, *From Opposition to Power,* chap. 2; see also John Fuh-Sheng Hsieh, "The SNTV System and Its Political Implication," in *Taiwan's Electoral Politics and Democratic Transition: Riding the Third Wave,* ed. Tien Hung-Mao (Armonk, N.Y.: M. E. Sharpe, 1996).

50. Lin Jih-Wen, "Vote Buying versus Noise-Making: Two Models of Electoral Competition under the Single Non-Transferable Vote Multi-Member District System," *Chinese Political Science Review* 30 (1998).

51. For example, during legislative elections in 1992, the lowest winning threshold in Taipei city (18 seats) was just over 21,000 votes, or 3.5% of the total vote. In Kaohsiung city (12 seats), the highest winning vote amounted to about 10% of the total votes cast. Andrew Nathan, *China's Transition* (New York: Columbia University Press, 1998), 114. After the Legislative Yuan was expanded to the current 225 seats in 1998, the average winning threshold decreased to 30,000 votes.

52. Emerson Niou and Peter Ordeshook, "A Game Theoretic Analysis of the Republic of China's Emerging Electoral System," *International Political Science Review* 13 (1992): 77.

53. In the 1992 Legislative Yuan elections, 330 candidates were fielded for 120 contested seats, or 278%. Calculated from figures cited in Nathan, *China's Transition,* 114.

54. For example, Huang Mei-Ling, director of the central DPP policy committee, explained that most legislators work completely independently of the central party. In early 1999, DPP headquarters drafted a resolution to encourage intraparty dialogue on policy matters in an effort to forge a united DPP in the legislature. Author interview (October 11, 1999). During a follow-up interview conducted a year later, Huang lamented that there had been little improvement in intraparty cooperation, particularly with respect to social policy reform. Author interview (October 2, 2000).

55. 1998 NHI Coalition, *Big Business Health Insurance, Citizens without Insurance* (Taipei: March 1998) [in Chinese].

56. Sidney Tarrow, *Power in Movement: Social Movements, Collective Action, and Politics* (Cambridge: Cambridge University Press, 1994).

57. Yun-Han Chu, *Crafting Democracy in Taiwan* (Taipei: Institute for National Policy Research, 1992), 124.

58. For example, primary care physicians strongly support a referral system based on differential copay percentage rates. Labor and women's groups, on the other hand, are adamantly opposed to any copay increases in addition to a referral system in which only the wealthy are able to "jump levels" and directly pay for and receive higher-quality care from the more expensive medical centers.

59. Paul Pierson, *Dismantling the Welfare State? Reagan, Thatcher, and the Politics of Retrenchment* (Cambridge: Cambridge University Press, 1994).

60. Dr. Shi Hsian-Yan explained that before the implementation of the NHI program, the association of primary care physicians was limited to the city of Taipei. After 1995, however, it was imperative that primary care physicians form an island-wide association. Author interview with Shi Hsian-Yan, president, National Primary Care Physicians Association (November 29, 1999).

61. Author interview with Shen Fu-Hsiung. See R. Kent Weaver, "The Politics of Blame Avoidance," *Journal of Public Policy* 6 (1986).

62. Author interview with Tsai Shu-Ling.

63. Author interview with Chang Hong-Jen, deputy minister, Department of Health, Executive Yuan (October 20, 1999).

64. Independent labor organizations such as CALL and the TLF are presently more inclined to cooperate with the KMT-sanctioned China Federation of Labor. Wu Young-Yie, a senior officer at CALL, stated that even though independent labor groups have always been at odds with the CFL, it has effectively represented labor interests in the health care policy arena. Author interview with Wu Young-Yie, Committee for Action on Labor Legislation (December 1, 1999).

65. Pierson, "New Politics," 146. See also Giandomenico Majone, *Evidence, Argument, and Persuasion in the Policy Process* (New Haven: Yale University Press, 1989), 151–52.

66. This senior official asked to remain anonymous.

7. DEMOCRACY AND THE IDEA OF SOCIAL WELFARE

1. Chung-In Moon, "Democratization and Globalization as Ideological and Political Foundations of Economic Policy," in *Democracy and the Korean Economy*, ed. Chung-In Moon and Jongryn Mo (Stanford: Hoover Institution Press, 1999), 9.

2. Kyong-Dong Kim, "Social Attitudes and Political Orientations of the Korean Middle Class," in *East Asian Middle Classes in Comparative Perspective*, ed. Hsin-Huang Hsiao (Taipei: Institute of Ethnology, Academia Sinica, 1999), 252.

3. Doh-Chull Shin and Richard Rose, *Responding to Economic Crisis: The 1998 New Korea Barometer Survey*, Studies in Public Policy no. 311 (Glasgow: Centre for the Study of Public Policy, University of Strathclyde, 1998), 35.

4. Doh-Chull Shin, *Mass Politics and Culture in Democratizing Korea* (Cambridge: Cambridge University Press, 1999), 21, 35.

5. Shin and Rose, *Responding to Economic Crisis*, 36.

6. David Lindauer et al., *The Strains of Economic Growth: Labor Unrest and Social Dissatisfaction in Korea* (Cambridge: Harvard University Press, 1997); Soonwon Kwon,

"Korea: Income and Wealth Distribution and Government Initiatives to Reduce Disparities," Korea Development Institute Working Paper no. 9008, June 1990; Hagen Koo, "The Political Economy of Income Distribution in South Korea: The Impact of the State's Industrialization Policies," *World Development* 12 (1984).

7. Cited in Ku Yeun-Wen, *Welfare Capitalism in Taiwan: State, Economy, and Social Policy* (New York: St. Martin's Press, 1997), 190.

8. *The 1994 Social Image Survey* (Taipei: Sun Yat-Sen Institute, Academia Sinica, 1994), 108 [in Chinese].

9. Fang Wang, "Support for a New Welfare State in Taiwan: Social Change, Political Dynamics, and Public Opinion," Ph.D. diss., University of Chicago, 1997, 322.

10. *1994 Social Image Survey*, 108.

11. Ibid.

12. Ku Yeun-Wen, *Welfare Capitalism*, 191.

13. Herbert Kitschelt, "Partisan Competition and Welfare State Retrenchment: When Do Politicians Choose Unpopular Policies?" in *The New Politics of the Welfare State*, ed. Paul Pierson (Oxford: Oxford University Press, 2001), 278–79.

14. One exception is Herbert Kitschelt, Zdenka Mansfeldova, Radoslaw Markowski, and Gabor Toka, *Post-Communist Party System: Competition, Representation, and Inter-party Cooperation* (Cambridge: Cambridge University Press, 1999).

15. John Fuh-Sheng Hsieh, "Continuity and Change in Taiwan's Electoral Politics," in *How Asia Votes*, ed. Hsieh and David Newman (New York: Chatham House, 2001).

16. Emerson Niou and Peter Ordeshook, "A Game Theoretic Analysis of the Republic of China's Emerging Electoral System," *International Political Science Review* 13 (1992): 68.

17. Tse-Min Lin, Yun-Han Chu, and Melvin Hinich, "Conflict Displacement and Regime Transition in Taiwan: A Spatial Analysis," *World Politics* 48 (1996): 465.

18. Dafydd Fell, "Party Platform Change in Taiwan's 1990s Elections," unpublished manuscript, London School of Oriental and African Studies, 2000.

19. Edwin Amenta and Theda Skocpol, "States and Social Policies," *Annual Review of Sociology* 12 (1985).

20. Paul Pierson, *Dismantling the Welfare State? Reagan, Thatcher, and the Politics of Retrenchment* (Cambridge: Cambridge University Press, 1993), 42.

21. Huck-Ju Kwon, *The Welfare State in Korea: The Politics of Legitimation* (New York: St. Martin's Press, 1999), 95–99.

22. Ku Yeun-Wen, *Welfare Capitalism*, 247–49.

23. Yun-Han Chu, *Crafting Democracy in Taiwan* (Taipei: Institute for National Policy Research, 1992).

24. Jongryn Mo, "Political Learning and Democratic Consolidation: Korean Industrial Relations, 1987–1992," *Comparative Political Studies* 29 (1996). See also Yin-Wah Chu, "Ideology and Organization in the Oppositional Movements of Taiwan and South Korea," *Social Movements, Conflict, and Change* 21 (1999).

25. Chu, *Crafting Democracy*, 104.

26. Mo, "Political Learning."

27. See Chan-Ung Park, "Institutional Legacies and State Power: The First State Health Insurance Movements in Great Britain, the United States, and Korea," Ph.D. diss., University of Chicago, 1997, 387–91.

28. Author interview with Lin Liang-Rong, Taiwan Labor Front (October 18, 1999).

29. Michael Hsin-Huang Hsiao, "The Labor Movement in Taiwan," in *Taiwan: Beyond the Economic Miracle*, ed. D. F. Simon and Michael Kau (Armonk, N.Y.: M. E. Sharpe, 1992), 151–67. See also Yin-Wah Chu, "Democracy and Organized Labor in Taiwan: The 1986 Transition," *Asian Survey* 36 (1996).

30. Author interview with Lin Liang-Rong.

31. Hagen Koo, *Korean Workers: The Culture and Politics of Class Formation* (Ithaca: Cornell University Press, 2001), 216.

32. Author interview with Woo-Hyun Yoon, director, Policy Division, Korean Confederation of Trade Unions (June 8, 2000).

33. Dietrich Rueschemeyer, John Stephens, and Evelyne Huber-Stephens, *Capitalist Development and Democracy* (Chicago: University of Chicago Press, 1992), 299.

34. Author interview with Shi Hsian-Yan, president, National Primary Care Physicians Association (November 29, 1999).

35. Author interview with Lee Yoong-Jung, Social Welfare Policy Research Division, Citizens' Coalition for Economic Justice (May 31, 2000).

36. See, for example, Gosta Esping-Andersen, *Three Worlds of Welfare Capitalism* (Princeton: Princeton University Press, 1991), 31.

37. Author interview with Lee Eun-Gong, Welfare Division, People's Solidarity for Participatory Democracy (June 7, 2000). During the interview, Ms. Lee showed me an entire wall of files, one for every legislator, past and present, including press releases, reports, voting records, and personal profiles. See also Andrew Eungi Kim, "Citizens' Coalition Movement and Consolidation of Democracy: 2000 General Elections in South Korea," *Journal of East Asian Studies* 1 (2001).

38. On these middle-class civic groups, see Bronwen Dalton and James Cotton, "New Social Movements and the Changing Nature of Political Opposition in South Korea," in *Political Oppositions in Industrializing Asia*, ed. Garry Rodan (London: Routledge Press, 1996).

39. Author interview with Lee Yoong-Jung, Social Welfare Policy Research Division, Citizens' Coalition for Economic Justice (May 31, 2000).

40. Author interview with Liu Chin-Hsin, Taiwan Labor Front, former DPP legislator (October 4, 2000).

8. DEFENDING DEMOCRACY

1. Adam Przeworski, "Minimalist Conceptions of Democracy: A Defense," in *Democracy's Value*, ed. Ian Shapiro and Casiano Hacker-Cordon (Cambridge: Cambridge University Press, 1999), 40.

2. Juan Linz and Alfred Stepan, *Problems of Democratic Transition and Consolidation* (Baltimore: Johns Hopkins University Press, 1996), 12–13; Adam Przeworski et al., "What Makes Democracies Endure?" *Journal of Democracy* 7 (1996): 43.

3. Nancy Birdsall, "Life Is Unfair: Inequality in the World," *Foreign Policy* 111 (1998); Andrew Hurrell and Ngaire Woods, "Globalisation and Inequality," *Millennium: Journal of International Studies* 24 (1995).

4. Evelyne Huber and John D. Stephens, *Development and the Crisis of the Welfare State* (Chicago: University of Chicago Press, 2001).

5. Rosa Mule, "Does Democracy Promote Equality?" *Democratization* 5 (1998).

6. Evelyne Huber, Dietrich Rueschemeyer, and John D. Stephens, "The Paradoxes of Contemporary Democracy: Formal, Participatory, and Social Dimensions," in *Transitions to Democracy*, ed. Lisa Anderson (New York: Columbia University Press, 1999).

7. Robert Dahl, *Polyarchy: Participation and Opposition* (New Haven: Yale University Press, 1971).

8. Jack Knight, *Institutions and Social Conflict* (Cambridge: Cambridge University Press, 1992), 40.

9. Geraint Parry and George Moyser, "More Participation, More Democracy?" in *Defining and Measuring Democracy*, ed. David Beetham (London: Sage, 1994), 49.

10. Przeworski, "Minimalist Conceptions," 45–46.

11. John Dunn, "Situating Democratic Political Accountability," in *Democracy: Accountability and Representation*, ed. Adam Przeworski, Susan Stokes, and Bernard Manin (Cambridge: Cambridge University Press, 1999), 334.

12. Kenneth Roberts, *Deepening Democracy? The Modern Left and Social Movements in Chile and Peru* (Palo Alto: Stanford University Press, 1998).

13. Kurt Weyland, *Democracy without Equity: The Failure of Reform in Brazil* (Pittsburgh: University of Pittsburgh Press, 1996); Margaret Keck, *The Workers' Party and Democratization in Brazil* (New Haven: Yale University Press, 1992).

14. Edward Gibson, "The Populist Road to Market Reform: Policy and Electoral Coalitions in Mexico and Argentina," *World Politics* 49 (1997): 362–63.

15. Omar Encarnacion, "Social Concertation in Democratic and Market Transitions: Comparative Lessons from Spain," *Comparative Political Studies* 30 (1997): 408–9.

16. See Robert Mattes and Hermann Thiel, "Consolidation and Public Opinion in South Africa," *Journal of Democracy* 9 (1998).

17. Deborah Brautigam, "Institutions, Economic Reform, and Democratic Consolidation in Mauritius," *Comparative Politics* 30 (1997).

18. Ethan Kapstein and Michael Mandelbaum, *Sustaining the Transition: The Social Safety Net in Post-Communist Europe* (New York: Council on Foreign Relations, 1997).

19. Gosta Esping-Andersen, *The Three Worlds of Welfare Capitalism* (Princeton: Princeton University Press, 1990), 16–18.

20. Roberts, *Deepening Democracy?;* Marcelo Cavarozzi, "The Left in South America: Politics as the Only Option," in *Social Democracy in Latin America: Prospects for Change*, ed. Menno Vellinga (Boulder: Westview Press, 1993); Daniel Chirot, ed., *The Crisis of Leninism and the Decline of the Left: The Revolutions of 1989* (Seattle: University of Washington Press, 1991).

21. Edwin Amenta and Theda Skocpol, "States and Social Policies," *American Review of Sociology* 12 (1986): 149.

22. Paul Pierson, "The New Politics of the Welfare State," *World Politics* 48 (1996): 147.

23. Paul Pierson, *Dismantling the Welfare State? Reagan, Thatcher, and the Politics of Retrenchment* (Cambridge: Cambridge University Press, 1993), 42.

24. Michael Atkinson and William Coleman, "Policy Networks, Communities, and Problems of Governance," *Governance* 5 (1992).

25. Sidney Tarrow, *Power in Movement: Social Movements, Collective Action, and Politics* (Cambridge: Cambridge University Press, 1994), 85.

26. Guillermo O'Donnell and Philippe Schmitter, *Transitions from Authoritarian Rule: Tentative Conclusions* (Baltimore: Johns Hopkins University Press, 1986).

27. Herbert Kitschelt, Zdenka Mansfeldova, Radoslaw Markowski, and Gabor Toka, *Post-Communist Party System: Competition, Representation, and Inter-party Cooperation* (Cambridge: Cambridge University Press, 1999), 384.

28. Douglass C. North, *Institutions, Institutional Change, and Economic Performance* (Cambridge: Cambridge University Press, 1990), 74.

29. Linz and Stepan, *Problems;* Gerardo Munck, "Review Article: Democratic Transitions in Comparative Perspective," *Comparative Politics* 26 (1994); Dankwart Rustow, "Transitions to Democracy: Toward a Dynamic Model," *Comparative Politics* 2 (1970).

30. Ko Shu-Ling, "Analysts Doubt Premier's Chances to Be President Chen's Next Running Mate," *Taipei Times* (August 19, 2003).

INDEX

Italic page numbers refer to tables.